To Mario,
May you find
your SELF
in
the Now!

James White

MY JOURNEY TO NOW

PLUS
TOOLS FOR THE SEEKER

A Spiritual Memoir

JAMES WESTLY

BALBOA
PRESS

A DIVISION OF HAY HOUSE

Balboa Press books may be ordered through booksellers or by contacting:

Balboa Press
A Division of Hay House
1663 Liberty Drive
Bloomington, IN 47403
www.balboapress.com
1 (877) 407-4847

Because of the dynamic nature of the Internet, any web addresses or links contained in this book may have changed since publication and may no longer be valid. The views expressed in this work are solely those of the author and do not necessarily reflect the views of the publisher, and the publisher hereby disclaims any responsibility for them.

The author of this book does not dispense medical advice or prescribe the use of any technique as a form of treatment for physical, emotional, or medical problems without the advice of a physician, either directly or indirectly. The intent of the author is only to offer information of a general nature to help you in your quest for emotional and spiritual well-being. In the event you use any of the information in this book for yourself, which is your constitutional right, the author and the publisher assume no responsibility for your actions.

Any people depicted in stock imagery provided by Thinkstock are models, and such images are being used for illustrative purposes only. Certain stock imagery © Thinkstock.

Printed in the United States of America.

ISBN: 978-1-4525-9620-4 (sc)
ISBN: 978-1-4525-9621-1 (e)

Balboa Press rev. date: 04/24/2014

To all those who seek to experience the essential truth of life. To dive below the surface to find its essence, its true meaning. If you are one of those, this is the unembellished story of my search for truth, along with a set of tools to help you set out on your own journey to Now.

—James Westly, 2014

"The journey is everything."

—Virginia Woolf

CONTENTS

BEING THERE

LEAVING THERE

TOOLS FOR THE SEEKER

FORWARD

This book recounts an extraordinary journey that begins for Westly back in 1977. He is at the time happily married and involved in a successful corporate business career in Philadelphia. But something is missing. He doesn't know quite what it is that he is searching for, but one day a small ad in the personals section of the newspaper catches his attention and starts him on a path that totally changes his life. In the months that follow he will set out on a journey of self-discovery that will within a year's time lead him to virtually withdraw from the world; to separate himself from his job, his house, his wife, his friends, and his material possessions. In the process he will join a retreat in northern California and make a new life for himself there, where he will begin a profound intellectual, emotional and physical transformation that will open up for him an entirely different way of living.

His account of his journey into this new world reads like a novel. He tells his story with a mixture of eloquence and insight that is both breathtaking and inspirational. The journey ends happily, but it is not without its moments of conflict, crisis and peril.

The book has a lot to offer the reader beyond the remarkable story of his personal journey. It's also highly provocative philosophically. It really makes a reader examine himself and his life. It also includes a separate practical guide called Tools for the Journey that should be of great interest to many readers.

I was quite impressed by it. If I were still a book editor I would take this one on without hesitation. I would also be happy to give any potential publisher a quote for the flap copy.

A brief word about myself: I am the author of one work of nonfiction and six novels in print in over a dozen languages. I am also a former magazine and book editor. In my years as a senior editor at LIFE Magazine and as an executive at the publishing houses of Atheneum, Doubleday and G.P. Putnam's, I worked with the widest variety of talents, including a substantial number of best-selling authors, academics, historians and novelists, among them Stephen Ambrose, Theodore H. White, Admiral Samuel Eliot Morison, Anthony Cave Brown, Joan Didion, Robert Ardrey, Edward Abbey, C.P.B. Bryan, Thomas Thompson, George Plimpton, Larry L. King, and Senator Eugene McCarthy.

—Tom Hyman 2013

PREFACE

Long before I could even read I wanted to know, to directly experience the true meaning and purpose of life. I had no ability to articulate this deep motivation. It existed in me as a feeling, a deep desire, a longing so strong and enduring that it exists to this day. In my thirty-fourth year, it was this drive that compelled me to divest myself of everything I had accomplished, everything I "owned", to join a secret community of like minds who were also seeking the answer to the one question I believe exists in each one of us, "Why do I exist? What is Life really about." I share this story to encourage those who have become aware of this question within themselves and are ready to seek their own unique answer. The tools I share at the end of the story are a generic spiritual practice that will open the door to anyone who is willing to do what it takes, and for whom the answers to these fundamental questions are more important than anything else.

—James Westly Phoenix, Arizona 2014

ACKNOWLEDGEMENTS

First, I wish to thank The Teacher (who will remain unnamed) and all the members of The School, both known and unknown to me, all of whom participated in the creation of the world- wide setting that made this journey possible.

I thank also those whose work paved the way historically, bringing the ideas expressed here to the attention of the Western world in the form of a teaching called The Fourth Way. Chief among these individuals is George Gurdjieff, the founder, his chief disciple, Peter Ouspensky, and his chief disciple, Rodney Collin, along with John Bennett and a host of others who have shared their wisdom and experience in world literature. All these people lived and sought long before me, creating a rich legacy of experience and insight.

Second, I offer my profound gratitude to Allura Westly, my life partner for her support, recognition and encouragement, without which I would not have recognized and developed my gifts.

I thank my parents for giving me a nurturing foundation and unconditional support for a quest they themselves did not understand.

I give special thanks to Tom Hyman, my writing teacher from Longridge Writers Group, who challenged the novel I was attempting to write, compelling me to look deeper within for the story that was asking to be told. His voluntary help, which far exceeded the requirements of writing instructor, has gone far to make possible the book you now hold in your hands.

Finally, my deep appreciation goes to all those individuals who have taken the time to read and comment upon my manuscript. Your validation has helped to encourage me in persisting to make this work a reality.

INTRODUCTION

This is the story of my life from 1977 to 1985, a time when I broke free from the restraints of ordinary middleclass American life, literally obliterating all I had acquired or accomplished in the first thirty-four years of my existence, to go in search of my destiny, to, in the words of poet Walt Whitman:

> To escape utterly from others' anchors and holds!
> To drive free! To love free! to dash reckless and dangerous!
> To court destruction with taunts, with invitations!
> To ascend, to leap to the heavens of the love indicated to me!
> To rise thither with my inebriate soul!
> To feed the remainder of life with one hour of fullness and freedom!
> With one brief hour of madness and joy.

GETTING THERE

CHAPTER ONE

The First Step

The worn two-lane tarmac unfolds in an unending straight line into the horizon's infinity. Twenty-five miles of rice paddies, a variegated green patchwork of flooded fields, extending north up the Sacramento River valley, toward Marysville.

It is mid-afternoon on a June Friday, 1978. I am driving my grandmother's old Chevy, accompanied by the Santa Barbara center director of the Fourth Way School I joined in August 1977. To say I am excited is an understatement. This is the fulfillment of a nine-month build. I am alert, intense, and radically alive. Ahead lies the fulfillment of a life-long dream. Hidden invisibly away in the Sierra Foothills is the school's private retreat, my Shangri-La. This is my first visit. One of many that will eventually lead to my total withdrawal from society. How I get there and where it takes me is the subject of this book.

The journey begins one ordinary Monday morning in Philadelphia, Pennsylvania. I live in a charming downtown neighborhood seven tree-lined blocks from my office in the Public Ledger Building, across from Independence Hall, where I work as a corporate insurance broker. I am two years back into a suit job having spent the past five years adventuring in the counter culture, seeking revolution through chemical consciousness expansion. When the revolution fails to materialize, I return to the corporate humdrum, disillusioned. At the age of thirty-four I have failed to find my life's meaning and purpose, and am beginning to feel it does not exist.

When I am four I have an intuitive knowing that I will participate in a significant change for humanity. It is my secret. I tell no one. I cannot. It is something deeper, beyond words. Besides, what four-year old can articulate such a notion? This knowing does, however, have a significant effect on my behaviors and choices through out life.

In high school I am rebel without a cause. At nineteen, I am Beat. By twenty-two an intellectual; at twenty-five a married businessman; at twenty-nine a hippie dropout. Now, at thirty-four I am a married businessman, again. Like many who join the counterculture, the need to pay the bills eventually reasserts itself. The weird thing for me is I return to the same firm I quit five years before. I feel like I have again arrived at Go on the Monopoly board of life and am depressed about having to go around again. It all seems so pointless. I have reached existential ennui.

Three weeks earlier I break a bone in my foot while playing Frisbee. I am on vacation at home, in a cast, so I hobble around the corner to the Middle Earth Bookstore to find something philosophical to read. The face of a Mid-Eastern mystic on the cover of a book called Is There "Life" on Earth, magnetizes my attention. It is a book about George Gurdjieff, a name that resonates, seems familiar. It will come to have profound significance for me.

I read the book and return the next day to buy Gurdjieff's masterwork: All and Everything; Beelzebub's Tales to His Grandson. An extraordinarily unique document, it defies description, save to say that to glean anything at all from this mysterious masterpiece requires intense concentration, and the learning of a new language, a language the author invents in the book. The author himself advises to read his book three times. First like a newspaper, second aloud to another person and third for meaning and comprehension. In all honesty, at this writing I have performed the first two tasks. The third awaits me.

I cannot put the book down. It consumes my every waking thought. I come home every night and read into the early morning hours. This is my state of mind on this particular Monday morning.

Mid-morning I make my routine visit to the men's room where it is my custom to read the newspaper. On this particular morning, all the sections of the paper are soaked, leaving the want ads. I go to the personals. Almost immediately the name Gurdjieff rivets my attention from a tiny two line ad that reads: "Gurdjieff-Ouspensky Centre, now accepting students", with a phone number. I run back to my office, call the number, arrange three introductory meetings and join. My life changes forever one ordinary morning, in the men's room. One never knows where or when lightning will strike.

In telling this tale, my journey to now, I intend to speak only from my point of perception and will name few names. Most characters will be identified by their role. Those roles, which are dominant and recurring, may be given fictitious names.

CHAPTER TWO

A New Beginning

Before attending the first of three introductory meetings, I am instructed to read Ouspensky's book, The Psychology of Man's Possible Evolution. I read it twice and take notes, thinking I will have to perform in some way, pass a test. The one thing important for me to mention at this point is this phrase that I took from the book: "Believe nothing, verify everything." To me this means I am not going to be sold an unsubstantiated belief.

The meeting is held in a private home a few blocks from my house. The leader is an articulate young woman who dresses like Alice in Wonderland. There are several others in the room who are obviously group members, and three or four who are, like me, prospective students. The leader expresses an idea, then other members follow up with what they call "angles of thought".

The presentation follows the format of Ouspensky's

book, the gist of which is that we exist as potential that can only be actualized through conscious labor and intentional suffering. They say:

"We are many 'I's and cannot do, everything happens. We have no will," they go on, "and are not unified beings, but rather are multi-brained individuals functioning as stimulus-response robots. We are many people inside. We contain a multitude and are living in an illusion of singularity."

There is a strange familiarity to everything they say, like I already know it, but do not know I know until this moment.

They speak for an hour then take a break. Before the break, a series of exercises are given to perform that, they say, will confirm the ideas discussed. We are asked to practice these when talking informally. They sound easy enough.

We are to not speak contractions, you know, like "I'm, isn't, wasn't weren't...etc." We also are not to use the word "I", but find a suitable substitution, like "this person". In addition, we are not to put hands in pockets or on hips. And, finally, we to refrain from expressing negative emotions.

We are told that when we violate an exercise, a member will make us aware of it by raising their hand in a karate chop motion. They call it a "photograph". The hand motion imitates a camera shutter, giving us a snapshot of our lack of awareness. What they do not say, but what becomes clear almost immediately, is following the exercise is more important than what we have to say.

Now, my ego is confident I will have no problem following the exercises. I am eager to interact with the members. I approach a small group of them, having what I think is an important something to say. I stride up, plunging my hands into my pockets, saying, "I can't believe..." Immediately several hands are waving in my face. My face flushes as I feel my mind wanting to insist on continuing to speak. They are not paying attention. I have something important to say. The outcome is paralysis. My ego is insulted over not being heard, and thoroughly humiliated over failing the exercise, revealing my automatic behavior.

My own lack of awareness is obvious and confusing. Just moments before I have a picture of myself as a very aware person. My mind resists changing this perception, rattling my ego's confidence. Every attempt to initiate conversation ends in this disaster. I am painfully in-the-moment.

I understand now why the members seem different, at times, weird. They are doing the exercises, maintaining a constant vigilance that brings intense deliberation into their speech and movement. Not using contractions or saying the word "I" makes for unusual speech patterns. The eyes of the older students project a peaceful vibration. It feels loving, safe and intense. It is physically visible. Their eyes appear indefinably different.

The demonstration is very effective. I am stunned by my failure to perform these seemingly simple tasks. I feel raw and humbled throughout the second half of the meeting. I also feel exhilarated. My life has been defined by the search for an entry point into life's mysteries. Until this moment everything I read; philosophy, metaphysics, classical literature, existentialism, The Masters of the Far East, tells about, but never reveals how, how to find and open the door to an experience of a deeper reality.

The Fourth Way seems to be the key. The Now moment

is the portal, the door. Accessing the Now moment requires me to maintain full attention on the one place and time life is happening, Here/Now. The price of admission is my mind. I must relinquish my habitual thought processes.

The evening is a watershed. The emotion of it is profoundly deep and positive. I feel my yearning for the key to life's meaning and purpose is closer than ever to being fulfilled. I am bouncing off the walls. To say I am excited, inspired, moved, activated is insufficient. I go home and try to convey the enormousness of this to my wife, who has no interest in such matters. I tell her what happened is the most important event of my life. I am sure she thinks me mad.

The second meeting, later that week, contains detailed information about our status as multi-brained beings. These brains are called centres. The meeting is lead by a different person, a bearded man who is the only person in the group with whom I feel kinship. I sense we have followed similar paths. The three other prospective students from my first meeting fail to attend, leaving me the focus of the group.

The gist of the meeting is that the centres, the various brains, do not do their work correctly. Each produces its own thoughts, and has its own desires and intentions. Each asserts itself as "I", taking the stage of surface consciousness momentarily, masquerading as the whole. Each thought calls itself "I", creating the illusion of wholeness, obscuring the truth, that each "I" is a part and does not represent the whole. Thus there is not one inner voice, but a multitude, many "I's".

There is the Instinctive Centre, concerned with the inner workings of the body, the Moving Centre, the brain of external motion, the Emotional Centre, the feeling brain and the Intellectual Centre, the thinking brain. Furthermore, each brain is subdivided into three levels of attention. There is the lowest level from which attention flows automatically, the second level where attention is drawn by some stimulus (external or internal) and the third level where attention is directed with effort. On top of that, each Centre operates at a different speed, the Emotional being the fastest, the Intellectual being the slowest. It all makes sense, but the amount and detail of the information is overwhelming.

The biggest challenge, however, is the break. I am determined not to repeat my previous humiliation. I approach socializing with caution. It is becoming more important for me to master the exercises, than to display my conversational brilliance. My focus of attention is on avoiding the automatic behaviors that will result in waving hands.

It feels awkward, stilted. Speech and body posture are closely watched as my ego works diligently to avoid the humiliating experiences of the previous meeting, then fails anyway. I enter a conversation with noble intentions, determined to hold the exercises, and then become more interested in what I am saying and less in how I am saying it. Without focused, intense, diligence, something else takes over. I watch helplessly as automatic phrases flow out of my mouth. Phrases I use in hundreds of conversations, phrases that are intended to make me look good, to inflate my worth. I am developing an Observer, a portion of my consciousness assigned to witness my behavior.

Now the failures are less devastating, though still humiliating. I find myself thanking the giver of a "photograph", then making a correction and continuing. It seems natural to be grateful for their assistance, their help in showing me my deficient awareness, while simultaneously my ego is humiliated over having failed. I am watching every bodily movement, every word that forms itself in my mind before it emerges as speech. Something new is arising within me that is separate from what I am coming to see as automatic behavior. I am becoming aware that I have automatic behavior. I used to think of myself as being in charge, now I discover I am mostly an automatic response. This is what Gurdjieff calls "The Terror of the Situation."

The third meeting takes place at a different location, in the Philadelphia suburbs. The directions are complex, and near the end, I get lost. I feel panicky, fearing I am failing some test, that if I do not find the house, I will lose an important opportunity. Finally I locate it, a multistoried brownstone mansion that feels European.

We again sit in a circle. A different man leads this meeting, a physician who is the center co-director. The subject is a complex presentation of information called Body Types. A diagram, consisting of a circle containing a triangle and an unusual six-pointed line figure is displayed, called an enneagram.

In the next two and a half hours I learn we are spiritual beings traveling in a body. The body we each inhabit, according to this theory, is a variation on one of seven themes. There are seven basic body types, which combine in an infinitude of lawful variations. Each type has a unique physical appearance and structure, a particular psychology that creates a predictable worldview, and a chief weakness, or chief feature.

The meeting culminates with my being given a Body

Type. They decide I am a certain type, the result of a series of observations they offer concerning my physical structure and stature, skin and hair coloring, personality and temperament. I am then given the opportunity to join the school. Apparently the only qualification for admission is to endure these three meetings and be willing to pay 10% of my gross income. I slap a $100 bill down on the table and say: "I'm in!!"

CHAPTER THREE

The "Work" Begins

I begin attending meetings twice a week. When I am not working or at a meeting, I am studying. I continue reading Beelzebub's Tales and The Fourth Way, a record of Ouspensky's lectures, on alternative nights. I am totally absorbed. Everything outside The Work becomes meaningless. My career, my marriage, and my social life are all eclipsed by my obsession with elevating my consciousness.

I discover I joined an international organization that maintains "teaching houses" in every major U.S. city, in many European cities, and Israel. The Philadelphia center consists of two houses and is led by a man, a practicing physician, and a woman, a chemist. They were sent to the city, along with a handful of other students, by The Teacher, who resides in a retreat in the foothills of the California Sierra Madre mountains.

The meetings are always concerned with some aspect of the knowledge, or the development of new tools to facilitate Self-Remembering, a state of awareness in which you experientially sense life from a deeper perspective.

The format is the same as the introductory meetings. Someone leads, introducing a topic or asking the group for a question, while the others offer "angles of thought". The concept is everyone has a perspective on the truth, an angle. All angles are aspects or facets of something larger. There is no argument or debate, each point-of-view is honored as an aspect of truth. The leader controls the conversation by having members raise their hands to be recognized.

The atmosphere in the room is meditative. Everyone concentrates on holding their entire awareness in the room, not allowing their minds to wander. When a topic is offered or a question asked, members focus their minds on the issue, listening internally for a connection.

At first, the process intimidates me. I study diligently between meetings, working to generate questions. During meetings I listen intently, but offer nothing, not feeling competent to contribute an 'angle'. Gradually, though, while listening, I begin to hear inner responses to the external dialogue. Out of the inner stillness of listening a new voice begins to arise. In the beginning I listen.

Intense listening is a focus of attention, requiring concentration. When you concentrate on a task, any task, it causes the mind to become quiet. The inner voices we call thinking become still, allowing more attention to emerge into the moment, intensifying the experience. During these first weeks I listen so intently my ears ring, becoming a barometer for my level of presence. Then, as my Here/Now focus deepens, I begin to hear 'angles'. Whatever the topic is, an 'angle' arises which has merit. When this happens, a new struggle ensues, causing me to lose focus.

When a worthy thought emerges from my inner stillness, I begin internally rehearsing what I will say. I fear raising my hand before I compose a complete thought, a near impossibility. This, of course, interferes with listening, and inevitably results in an even weirder occurrence. As I sit struggling to piece together my speech, someone else raises their hand and gives his or her version of my thought. This does not happen occasionally, it occurs with reliable consistency. Every time I get stuck in paralysis attempting to compose a speech, someone else rises and seizes my moment.

At first I am puzzled. How can this be? I write it off as coincidence. When it occurs again, and then again, I become paranoid. Is someone reading my thoughts? Then I get it.

One evening the discussion is around how our mind is not who we are, but a powerful instrument we possess. One of its less recognized capabilities is that it is a receiver of thought, like a radio set. In my work on inner self-observation I have already begun to verify this experientially. I am coming to realize my thoughts are not necessarily my own, but indeed appear to just show up. During this talk, someone mentions that thoughts are circulated routinely between the physical and the non-physical world. Any thought given out in a meeting is given to more than one person to increase the likelihood of it being expressed. Of course! I naively think my mind is my private domain, that I "think" all my thoughts. Actually I am receiving thoughts all the time. This takes the idea of connection to a whole new level.

Finally, after weeks of struggle, I get it that part of being in the moment is proceeding one step at a time. In this case that means, the idea emerges out of my inner stillness, I raise my hand, and speak the thought one-word-at-a-time as it emerges. I begin speaking, not knowing what I am going to say until I say it. This gives deeper meaning to the idea of Being in the Now.

The result is intensely liberating and astonishing. What comes out of me is far superior to anything my mind could produce. It is a whole new dimension of awareness. The energy of it is phenomenal. I open the door and something larger comes through. All I have to 'do' is give up thinking and find consistent inner stillness.

Please know this is a gradual process. I am not suddenly struck by lightning and God speaks. I struggle for many years, progressively becoming more adept, until I am able to lead meetings with no preparation. Each time is an individual act of courage, a letting go of the illusion of control and trusting. Now, after 30+ years practice, I am able to listen and flow with what comes. The formerly soft, faint voice of my inner connection is now strong, clear and intimate.

The meetings cover many topics. The Fourth Way states mankind is a multi-brained being that has greater potential for conscious awareness than it is currently experiencing. The path is the unification of consciousness through present moment awareness. This is approached through studying the "machine", purifying it of "wrong work" and making intensive intentional internal efforts to concentrate all one's attention into the Now, considered a portal to a deeper reality. Experiential verification is the process. What lies on the other side of the door is an inexpressible mystery. It cannot be described. Thought cannot contain it. Words cannot speak it. The mind cannot know it. It can only be experienced. "Price of admission, your mind." (Herman Hesse, Steppenwolf)

Students study the literature of the system, reading the works of George Gurdjieff, Peter Ouspensky, Rodney Collin and other Fourth Way writers to glean practical knowledge, wisdom they can put into effect to facilitate the alignment of their consciousness with the present moment.

The group also studies the works of various other historical bright lights that are identified by The Teacher as advanced souls. The list reads like a study guide for a PhD in the Humanities. Their work is read and interpreted through the lens of The Fourth Way.

Shakespeare is one of those luminaries. Having enjoyed his iambic pentameter since high school, I start memorizing his sonnets, seeing esoteric ideas in many of them. Take these lines for example:

"When I consider everything that grows,
Holds in perfection but a little moment,
That this huge stage presenteth naught but shows,
Whereon the stars in secret influence comment."

They are a reminder of the preciousness of the moment and a reference to the larger picture ("the stars in secret influence comment"). I begin committing his sonnets to memory, then reciting them mentally as a method of putting something against the constant flow of automatic thought continuously flooding my brain.

The meetings alternate between the downtown house and the suburban mansion. Different students take turns leading them. They last three hours, with a refreshment break midway. In the second half of the meeting, the students are divided into small groups that are led by different members, giving everyone an opportunity to develop leadership skills. After the meeting we adjourn to a local restaurant where the discussion continues informally.

To say I am consumed would be an understatement. I feel, for the first time in my life, I am connected to something that will answer my burning questions about the purpose of life and offer practical tools to play its game with conscious awareness. I have a passion for this like nothing else I have ever encountered.

CHAPTER FOUR

Meeting The Teacher

Six weeks into my studies a teaching event occurs. Our center directors tell us The Teacher is traveling to the New York center to conduct a meeting and we are all invited. Everyone is abuzz.

I drive to the teaching house on Long Island, arriving Friday afternoon. The house is an enormous made over barn sitting on four acres of gardens and orchards. I pitch my tent in a small wood behind the house and go to the kitchen to help and socialize. Late in the afternoon there is a tea party on the lawn. Everyone dresses in their finery. People are arriving all day long. I see several California license plates. Astonished, I realize these students had made the effort to drive three thousand miles to hear The Teacher speak.

Now, I am one of those people who have interests that do not fall into the category of ordinary concerns. A philosopher by nature, I rarely meet anyone I can really talk with about my deepest interests, and then, only one-at-a-time at widely spaced intervals. That afternoon, standing on a slight rise in a lush Long Island garden, I gaze upon two hundred like minds. I have come home. I feel that spiritual connection now, writing these words thirty-seven years later.

We dine in the orchard that evening to the accompaniment of classical music. As I stand at the edge of the orchard, wine glass in hand, a fellow student comes over, the bearded man who led my second perspective meeting. We have become friends. All the people there are working hard internally to keep their attention focused in The Now, creating a meditative atmosphere. Our minds are more still than noisy. My friend points to some farm laborers across the field a hundred yards away.

"You can be there, with them, now!" he says. "Just project your attention using your creative imagination and you'll be there."

I do what he suggests and find myself next to the workers, feeling them, almost smelling them. The experience is visual and kinesthetic. You might call it a mind expansion exercise. It deepens my presence. I know this now because I remember it vividly to this day. All vivid memories are traces of presence. This book is not being written from physical notes, but from my vivid memories, my moments of connection to the Now.

Next day is the meeting. It is held in a large two-story room with an exposed stairway running up one wall. At the top of the stairs is a door. The room is filled to capacity, so I decide to sit on the stairs halfway up, giving me an overview of the event.

I am sitting on the steps waiting for the meeting to begin when I feel a hand on my shoulder. I turn to find The Teacher speaking to me. I can tell he is speaking because his lips are moving, but I can barely hear him. There is a loud rushing sound in my head. He repeats: "You have a good seat here." I say: "Oh", a word we are working not to say, embarrassing myself. His face lights up with a brilliant smile surrounded by a bright light. This brief moment illuminates my entire day. I have little recollection of the meeting or the rest of the day, this man's presence creates such an intense, unforgettable experience.

CHAPTER FIVE

My Studies Continue

That winter I settle into a pattern of work, study and attending meetings. I work in business, something I am good at but have no passion for. It does not match what The Work calls my Essence. I am not proud of what I do to sustain my existence. In fact, it verifies for me the idea that life happens, we do not "Do". The insurance business happened to me. I was almost in the airline business, but a twist of fate brought me here.

The 'twist' I speak of is my own automatic behavior. In the school they call it Inner Considering. You internally consider other people. You worry about how they see you or what they think of you. Ten years before, I am fresh out of college looking for a career direction while attending graduate school. I meet a man in graduate school who works for a local airline. We become friends and he tells me of a job opportunity at the airline. I interview and am told I have the job but will have to wait six months until a hiring freeze is lifted. Since I need an income immediately, I continue my work search and eventually find an entry-level position with an insurance company. When the six months pass, my friend comes to me with the job, assistant to the president, but I decline, feeling a misplaced sense of loyalty to the man who hired me at the insurance company. I want to work for the airline, but I give my power away to Inner Considering.

Inner Considering is one of six obstacles to present-moment awareness identified by the teaching. Each is a mental process that takes attention away from the moment. Observing these obstacles in others and myself becomes a part of my core practice. Every day, to this very moment, I am aware of the operation of these mechanisms in my psychology.

Now the day is no longer something to get through, but is rich with opportunity to uncover my true Self through sometimes painful discoveries of my non-self. I discover many unpleasant things about my ego. For instance, how I lie to impress others, telling little stories about my life experiences that are not true. I notice how my mind wanders continuously while performing mundane tasks. I realize how I place my sense of identity in my possessions, my clothes, and my job.

The deeper I travel into The Work, the more I realize the depth of my unconsciousness. Everything about me is suspect, must be disassembled and reconstructed. Self-observation, a major Work tool, reveals how my persona is constructed from external influences. I unconsciously model (learn through imitation) my personality from all the influential people in my life, characteristics both deep and superficial. I debate like my stepfather (need to be right), am defensive like my mother, have their attitude about money (or the lack of it), imitate this person's laugh, tell that person's joke, nothing is my own. What about me is real?

Then something amazing happens. One morning at work I am writing routine follow-up memos. Without warning, my awareness shifts to a point about four feet above and behind me. I find myself watching my body continue to write the memos. It continues performing this routine task while my consciousness hovers outside and above, watching. I have no idea what is being written. It is like watching a stranger. I feel completely detached from its ordinary functioning. Clearly, I am not my body. It lasts no more than a minute, possibly less.

It is a spontaneous occurrence. The Work is nowhere in my thoughts. I am not 'thinking' about consciousness, or trying to "do" anything. I mention it at the next meeting and am told that conscious influence, the school's metaphor for a larger reality or a higher power, may gift someone beginning The Work in such a way. For me, it confirms I am a traveler in a body. Something plucked me out of my physical existence for a moment to show me a deeper reality.

CHAPTER SIX

San Francisco Here I Come

Just prior to meeting The School, I applied for entry into a photography school in Santa Barbara, California. They accepted me, and I planned to sell my house and finance my schooling with the proceeds. Photography was my consuming passion before finding The Work. I put the house on the market just a few weeks before The School entered my life. Now it all appears to have been part of a larger plan designed to bring me closer to the heart of the school in California. It feels like some larger intention known only to my subconscious, or my Soul, is coordinating my life.

In June 1978 my house sells and I make preparations to move to Santa Barbara. I fly to San Francisco to visit my family in Sonoma, a small town forty miles north of The City. There I borrow my grandmother's car and drive to one of the school's teaching houses in San Francisco.

I arrive at an address in the Mission District, walk to the door, turn the knob and enter, unannounced. Teaching houses are never locked. Inside I find friendly faces, some of whom I know from New York. The school is an extraordinary support system. It amazes me to find friends in strangers three thousand miles from home. A very nice older lady makes me comfortable, offers refreshment and chats with me.

A few hours later we drive to a large auditorium across the bay where about five hundred students gather to hear The Teacher speak. I follow a car full of students through swirling late afternoon traffic to the Oakland hills. The car I am following seems to be driving as fast as possible, almost as if they are trying to shake me, knowing I would not make it to the meeting if I lost them. It is similar to the test of getting lost going to my third perspective meeting. I struggle with not taking the situation personally. My ego wants to be angry, but I persist, finding my sense of humor and adventure. I have traveled three thousand miles since finding that two-line want ad. I sold my property and left my position, all driven by an intense passion for spiritual evolution, that elusive something buried deep within.

A beautiful meeting hall on a courtyard emerges as I walk up the broad steps from the parking lot. There is a food service area on one side toward which I gravitate. For me the best way to meet people is to volunteer in the kitchen.

The courtyard is crowded with hundreds of finely attired students, talking in groups while not using the words "I" or "Oh" or contractions, not putting their hands in their pockets or on their hips, allowing one person to speak at a time without interruption, and listening intently to each other. Normally in a crowd this size the noise would be deafening, driven by competitive conversation. Here there is a low murmur. Overheard bits of conversation contain those unusual sentence structures peculiar to students, giving the whole scene a surrealistic ambiance.

I contact the Santa Barbara center before arriving, and arrange to meet one of their members at the meeting, intending to return with them to Santa Barbara. I am going there to stay in the teaching house to find housing for my move to California. I ask those around me if they know my contact, and am eventually introduced to the woman who is the Santa Barbara center co-director.

The meeting is an exercise in group-focused attention. It is the largest I have ever attended. The Teacher appears at the head of the room on a stage with six older students. He begins speaking about Self-Remembering, the core practice of the teaching. A profound stillness pervades the room. All present are actively working to focus their attention Here/Now. Every mind is focused on the topic, internally listening for the privilege of receiving a thought worthy of expression.

It also is an ego thing. The ego adapts to new environments, constantly searching for new identities. At the very least, if you raise your hand, are recognized, and say something significant, your fellow students will hold you in high esteem. Also, a professional court reporter, a student, is sitting at the front of the room taking notes. These notes are then edited and eventually published in the school's monthly journal. Your comments may be published, making you famous, raising you even higher in the eyes of others. There are older students in the room who are good at speaking in meetings and have been published. They are school celebrities.

The discussion of Self-Remembering offers clues and tools for practice. The stillness in the room deepens. My ears are ringing loudly, my indicator of Presence. I feel a growing connection to something larger for the first time in my life. What is being shared is practical and life changing. It has a powerful positive effect upon me.

I serve food during the break then attend the second half. People count off one through eight and reassemble into small groups. A leader from the stage goes around appointing group leaders. My small group is larger then the entire group I meet with in Philadelphia. Many of the people I meet have been students for seven or more years. I am again awed, as I was in Long Island, by the presence of so many interested in something beyond the superficial. I feel I belong. Ten thirty that evening I head south with the lady from Santa Barbara, arriving at the teaching house in the small hours of the morning.

CHAPTER SEVEN

Santa Barbara

I awake the next morning on the couch of a pleasant two-story house in Old Santa Barbara. I have a week to find a place to live. I plan to travel to The Retreat in Northern California on Friday, having made arrangements to be accompanied by the lady center director.

A quick review of the Santa Barbara possibilities makes it clear I cannot afford the town. Looking in the towns to the south, in two days I find a property close to the beach in Oxnard Shores. None of the complex details of this whole uprooting process daunt or frustrate the extreme excitement I feel at the prospect of attaining the heart of the school, the Teacher's home.

Wednesday night we all travel to Los Angeles to attend a large prospective student meeting, the one on body types. I sit on the stage as a representative of my type, even giving "angles of thought" on what it means to live in my particular vehicle, my type.

Friday morning the center director and I get into my grandmother's old Chevy and spend the day driving north up through the San Joaquin Valley, past Sacramento, over the rice paddies to Marysville, then up into the Sierra Madre foothills.

During the seven-hour trip she tells me the history of the retreat. It was founded in 1971 after an extensive search for a property with the right "vibration". The Teacher makes the decision to buy the property based on how it feels to him intuitively. The ground there is red, indicating high iron soil content, making it an electro-magnetic vortex, a place that will support and empower spiritual work. It starts as 600 acres of undeveloped Ponderosa and Redwood forest with a log cabin and a barn at its center. Since then 400 acres have been cleared, terraced and planted with wine grapes, all under the guidance of a German wine master who joined the school. Student architects are developing plans for a grand winery building. The log cabin has been remodeled and added onto several times, turning it into a dining hall, meeting room and library, with an upstairs dining room for elegant formal dinners with the Teacher. A large meeting and concert hall is currently under construction.

Students from all over the world are constantly visiting, contributing their labor to the various projects, working in the vineyard, doing carpentry on the new building, or washing dishes in the kitchen. Contributing to the nurturance of the organization and the furtherance of the teaching is considered a requisite aspect of the evolutionary process. There is work on oneself, the first line, helping others, the second line and work to promote The Work and The School, the third line. Maintaining a balanced relationship between the three is considered essential. Part of the mythology of the school is that the retreat is to be a safe haven from Armageddon.

CHAPTER EIGHT

On to Shangri-La

The old Chevy labors up the grade out of Marysville, leaving behind Philadelphia, with my marriage, house and career. They are nowhere to be found in any corner of my inner world. At about one thousand feet elevation we break through the fog layer sitting like a lid on the valley below, emerging into an enchanting world of Ponderosa pines and Sierra peaks, set ablaze by the setting sun. The worn two-lane pavement snakes around tight corners, climbing higher and higher, leaving behind the mundane world of thought, moving into the magic world of Presence.

We come to a T-intersection. At the top of the T is a post office. There are no other buildings. Taking the turn onto the leg of the T we pass a field, then a small general store and gas station. The road then begins winding along a streambed into the woods, passing a few widely scattered, ramshackle houses and mobile homes. Leaving these behind, the road narrows to one lane filled with potholes. The forest closes in, becoming dark and windy as we climb through tall pines. Suddenly, rounding a corner, the landscape opens to terraced hillsides thick with well-tended grape vines. We have passed through a wormhole into another dimension.

The pavement improves as we drive along the edge of the property, coming to a charming well kept cottage with beautiful gardens, and finally to an entry road marked with a sign: "Private Monastery".

We turn onto a manicured property. Everywhere you look there is beauty and order. Behind a row of sentinel Ponderosas rise rippling hills of vineyard. The road curves back around past the cottage, the Teacher's house, and down a little slope, past a fifteen foot high statue of the Greek God Poseidon, which stands at the entry to a small trailer park containing a collection of Air Stream trailers, all surrounded by flowers. The road meanders further, vineyards on both sides, climbs the hill past an old barn, next to a yard filled with backhoes and bulldozers, up to a cradle in the hillside holding a rambling three level structure called The Lodge. Not a soul is in sight. We have not seen anyone since entering the property. There is an eerie, non-threatening stillness.

We park in a circle at the front of the building and enter the lowest level, containing a large cloakroom and restroom facilities, then up a stairway that emerges onto a mezzanine with windows looking back down the slope. The atmosphere is saturated with a palpable sense of what I have come to know as Presence. There is a deep stillness, broken by a single soft female voice speaking wisdom. Around the corner a large room opens to reveal over a hundred highly focused students. The stillness is deafening. The leader is discussing an obstacle to conscious awareness. This is it, a conscious community, working together 24/7, supporting each other's efforts to spiritually develop.

CHAPTER NINE

The Retreat

I stand listening as the meeting reaches its conclusion. It has taken me ten months, three thousand miles and a ten-hour drive to reach this sacred place. My awareness is so intense everything seems to glow with live energy. The disciplines being practiced by the beings in the room are clearly visible. I feel more vital than I have ever felt in my entire life, but it is not excitement in the conventional sense. It is more like every cell in my body is vibrating at a higher pitch. I am intensely calm, vibrantly alive.

The meeting adjourns and the still picture comes alive. The students rearrange the room, turning it from a meeting hall into a dining room. Eight-foot long tables and chairs appear and are put in place, covered with linen table clothes. Magnificent flower arrangements appear on each table. A huge flagstone fireplace dominates the center of the outside wall. Windows look out onto the mezzanine, the windows of which look down the vineyard slope. Behind the fireplace wall other windows reveal a patio dug into the hillside with lawn sloping down to the circle where I left my car.

Out on the mezzanine a wine bar is set up, as Mozart softly enchants the air. My traveling companion takes me around, introducing me. I return to my car, move my suitcase and sleeping bag into the dressing room, then drive the car half way down the hill to a parking lot and slowly walk back up the hill, drinking in the views.

In the dressing room I change into a suit and tie and re-emerge onto the mezzanine which is now crowded with students quietly communicating over glasses of fine wine. I purchase a glass along with a dinner ticket, make a table reservation and go out on the patio to feel the place.

I drink in the peace and serenity, the heightened state of awareness, as I sip my wine. Gazing down the terraced slope before me, I marvel at how the light of the setting sun turns the grape leaves into green gold. In the distance the sunset turns the cloud cover over the valley to crimson, reminding me of the world beneath, deepening the feeling of having found the way to Presence.

The patio is crowded with students. As I move among them, many greet me. Each has a unique story as to how they met the school and found their way here to this enchanting place. They are from all over the country, Europe and Israel. Each one is driven by what the school calls a Magnetic Center, a calling within that eventually draws them to the school. Some are retreat residents, others, are visitors like myself. This remote, hard to find, location receives guests daily from around the world, students who spend their vacations working in the vineyard.

Conversations are around various aspects of the Teaching, like: "What is your body type and center of gravity? Where did you join? How long have you been in the school and how did you find it?"

Students share new information given by The Teacher on some aspect of The Work, while others converse on some new connection they have found in the work of one of the historical individuals The Teacher has identified as conscious beings. These include such names as: Abraham Lincoln, Walt Whitman, Benjamin Franklin, William Shakespeare, Johann Goethe, Rainer Marie Rilke, Rumi, Aristotle, Epictetus, Marcus Aurelius and many others. The list reads like a syllabus for a PhD in philosophy.

Each student is a highly unique individual, someone who has found dissatisfaction with the surface reality of modern culture and has developed the strength to seek and follow a conscious alternative. Many are ex-hippies. All have dedicated their lives to the evolution of their consciousness.

I while away the delicious evening out on the patio under the stars with a whole bunch of new friends, people who have managed to find their way to this place. That fact alone makes them special. Eventually it is my turn to dine.

I sit at a long table with seven other students. Laid out before me is a formal setting of fine china, sterling silver and crystal water goblets. When everyone is seated and settled, before the service begins, a lovely young woman with a lilting Irish accent reads a Shakespearian sonnet. Then the low hum of polite, non-intrusive conversation resumes, gently overlaid with classical music, as fellow students serve a delicious gourmet meal. Everybody takes a turn serving. Those who are served at the first seating became the servers at the second seating.

Finally the evening comes to an end and The Lodge is transformed into its final function of the day, rest. The long tables in the main room are folded and set aside. Students go down to the dressing rooms and change into sleep clothes, take out sleeping bags and find a spot on the floor to sleep.

I am the last one up. It is hard for me to let go of the evening. I finally go downstairs, change, and bring my sleeping bag upstairs to find a spot. I look around the mezzanine and am amazed to see the couch unoccupied. I foolishly think someone is watching out for me, to have everybody else sleep on the floor and leave me the couch. I have feelings of gratitude to conscious influence as I slip into an exhausted sleep.

I awake at dawn the next morning being gently shaken by a sweet-faced young woman who politely informs me that sleeping on the couch is against the rules as it will break down the cushions.

Bam!! Not twenty-four hours here and my unconscious behavior betrays me. Scurrying off to the dressing room I change clothes and return upstairs. Breakfast is meditative. Many read something from The Work literature taken from the well-stocked library. What they read becomes their practice for the day.

At 7:00 a.m. the vineyard crew meets on the mezzanine to plan the day's activities. It is June and the growing season is in full swing. On another part of the property, land is still being cleared by a young man who drives a D-8 bulldozer the size of a house. His expertise in handling this huge machine is performance art!

Since there are a large number of visitors, the vineyard manager, a muscular red headed man, proposes a tour of the property. We all pile onto the back of a flatbed truck in front of The Lodge and roll down the hill to the rambling old barn in the middle of the vineyard. It is a beehive of activity.

This building performs several functions. First there is the auto shop, run by a very intense soft-spoken man who is absolutely mystical with machinery. Everyone calls him Doctor Don. He and his crew service every vehicle, including the D-8, several backhoes and a Bobcat. Then there is an extensive woodshop, a metal shop and an antique restoration operation. The Teacher likes to find rare antiques and have them made better than new. They are working on an inlaid wood Steinway piano built around the turn of the century for a member of British royalty. It is eventually to be housed in a new concert/meeting hall being built on another part of the property scheduled for Fall completion.

Next stop is a drive through of The Court of the Caravans, a small collection of a dozen or so Air Stream trailers arranged in a circle around well manicured flowerbeds. Then back out past the Poseidon statue and on to the house at the entrance of the property called the Blake Cottage (named after the English poet William Blake), which, in addition to being The Teacher's residence (he is currently away traveling), also houses the pressroom that publishes The School's monthly journal using archival paper and hand set type.

The crew is entirely staffed by a type that is passive and meticulous, perfect for the tedious demanding work required for type setting. In ordinary life, pressrooms are dirty and chaotic. Here the opposite is true. All is meticulously clean, neat and organized. The staff is neatly dressed and wearing aprons. No ink splatters are found anywhere. Classical music creates a meditative atmosphere as each letter is intentionally selected and set into the type frame. They are busy printing the quote of the day onto small cards that are made available at lunch.

Next we bounce over dirt roads through the vineyard up to the winery knoll where a massive circular concrete foundation and wine cellar are in the early stages of construction. Here we meet a tall blond man who is the construction manager. He gives us a tour and answers our questions, describing the architect's grand vision of an inflated plastic dome anchored to the foundation that will house the wine production area. The dome is to be a temporary structure until a neo-classical Greek concrete structure is constructed.

The next stop takes us back across the vineyard and down a wooded draw to the Rembrandt Cottage, a quaint little house nestled in a pine grove. Inside are several artists all practicing their craft. They are "on salary" to produce art for the school and wash dishes. The dish washing is to keep them humble.

I meet an intensely focused man there who is an exquisite watercolorist and miniaturist. Beside him stands a tall, lanky fellow doing an oil portrait of a Greek god. The Teacher only values and supports the classics. He has no interest in modern art at this time.

In the next room a petite young woman is painting portraits of Gurdjieff and Ouspensky on small porcelain ovals that are eventually printed on bookmarks made in the pressroom.

Another man is studying and experimenting on how to gold leaf sculpture and ornate furniture carvings. He is using nitric acid and other toxic chemicals in what almost appears to be an alchemical process.

We hang out there for some time. I make friends with the watercolorist. Then we have a wild ride through the woods to our final destination, the general store. Inside I meet a delightful middle-aged lady whose store stocks everything from used clothing, to toiletry needs, snacks and esoteric books about The Work. There is also a nail tech and a hair stylist working there. Vineyard workers and visitors mingle here, some to buy a midmorning snack, others to find a rare piece of beautiful antique jewelry or a treasured book to take home. I buy a miniature pocket edition of Shakespeare's sonnets. Afterwards I walk back up the hill to The Lodge for lunch, which is served on a deck behind the building overlooking the vineyard slope.

That afternoon is my time. Wandering over the property, I climb up the hill above The Lodge to discover an orchard in a hollow behind three Ponderosa sentinels. The top of the hill reveals a panorama of snow capped Sierra Madre peaks looming a few miles away. It is Heaven.

My desire to live and work in this place outweighs all other considerations. It is a pure, simple, meditative life. You devote your entire existence to serving The School. Sure, people still have egos, but at least they are working on them. Students are not shy about 'photographing' someone (offering them an observation about themselves), making it difficult for the ego to hide. It is a 24/7/365 awareness training.

The commitment is total. You have to burn the boats (Cortez, 15th Century Spanish explorer, landed on the shores of what is now Mexico and had his men burn their ships before going off to conquer the Aztec empire). At this moment I am tied to a string that will soon pull me back to Philadelphia, my house, my career, and my marriage (my boats). Clearly the task is to free myself from these attachments, eliminating all possibility of a return to something I have outgrown.

Then, going 'on salary' is not something you decide to do. You have to earn an invitation. That means being in striking distance of the heart of the school. I have everything in place. My house is sold and a place is rented near Santa Barbara. In one week I will return to 'the world' to activate my final withdrawal from a nine-year encounter with a city I love. None of it matters to me now. Finding this place, and tasting my longing to join this community, does nothing but deepen my commitment to one day finding myself living on this sacred ground.

That evening is even more delicious than the first. There is a concert. Professional chamber musicians are regularly hired to perform at The Retreat. This evening it is a string quartet. The main room of The Lodge is cleared out. The hearth becomes a stage facing rows of chairs.

The room overflows with students who all listen with intensity and rapt attention then applaud gently, politely. The understanding is that the performance generates emotional energy, energy used to elevate consciousness. The intention of receiving this energy is to retain it, not spew it back with standing ovations and bravos. I imagine it must be strange for performers who base their worth on audience feedback. Afterward, there is wine and dinner into the late evening. All are fed as students take turns serving then being served.

The following Monday I present myself to the ranch manager ready for work. He is a craggy middle-aged man, a former law enforcement officer. His stern exterior appearance is offset by the warm heart energy emanating from his eyes. He gives me different work assignments each day.

Every day that week I work from dawn to dark like a person 'on salary', enjoying the camaraderie that naturally arises between people who share a common vision. I dig ditches, prune in the vineyard and wash dishes in the kitchen. At day's end there is wine on the patio and fine dining at The Lodge. While these may not sound like vacation activities, it is joyful for me, every bit of it. I am making some small contribution to the building of a special community.

That Friday, after breakfast I take a long look around the property, the vineyards, the gardens, the rolling hills, the mountain peaks, the valley fog below, the industrious students and bid it all a fond farewell, knowing I will return soon.

Driving past the "Private Monastery" sign, I head back down the wormhole to "normal" reality. Out past the general store, the little post office, and down the mountain into the fog- covered underworld. I return my grandmother's old Chevy to her in Sonoma and pick up my younger brother who is returning with me to Philadelphia to help with my move to Oxnard.

CHAPTER TEN

Uprooting

B ack in Philadelphia, I set about dismantling the life I created there. Returning to work, I give two weeks notice of my departure. I say goodbye to those friends I still have contact with, to my lovely neighborhood and release every attachment I developed to the life I once lived there. This is not a wrenching experience, but a joyful letting go. Nothing is difficult.

Everything falls easily into place. The house sale closes. I pay off my mortgage and all other debts, leaving me a bankroll to fund my adventure into the unknown. This is the moment I let go of the illusions of stability and certainty. Everything I built and nurtured here is washed clean. Career, home, social network, identity with place, all carefully dismantled, sold or given away.

Surface facts are, I am going off to attend a prestigious photography school to further develop my skills and start a new career, but as you will see, it is all a ruse to shake me loose from everything I hold dear. All the stagnation, the entropic misery I felt before meeting the school, disappears in my quest for consciousness. I feel new, raw, and alive! All that was my identity is dissolved, made meaningless in the face of the possibilities that lay ahead. Any "rational" person would think me mad. I had it all, home, career, marriage. To leave it all in pursuit of some ephemeral dream of higher consciousness would be considered sheer madness by most.

These words from Walt Whitman sum it up:

"One hour to madness and joy! O furious. O confine me not!
O to drink the mystic deliria deeper than any other man!
O to return to Paradise!
O to speed where there is space enough and air enough at last!
To be absolved from previous ties and conventions!
To find a new unthought-of nonchalance with the best of Nature!
To have the feeling today or any day I am sufficient as I AM.
To escape utterly from other's anchors and holds!
To feed the remainder of life with one hour of fullness and freedom!
With one brief hour of madness and joy."

A moving van is rented and filled with my worldly goods. It is July by now and the country is having a heat wave, so we decide to travel at night. We (me, my wife, brother and two cats) set out at dusk on the day of departure. I look back once in fond farewell to the place I called home and our little caravan (van and car) drive off into the sunset.

The journey is a blur of night driving and sleeping in motels during the day. My brother and I take turns driving the truck. Four days later finds us collapsed in an exhausted heap on the floor of our beach house in Oxnard.

CHAPTER ELEVEN

Southern California

I spend the summer and fall of '78 in limbo. The only thing that structures my life is The School. I am a member of the Santa Barbara Center where I attend Wednesday night meetings. On Fridays we travel to Los Angles to attend the meeting of that center.

It is a time of deepening study and involvement with the school community. I spend my days reading, observing my inner world and noting the connections I make between The Work and the behaviors of people around me.

The Los Angeles Center is housed in Liberace's (50's television star) old house with a swimming pool shaped like a grand piano. It is mainly comprised of older students who have settled into communal life. They hold jobs and have careers. Many have been in the school for several years and have lived at The Retreat. I begin to see that this too can be a place to settle into and live a routine existence. There is a part in all of us that seeks sameness, finding a sense of security in it. They settle for life in the school without appearing to look for the next step in their personal evolution. I vow to myself then to not let that happen to me.

I visit The Retreat and drive to the San Francisco Bay Area to attend big meetings led by The Teacher. He remains a remote figurehead for me at this stage, a tall full bearded man who has an other-worldly air about him, an emanation of some indefinable, something that is, nonetheless, observable. Students who have had close contact with him all have stories demonstrating his level of awareness, extraordinary intuition or profound memory for detail (a sign of presence).

Memory is considered an element of consciousness. In a moment of deep connection to the Now, all attention is here/now focused, "creating memory". It makes sense. If a person's consciousness is fragmented and only partially focused here/now, the events of the moment pass by unnoticed. We all have strong memories, but the more I study my own consciousness and that of others, the more I become aware that the critical factor is presence. Whatever we are there for, present to, is what we remember.

For most people trauma is the main memory maker. If you have ever been in an auto accident you know what I mean. A routine unremembered moment is transformed into a story you tell the rest of your life, by a break in the routine of automatic functioning. Why? Attention is completely captured by the traumatic event. Suddenly the something you were rushing toward ceases being important. Your entire focus is riveted on an unexpected discontinuity in the event stream of your personal life.

This is clearly brought home to me when I watch a televised interview with Christopher Reeves, the actor who once played Superman in the movies. Reeves, a horseback-riding enthusiast, is competing in a horse show, when he falls and breaks his neck, rendering him quadriplegic.

The interviewer says: "Chris, you were an excellent horseman. How come you fell?"

His reply stunned me.

He said: "My mind was on the next jump, I was not in the moment."

The next jump is a fraction of a second away in this fast moving sport. The lesson this story tells is staggering. Because he was not fully focused, Reeves suffered a severe, life-changing, trauma.

The most significant thing that occurs during my time in Southern California is the resolution, or the beginning of the dissolution, of my marriage. I have not mentioned much about this aspect of my personal life to this point. You may recall, when I first meet the school, I tell my wife this is the most important event of my life. From that moment on I work mightily to "sell" her The School, to get her to see the importance of the teaching, not only to justify my commitment, but also to persuade her to join me in this adventurous endeavor.

All to no avail. She calls The Retreat Disneyland, and undoubtedly secretly thinks I have lost my mind, something I am, in fact, consciously working to do. I try to involve her socially by getting dinner invitations from student couples. I work to persuade her of the power of the ideas and the necessity for inner work, but nothing will take. She does not have a Magnetic Centre, that inner draw to consciousness.

The more deeply I immerse myself in The Work, the less I am able to tolerate having a life outside it. The Santa Barbara teaching house enhances this feeling. The students have managed to rent a totally charming high-end mountain retreat, a cabin in the mountains perched on a cliff overlooking the town. The romantic ideal of living in this house while studying and applying ancient wisdom becomes more and more appealing.

While we remain good friends, our relationship grows more and more distant. I am consumed with The Work, it occupies most of my waking hours, but I cannot share this passion with my wife. As the space it occupies in my inner world grows, I have less and less to share with her.

My feelings finally come to a head at the end of the summer. I take her for a walk to the beach a few blocks from the house. I tell her I want to move into the teaching house, that I can no longer live in a relationship where I cannot share my passion, where that passion is not respected. This request shatters what is left of our relationship. We resolve to part, but she asks that I not leave until she finds work. Agreeing, I postpone my plans.

During one of my visits to The Retreat, the ranch manager comes over to me.

"The Teacher asked me to tell you something," he says. This sets my heart racing. "He gave you a ladder photograph for a student living in the Carmel centre. It is recommended you contact this person and visit him. You are on the same ladder as he and you may find it beneficial to meet him."

Being on somebody's 'ladder' is an indication that we are following similar paths. That person might in some way help me walk my path, or make different decisions.

I make a series of phone calls and eventually set up an appointment to meet him at a restaurant in Carmel Valley. When I ask how we will identify each other, he tells me to rely on my intuitive sense. I will just know. I will instinctively recognize him.

I arrive at the appointed time after a five hour drive, filled with an uncomfortable anticipation. The voice that greeted me on the phone was not incredibly friendly, but at least he agreed to the meeting. I get a table and closely scrutinize every face that enters, not knowing quite what to expect. Will he resemble me? What is it about him that puts me on his "ladder"?

Sure enough I recognize him when he finally arrives. He has student eyes. I discover what we have in common is a deep interest in the art of photography. He relates to me how he had a fantasy about being The School photographer. He was identified with this role. It was the source of his sense of self. The Teacher saw this attachment and took various actions to help him release it, one of which was to completely ignore his efforts to contribute his photographic talents to the school. The intuitive shocker for me is never having told anyone at The Retreat about my plans to attend photography school.

Identification is considered by The Work to be a major obstacle to the awakening of consciousness. It is a process whereby the mind invests a sense of identity into almost anything. We identify with possessions, social roles, careers, physical appearance, relationships, in short, with almost everything we encounter in our incarnated life, including, especially, the negatives.

In my current life as a psychotherapist, I once had a therapy client say to me:

"James, you want me to give up my pain? I wouldn't know who I was!"

The patient was identified with the overwhelming pain of her childhood and had been obsessing about it her entire life. The message from The Work is that none of this is true identity. All of these attachments stand in the way of self-realization, or enlightenment.

At the end of the conversation I realize my intent to attend the photography school is a roadblock to my evolutionary growth, and a distraction from my intention to live at The Retreat. My memory flashes back to that moment standing on the hillside above The Lodge burning with desire to be a part of that community.

I see that my intention to attend the photography school is a ruse my Soul has concocted to dislodge me from my deep connection to Philadelphia. The timing is exquisite. My efforts to gain admission to the school preceded my involvement with The Work, loosening my identification with my Philadelphia home, as well as providing my wife a logical reason for the move. I return to Santa Barbara that afternoon and withdraw my enrollment from the photography school.

CHAPTER TWELVE

Retreat "Vacation"

August 1978 celebrated my first anniversary in The Work. In that one year, I completely dismantled my life, sold my home, left a lucrative career and moved across the continent. My present to myself is to celebrate this dramatic change and spend two weeks at The Retreat. The performance center being built there is due to be completed and I want to be there for the completion. It will be a time of intense effort. Completions contain enormous energy. I want to have that experience.

One of the ways The School works to engender greater degrees of presence, and help students break automatic habits and patterns, is to offer them the opportunity to push beyond their self-imposed endurance limitations. It is a principle in The Work, to push your personal envelope.

The performance center, named Town Hall, offers such an opportunity. Let me be clear, anyone who undertakes to make such efforts does so voluntarily. There is never any coercion or manipulation. To make the deadline real, a formal concert, featuring professional classical musicians, is scheduled for the proposed completion date.

When I arrive the construction project is in full swing 24/7. My "vacation" consists of me pushing myself as hard as I can day and night, sleeping only when absolutely necessary, not even taking time off to go to dinner at The Lodge. The kitchen sends take-out containers for meals that are eaten on the construction site. Sometimes we go to breakfast in our work clothes after working through the night.

This kind of effort produces euphoria. The brain begins producing extraordinary endorphin levels. Every move you make has to arise out of conscious exertion, as the automatic response is to fall instantly asleep. The momentum is huge. The Teacher is constantly on site, encouraging us with the intensity of his presence. There is no frenetic pressure like you might find in ordinary life. In its place is still, focused, effort.

I have an extraordinary moment of elevated awareness one afternoon when, while taking a break, The Teacher arrives from his residence. When I see him, my automatic response is to get back to work, to appear busy, like the boss has arrived. Then I have what we call a Work "I". This is a thought that encourages one to go against one's automatic tendencies. It says:

"The Teacher wants you to work against Inner Considering. Keep taking your break."

(Inner Considering is the mind's automatic tendency to worry about what others are thinking of you, giving your power away to them.)

I remain still and watch as he approaches, endeavoring to root my full attention into the moment. As he draws closer he glances in my direction. A brilliant beam of light flashes out of his eyes, like sunlight sparkling through a diamond. It enters my vision and penetrates my Soul. I have never forgotten that moment.

The work intensifies as the concert date draws near. It is a race to the finish line. The night before the day of the opening I am glazing windows, setting heavy double pane panels into beautiful mahogany frames. It is 3:00 a.m. The work requires intense intentionality.

As I labor, a shadow falls over my workspace. I look up to discover The Teacher gazing down on me with a smile. The instant our eyes meet a single word powerfully enters my mind. "Father" it speaks. Nothing else happens. I do not move, neither does he. It is completely a mental event. I know immediately it has come from him. There is no doubt in my mind. His demeanor does not change. At the physical level it is a non-event, yet it creates powerful memory for me, a memory that remains to this day thirty-six years later.

We continue working through the dawn. No one goes to breakfast. To say the energy is intense would be an understatement. The windows I glaze are set in place that morning and the final preparations and cleanup begin. The concert is to start at seven that evening. At 6:30 p.m. we were still making the final adjustments, putting rows of chairs and bouquets of exquisite flowers in place as elegantly dressed students line up outside the door. The final touches are completed and the work crew exits out the back door the very same moment the front door opens to admit the concert attendees.

Exhausted, we migrate to the dressing room at The Lodge, shower, put on suits and dresses and go to the wine bar for refreshment. The students who worked so hard to finish are not invited to the first concert. We are to attend the following night.

As I stand outside on the patio sipping wine and talking to a friend, a wave of exhaustion comes over me. The emotional energy sustaining my participation in the project drains away, leaving me depleted. I have pushed myself way beyond what I thought possible. My body craves sleep, but emotionally I am wired, awake and irritable. The demon low self-esteem comes up to bite me in the behind. Is this what I came for? Am I crazy to work so hard on a vacation I paid for, and for what? I drink more wine.

I realize that coming to The Retreat and making all this effort is about the journey, the experience itself, not the completion. Once it is over, it is time to go to the next situation, letting go of any expectations of reaching some imagined epiphany, some transcendent nirvana I "thought" I would reach by exerting myself in this way. In any creative endeavor, it is the act of creation itself that is fulfilling. Once the project is done, it is time to move on. The journey is everything.

CHAPTER THIRTEEN

Moving Closer

On my return to Oxnard, I confront my next situation. I have been on vacation since moving from Philadelphia. I rented a beach house; purchased a new car; and took numerous trips, most of them to The Retreat. My bank account is dwindling and I need to do something about it.

In October I find work with a small insurance agency in Santa Barbara. I feel stalled. My need to be in Southern California ceased to exist once I let go of my intention to attend the photography school. My attention turns once more to the goal of moving closer to The Retreat. San Francisco seems to be the next likely step.

As I sit in my office one morning at work, my intuition instructs me to call an old business associate in Philadelphia. I tell him of my situation and my intention to move to San Francisco. He tells me that a mutual business acquaintance of ours has moved to Los Angeles and is the West Coast manager for AIG, a large insurance company, and is looking for a manager to run his San Francisco office. I contact him, interview and am hired. Not only am I hired, my wife is hired too to head Human Relations.

More and more things like this have been happening to me since I entered The Work. I connect to an indefinable something that is very supportive of me pursuing my personal evolution. It confirms for me my growing connection to a larger reality. The school calls it conscious influence. The theory is that once a person begins to awaken, to become more conscious, more aware, the invisible forces that surround us respond. Almost from the moment I formulate the thought to seek employment in San Francisco, a way opens to make it happen. Within weeks a moving company arrives at my Oxnard beach house, packs my worldly goods and ships them off to my new apartment in the Bay Area.

CHAPTER FOURTEEN

The San Francisco Centre

Life in Oxnard is drowsy, slow, and introspective. San Francisco, on the other hand, is vibrant, external and fast paced. One of the things I learn from The School is to trust in my ability to handle in-the-moment challenges, to take on new situations without knowing ahead how I will handle them, trusting I will be able to do so. I have had no direct experience managing an insurance company department. I exaggerated my expertise in the interview in the expectation that, if I proceed with confidence, without fear of failure, listening to my inner guidance, my intuition, I will succeed.

Taking this kind of risk brings you to the edge, where you are compelled to operate at maximum capacity, to be fully in-the-moment. I am again stretching, reaching beyond my mind's fear, operating from a state of presence, relying on my inner direction to guide me moment-by-moment, task-by-task. The experience is exhilarating.

I plunge into involvement with the Centre. The male director is my old leader from Philadelphia, the physician. He is conservative, soft spoken, focused, and low-keyed. The female director is a legend in The School, a complete opposite. She is a wild, out spoken, outside the box, charismatic leader. I seek out involvement and ask for a job, something I can do to support the centre.

My first assignment is something I would normally refuse, but I am determined to say "yes" to every opportunity. I am asked to be the center bouncer.

To maintain membership in the school each student is required to make teaching payments, which are, at a minimum, 10% of gross income. There are, of course, especially in a centre with hundreds of students, those who fail to make their payments on a timely basis. When they fall two months behind, they are not allowed to attend meetings. Someone has to enforce that rule. That someone is me. Each meeting the centre bookkeeper presents me with a list of those who are behind. I am to find and encounter them, reminding them of their need to make payments in order to remain in the school, and, if they are too far behind, to ask them to leave the meeting.

I resolve to be compassionate, understanding, and yet firm. It is intensive work on Inner Considering, the mind's fear of what others will think. I work to make each encounter a positive experience. When I engage a student on this matter I use it as an opportunity to make practical use of Work ideas. I engage in deep inner listening to bring forth the words, facial expressions and tone of voice that will be most appropriate to that individual. The results at times amaze me. I even make a friend or two in the process.

Every other weekend I travel to The Retreat, where I present myself to the farm manager for work. I learn, from speaking to other students, that if I want to make a strong positive impression, I should visit on a consistent basis and find a steady job to return to each time.

Within a month such an opportunity occurs. I am asked to give the trash collector a weekend off every two weeks. Contrary to how it may sound, I actually enjoy the work. I drive a truck around to all the locations on The Retreat collecting trash, and am able to see what everybody is doing.

So, now I am set. During the week I am a high-flying business executive and on the weekends I collect garbage. What a contrast! This series of events aligns with all the other odd "coincidences" I have increasingly experienced since joining the school. There will be others as this story unfolds. In a certain way it verifies the theory that, when an individual decides to opt for spiritual evolution in lieu of the material world, they attract the attention of the unseen world, called Higher Forces by The School. It seems appropriate that I am given the "lowly" task of collecting trash in the face of having just acquired a fancy executive job. I am learning to release my identification with my function or job, and understand that every task is essential. Taking out the garbage is as essential as making executive decisions. Cessation of either activity will eventually bring an organization to a halt. They are thus equally important.

My life continues to accelerate. I am eventually taken off the bouncer job for the San Francisco Centre and asked to coordinate and lead prospective student meetings. This means that, in addition to attending regular meetings, I am to facilitate the gatherings where new students are introduced to The School.

Life is intense on every level, leaving little room for personal matters, like my marriage, which is essentially over. My wife moved to San Francisco with me to work for the same company and we continue to live together. My involvement with the school is so consuming, however, we rarely see each other. We are simply roommates. My eye is set on the prize of being invited to live and work at The Retreat. Even with the advent of the best position I have ever had in the insurance business, it pales in comparison to the intensity of my intentions for conscious evolution.

That spring our company puts on an employee retreat at a hotel in Monterey. My wife has a company friend who is going also and I invite him to ride with us. They both enjoy playing tennis and spend the weekend with each other. It is the beginning of what I hope for, a new relationship for her, taking her attention in another direction. I do what I can to facilitate that relationship. Everything is falling into place for my departure. All I need now is that invitation and I will disappear into the foothills, having divested myself of all worldly connections and distractions.

One day in June, while visiting The Retreat, the ranch manager approaches me.

"James. I have shared with The Teacher my observations of your consistent efforts. He instructed me to ask you to come on 'salary'."

My immediate internal reaction was resistant.

"I'm not ready!" it says.

Now I see it was fear. This would be the final release of my material existence, my death to the outer world. I asked for and was granted six months to put my affairs in order. I agree to go on 'salary' in January the following year, and am told I will work in the vineyard.

My heart is leaping in my throat. I have succeeded. Soon I would be a member of this very special community. My Soul is delighted, my ego, not so much. I have been at The Retreat in the winter. The thought of working outdoors in cold, fog, rain and sometimes snow is daunting to my body. For the most part, though, I proceed with my preparations in excited anticipation of my imminent escape from ordinary life.

CHAPTER FIFTEEN

A Huge Shock—Mr. Wright

A few months after my arrival at the San Francisco Centre, a female student approaches me during a meeting intermission. She offers me friendship, having learned I do not live in a teaching house. I begin visiting her and going out to coffee a few nights a week. This is not a romance, but a friendship. I do not buy her drinks or meals. We just meet, have an occasional drink, and enjoy discussing The Work. Occasionally we travel to The Retreat together.

One weekend in August we make that journey and stay late Sunday evening to enjoy a concert and dinner at The Lodge before beginning our return journey. It is after midnight when we set out. She volunteers to drive my car.

Around 2:00 a.m. we are cruising down the Berkley freeway at 55 mph, the national speed limit at the time. The road is completely without traffic. As we pass an on-ramp, I notice a parked highway patrol car. The officer appears to be intently watching the empty road.

A little further down the road, I am leaning on the center counsel reciting poetry to her to keep her awake when we are struck from behind with tremendous force. My head slams down into the counsel where it strikes an edge, partially ripping off my ear, stunning me. The car is forced off the road by the impact and bounces down a steep grassy slope.

I regain consciousness to the smell of gasoline. I am dazed. For a moment, I do not know where we are or what is occurring.

"Where are we? What just happened?" I shakily ask. "What hit us, a truck?"

"We are on the way home from The Retreat," she replies. "Just before the crash I looked in the mirror and saw head lights way back, a mile or so. A minute later, just before they hit us, I looked again and they were a few feet away."

In deep shock I crawl out the passenger door and go around to extract my friend from the driver's seat. She says her back hurts and she is afraid to move. I insist, citing my fear the gasoline smell will become an explosion. Together we crawl up the slope to distance ourselves from the car.

My first thought is: "If you are ever going to do The Work, now is the time."

There are no resistant emotions, no "This isn't happening!" I feel strangely calm, entirely focusing on the needs of the moment.

I look back at my crumpled car: "So much for that identification," I say to myself. (I had been pondering whether to take my car with me when I move to The Retreat or sell it.)

"We need to find help." I say.

As I speak, flashing lights appear at the top of the embankment.

Curious, I think. How did they get here so soon? How did they even know this has happened? Then I remembered seeing the patrol car.

Moments later we are surrounded by EMTs and highway patrol officers. I am bandaged up. She is gently lifted onto a back-board. We are loaded into an ambulance and taken to a nearby hospital. As this is happening, I notice a second ambulance apparently tending to the other driver.

My friend and I are placed into a room and left alone while the ER staff works on him, who is apparently in worse shape. She starts to shake. Some sort of hypothermia is setting in. I can't find a blanket, so I crawl up on the gurney and cover her with my body, projecting heat from my solar plexus until she stabilizes.

Later, I go out into the hall to look for help and encounter one of the highway patrolmen. He is looking at me curiously, watching me closely, seemingly puzzled by my behavior. The blow has catapulted me into an elevated state of consciousness. One of the intentions of The Work is to learn to transform the energy of shocks into higher awareness. I apparently am not behaving like an ordinary accident victim. Oddly enough, I am feeling a sense of gratitude for what the shock has produced in me.

I walk to the doorway of the next treatment room and watch as they work to save the life of the person who hit us. The officer closely watches me. He asks me how I feel and seems curious to know why I am not enraged at the perpetrator. He asks my relationship to my traveling companion. I guess he is concerned I might attack the man.

I take him aside and ask him to give me the information on the driver. I find out his name is Mr. Wright. The reason help arrived so soon is he murdered a family of four a few hours earlier and the authorities were in hot pursuit. He was driving a large American car flat out, around 125 mph, when he struck us. We actually stopped him, enabling his apprehension. That explained the patrol car I saw just before the accident.

A while later I am taken to a small operating room where I meet an Oriental physician, a plastic surgeon, who sews my ear back on so precisely that today there is no scar. Meanwhile, my friend is taken to x-ray where it is determined she has suffered a compression fracture of one of her vertebrae. I find her in traction hours later after my surgery. She is groggy from pain medication.

Shortly after dawn, I call a student couple I know in San Francisco, advise them of the situation, asking them to retrieve me. What is odd about this is I do not call my wife for help. My thoughts at the time are that I would be more likely to find a calm head with students. I feel my wife will not cope well and do not want to burden her. My mind is incredibly clear. The elevated awareness created by the shock of the accident persists after the medical shock wears off. I feel euphoric, focused and clear, with no resistance to what has happened. It is an alteration of consciousness that lasts for weeks.

The student couple picks me up at the hospital and takes me to breakfast. I am still wearing my bloodstained sport coat and dress shirt. It feels like a badge of honor. Something special has happened to me. During the meal the euphoria takes over. I am unable to contain the energy. I babble on and on to them until I notice they are just staring at me. I realize my ego is using the energy. I pause and refocus.

They take me to the teaching house where I pick up my friend's car and drive home to tell my wife what happened. Finally I rest. I sleep all day and awake still in an elevated state. That night I go to a large Bay Area meeting with my bandaged ear, and participate.

That week I make daily trips to the hospital to visit my friend. The shock has bonded us. There is intimacy in shared trauma. We both feel brushed by the wings of Death. Our conversations are all around how to continue using The Work to transform the shock into consciousness, and the significance of the accident. In the realm of conscious awareness there are no accidents. Everything has a meaning and purpose. We spend hours discussing what we think it all means.

A week later I drive behind the ambulance bringing her back to the teaching house, where I have arranged a hospital bed in a private room off the kitchen. I feel responsible. I want to take care of her. We become a couple. I move out of my apartment and into the teaching house, sleeping on the floor of the breakfast nook on a futon. One more step closer toward complete release of the life I am intent on leaving behind.

My relationship to and perception of every aspect of my life is changed by this event, especially coming so soon before my anticipated departure from life in the world. I continue in a kind of free floating, detached, euphoria. All the things of life I "cared" about are no longer important to me. A time will come soon where I will no longer have to deal with them. I meet my responsibilities without the usual stress or worry, while I continue to make preparations for departure. My wife is now in her new relationship. We see each other occasionally at work. I spend all my free time with my friend. We both feel we are in a 'fated' situation, one ordained by higher forces, giving the "accident" and the relationship enormous symbolic significance.

CHAPTER SIXTEEN

Final Preparations

I continue with my departure preparations, letting go of worldly goods, freeing myself of their burden. My wife agrees to keep my furniture. I give my photography darkroom away to my brother and his wife. My friend's brother, an Alaskan bush pilot, comes to visit. I give him my motorcycle and leathers, the costuming of my previous ego. I have been a serious art photographer for fourteen years, another old ego. I destroy all the prints and negatives I have created, my intention being to release all connection to the life I lived prior to entering The Work.

Part of my furniture is an antique round oak dining room table and chairs. Several of the chairs have been in need of repair for several years, one of those things I never got around to doing. But I hung onto them. I loved the set. As I am cleaning my belongings out of my old home, my wife confronts me with the chairs.

"You've been saying you would fix them forever! You're leaving! Do something with them. I don't want them around."

I go downstairs to the storage closet, pull out the chairs, take them out to the sidewalk, find a sledgehammer, and began to violently destroy them. Releasing my attachment to them with each hammer blow. Oddly enough, just at that moment, a student friend appears.

"What are you doing?"

When I explain, he grins, "Let me try it."

I watch as he gleefully shatters my old attachments. After years of procrastination, after having carried them from Philadelphia to Oxnard to San Francisco, I am finally letting go of something I would never find the time to do. I am releasing more than stuff, I am releasing old personalities, false selves, making space for new creations, new selves I will consciously manifest. I have dental work done and buy clothing for my new life, work clothes and a tuxedo. There will be frequent occasions at The Retreat where the tuxedo will be useful, more than I currently know.

By early October I am ready to go, though still having trepidations about winter in the vineyard. One weekend, while visiting The Retreat, my old centre director from Santa Barbara comes over to me. He is now working there as the purchasing manager.

"The ranch manager told me you are coming on salary in January."

"Yes. Working in the vineyard will be my assignment."

"How would you like to work in the office? We need a driver, now."

"NOW!? Well," I ponder, "Two weeks notice will be necessary."

"We can wait that long, but no longer. OK! The job is yours. Come over to the office this afternoon. We will show you around."

Suddenly my leisurely departure turns into a whirlwind of activity. Monday morning I board a plane to the Los Angeles office of my boss, unannounced, and give him two weeks notice. My story is that a vineyard/winery that I have invested in for years has asked me to come be their purchasing agent. I have been very successful in my ten months there, and he is a friend. He is, of course, sad to see me leave, but I assure him my assistant is now fully capable of assuming my position.

Tuesday through Thursday I work out the details of my business, passing responsibility to my chief underwriter. I recommend him to replace me. Thursday the president of the AIG subsidiary I work for visits the San Francisco office, a long planned event. I arrange a lunch for him with the heads of the major brokerage firms, along with some his old business friends.

It begins late and turns into a party with about twelve people at the table. After several rounds of drinks, while we are ordering our meal, the president says:

"James, since you're going off to be in the wine business, why don't you order the wine."

I have had a few drinks. I feel a twinkle in my eye as I look at my successor and order two bottles of the most expensive wine on the menu. It is a big hit, and we have several more rounds of the two-bottle order as the evening progresses. Each round costs $100. Finally the check comes and I watch with inward amusement as his eyes fall on the bottom line. His pupils dilate. He consults his friend next to him. They locate the cause. Not once do they look in my direction. I can see the wheels turning as he signs the check without flinching.

If I were not planning to leave I would never pull such a prank. Ultimately it does not hurt him and we both find amusement in it. He takes me aside the following morning at the office, and, with a little smile, tells me how we took the entire staff of a large brokerage house out to dinner. He obviously made an adjustment to his expense account report.

That weekend I stay home, making final preparations. I visit my family in Sonoma, advising them of my departure. They are accepting of my decision to leave, though they probably think I am loony.

The final week I pay all my bills for the last time, clearing all my debts, pick up my new tux and shop for work clothes and boots, outfitting myself for my next adventure. I am left with a few thousand dollars to supplement the $75 a month I will be earning "on salary".

My final evening is strange and empty. I no longer have a wife, a job or a place to live. My friend, now my relationship, is invited to a house dinner being given for some visiting student dignitary, but I am not invited. I feel alone. I have released all my connections to this outer world and am headed for what almost seems like another dimension. My friend is still recovering from her broken back and plans to stay in San Francisco for a while. We talk about her joining me later at The Retreat.

Saturday morning I load my clothes and books into the back seat of her car and set off on a one-way trip to a new life. The ride seems more significant than usual. I savor every moment of it. I have arranged to rent a small room in an out-building of a house owned by students. I arrive there, unload and put away my belongings. There are concerts on both nights. I wear my new tuxedo each time to celebrate my new life.

I have done it! Completely vanished from the world. I am to be found only by those who know of this place. I stand in The Lodge mezzanine Sunday evening in my tux, watching all of the visitors head home. Someone comes over to me to ask me how it feels, watching them leave. I am in awe. I no longer have anywhere to go. The Retreat is my home.

BEING THERE

CHAPTER SEVENTEEN

Beginning My New Life

M onday morning I rise at 5:00 a.m. and drive to The Lodge for breakfast. I choose a book from the library and join the breakfast club, a hardy few who rise early to have a meditative meal before engaging in the day's activities. A fire is burning in the huge stone fireplace that dominates one wall of the dining room. A different member of the club prepares the meal each day.

The workday begins at 7:00 a.m. Just before I leave to go to the office, I am approached by the vineyard manager, a ruddy muscular fellow with red hair and a no nonsense personality. He tells me his truck needs a starter and wants to make sure I pick it up on my travels that day.

I drive off the property, down the hill two miles to a private home that has been converted into office space. The two-car garage is turned into a large accounting room, the living room houses reception and telephone switchboard. The school's corporate secretary, a former stockbroker, and the treasurer, a former CFO of a large corporation, occupy one bedroom. Another bedroom houses a mainframe computer, and the master bedroom is the purchasing office, with three desks and a table crammed into a tiny space.

The purchasing staff consists of the manager, a dispatcher, a secretary, and a driver. The dispatcher takes me aside and gives me a list of vendors with their addresses and a map of the city of Sacramento marked with the vendor locations. I am told no one has made this trip in two weeks and there is a considerable backlog. No pressure.

My mission that day is to drive the seventy miles to Sacramento, find all the vendors and collect the orders placed there. I am to make frequent calls back to the dispatcher who will coach me through whatever challenges I encounter and add items to my already long list. The secretary gives me a driver's wallet with two hundred dollars cash to be used for the occasional cash purchases. I am allotted five dollars for lunch. She lets me know I need to balance my receipts and whatever cash remains, and will be personally charged for any discrepancies. She is an i-dotter, t-crosser, detail oriented type of person. I am then taken outside to an aging yellow Chevrolet pickup with a pipe rack, and sent on my way.

I drive off the property and head down the mountain, plunging into the winter fog like a submerging submarine, venturing out from Shangri-La to bring home needed supplies. I feel important and alive. As I wind down the twisting road, my thoughts flash back just three days to the life I left in San Francisco. No longer am I office bound to labor for a multi-billion dollar international corporation, a cog in an immense wheel. I am also no longer privy to a large salary and an unlimited expense account. The contrast is extreme. I have traded it all in for $75 a month plus food and an old Chevy pickup.

The entire day is spent going from warehouse to warehouse, collecting plumbing and electrical supplies, building materials, irrigation equipment, tools and spare parts. I am the visible representative of The School, a curious mystery to most of the vendors who are all quite happy to have a share of the $1,000,000 + spent annually. My learning curve is negotiating the highways and byways of Sacramento, and how to effectively pile as much into and onto the truck as possible. From 9:00 a.m. to 6:00 p.m. I labor thus, racing to successfully complete the list. By the end of the day the truck is so loaded down you can hardly see it.

The auto parts store is the last stop on the list. I pull up to the door at 6:15, fifteen minutes past closing time. I look through the door, and bang on it to get their attention. They just point to the clock. First day on the job and I am in trouble. The vineyard manager had been emphatic about the starter for his truck. Now, already, I am in hot water with him. I call my dispatcher, who makes it out to be no big deal, and head home. He instructs me to meet him at the office in the morning to show me the unloading procedure. It is 8:00 p.m. by the time I return to The Retreat, exhausted. I drive to the lodge for food, eat and retire.

The next morning I am at The Lodge for breakfast and the subsequent vineyard workers meeting. The vineyard manager is in my face immediately.

"You got my starter, right?" he demands.

"The list was too long," I reply, "I missed closing time by fifteen minutes", returning his intense gaze. "We will get it today in Marysville."

I am working internally not to identify with my failure, not to be defensive or make excuses. I can see he is working internally also. We glare at each other momentarily in front of the entire crew, then shift. A friend of mine, The Retreat gardener, who I know from Santa Barbara, chimes in with a grin:

"Off to a good start, eh, James?"

This is the beginning of what I come to call the "where is my ...". Being the guy who brings back what is needed is a two-edged sword. When I succeed, I am Santa Claus. I receive smiles and thanks. When I fail, I am the disappointer, and receive frowns and frustration.

I drive off to the office in my overloaded truck and pick up the dispatcher. We drive back to the property and pull up to a sheet metal shed behind the barn. Inside is a long rough counter measured off into boxes labeled for the various departments, i.e. plumbing, electrical, shop, vineyard, winery construction, maintenance...etc. Each item is off loaded, checked off on a master list and placed in the box of the appropriate department. Any discrepancies are noted. All in all, a very tedious process.

As we work, people filter in to pick up their materials and either express their delight in finally receiving their requested items, or their frustration with having to continue waiting. Afterward we return to the office, complete paperwork, matching receipts to purchase orders, and compile a list for that day's trip to Marysville, a county center 30 miles down the hill.

This is the pattern: weekdays away all day, returning late, unloading, to do it all again the next day. Monday, Wednesday, and Friday I go to Marysville. Tuesday and Thursday to Sacramento. The pace is demanding and exhausting. I find out from my coworkers I have signed up for the biggest burnout job there. I am told no one lasts longer than eighteen months. People are already taking bets on how long I will last. I feel challenged and daunted by this information. I burned all my bridges to get here and am determined to stay as long as possible. There is no going back.

About 45 days into the transition, I have a strange experience. I am in Sacramento when I call in to the dispatcher. I have taken a tire from The Teacher's Rolls Royce in to be repaired. The Teacher calls the dispatcher, instructing him to ask me to bring him the tire in San Francisco that afternoon where he will be having dinner at Ernie's restaurant, a high end Italian eatery.

The irony is that I was in that same restaurant barely two months ago. My chief underwriter took me there for a farewell dinner my last week on the job. It feels surreal as I roll the tire down the street to the waiting Rolls. The last time I was at this restaurant I was a sharp suited patron. Now I am a work booted outsider looking in. The contrast is profound. It is as though I have stepped through the looking glass and am looking back through, unable to turn back. I have no regrets, no desire to return, just a strange feeling of disconnection.

Even though I am operating in a haze of exhaustion, I continue to feel exhilarated just in the knowledge that I am part of something very special, mystical even. The place itself is stunningly beautiful. The school teaches that beauty is food, the consumption of which feeds the growth of higher states of awareness. So, in the midst of struggling with exhaustion, I drive to The Lodge at dawn just in time to catch wild deer grazing on the mist-shrouded lawn. Daily experiences like this raise my spirits and energize me to keep moving, placing one foot before the other, literally. It gives a whole new meaning to the phrase: living in-the-moment.

My life has a simplicity I have never experienced as an adult. No mortgage, bills, feared bosses, just the simplicity of performing the task at hand, and the satisfaction of playing a role in the building of a conscious community.

There are concerts every weekend, beautiful music that feeds the Soul. Sunday is a day off. Brunch is served at The Lodge. We dress for the occasion and sip Mimosas on the patio looking down the vineyard slope. There are always visiting students from all over the planet to provide stimulating conversation and fresh perspectives, altogether a precious experience.

CHAPTER EIGHTEEN

Marriage

On occasional weekends I drive to San Francisco to visit my girl friend. Our relationship continues to develop and in the spring of 1980 she moves to The Retreat. We take a room together in the house I live next to and begin talking of marriage. We consider the accident a fated event that has bound us together.

Her arrival brings me into the social whirl of the community. She is friends with an elderly gregarious woman who is close to The Teacher. This woman is The Retreat's queen mother and holds court at The Lodge every weekend. Everything about her is large, flamboyant, and grandiose. She routinely invites us to her table on weekends after concerts. We spend time with her at her home. We are her favorite couple.

That spring my girl friend's parents and mine come to visit The Retreat. We meet them in Marysville and take them on a tour of the property, then back to town for lunch. Her parents offer to give us a wedding in Alaska, inviting my parents and offering to pay their way. They decline.

My father is fascinated to find out that her father is a gold miner there, romanticizing the occupation. Her father quips back: "There's a difference between looking for gold and mining it. One is a romantic search, the other is hard work." I cannot fail to connect his comment to my own search for esoteric knowledge and the hard work entailed in developing higher consciousness.

My fiance is a goldsmith, a jeweler. She designs, creates and repairs jewelry for the students. She is a consummate artist. She creates our wedding rings. We become something of an "it" couple. In June we are married in the Tea Room of Town Hall on a Saturday afternoon. The concert that evening is in our honor and we have dinner on the grassy knoll outside The Lodge while the Irish actress with a lilting voice reads Shakespeare's sonnet Forty-Four.

"If the dull substance of my flesh were thought,
Injurious distance would not stop my way;
For then, despite of space, I would be brought,
From limits far remote, where thou dost stay.
No matter then, although my foot did stand,
Upon the farthest earth removed from thee;
For nimble thought can jump both sea and land,
As soon as think the place where he would be.
But ah, thought kills me, that I am not thought,
To leap large lengths of miles when thou art gone,

But that so much of earth and water wrought,
I must attend time's leisure with my moan;
Receiving naught by elements so slow
But heavy tears, badges of either's woes.

There are several meanings to this work. On the surface it is an ode to an absent lover. At another level, it is the spiritual seeker's lament to their divine Self, the absent "thou", and an expression of the desire to acquire the transformative powers of higher consciousness.

In August that year we travel to Alaska to visit her family who give us a wedding in an Alaskan ghost town named Flat. Her father and uncle are gold miners. They were raised in Flat when it was a thriving gold rush community in the mid 1900s. Her father went off to college to become a geologist and returned to invent a successful method of re-mining the tailing piles (piles of discarded ore). They spend their summers in Flat working the mine and winter at their home in Seattle.

We fly out of San Francisco to Anchorage past a still erupting Mt. St. Helens. Her bush pilot brother meets us there and loads us into a four-seat, single engine Cessna. The massive Alaskan range looms above the city, a towering wall of granite, ice and flowing glaciers.

"Looks a little heavy," he comments as he piles the baggage into the tiny high winged aircraft.

"I want you to lean forward when I say so as we take off. It moves the center of gravity forward. We need to move as much weight forward as possible to attain lift off," he casually says. I find the remark quite alarming. I look at the tiny plane and then at the towering mountains. I had flown private before, even had a license at one time, but am wishing there is something a little more substantial to take us over that looming wall of stone and ice.

We taxi onto the runway. He revs the engine and we roll down the concrete strip slowly gaining speed. Three quarters of the way down he shouts: "Now!! Lean forward as far as you can!!"

We bounce into flight just as the end of the strip disappears beneath us. It is the wildest plane ride I have ever had. Ahead rises a solid wall of granite, snow, glacial ice and razor sharp ridges that soar thousands of feet above the town. He banks the plane, heading toward a break in the wall. He tells us:

"This plane cannot fly high enough to go over the Range. We must go through it. There are a series of passes that will take us there."

I look down at the raw, savage, wilderness below us. No roads, no buildings, just forested mountains that transition into rivers of ice punctuated with pools of brilliant blue glacier water and unforgiving peaks of jagged stone. Nothing stands between us and this savage wasteland. Just a few bits of sheet metal and plastic, pulled along by a tiny four-cylinder engine.

Weaving through mountain passes, between soaring peaks, we are given a custom tour of The Range, winding through a connecting series of passes, circling magnificent peaks. In the middle of circling a peak at close range, the engine door flies open. Without any sense of alarm in his voice, her brother begins to tell us it might be necessary to land somewhere to close the door. He instructs us to begin searching the ground for a suitable landing site. His tone of voice is casual, as if this kind of event is no big deal, or he is messing with us. I am not feeling so nonchalant. In fact, I am rather frightened.

"Is it that big a deal, that little door being open? Can't we just continue without stopping to fix it?" I say.

The idea of landing in wild terrain and taking off again is inconceivable.

"OK," he smiles, "I guess it can wait."

The jagged peaks dissolve into a rolling plateau of forested hills, streams and valleys. We descend to a few hundred feet, enjoying the beautiful terrain unfolding below us. The pilot is watching the ground carefully. Suddenly he banks the plane into a steep dive shouting, "Look! There's a grizzly bear. Watch what happens when we buzz him."

He pulls the plane sharply out of the dive just over the bear, which begins running across the landscape in a panic. He laughingly tells us a story about how a pilot had once done this and then crashed. The bear he buzzed followed him and attacked the plane, killing the pilot who had survived the crash. I realize I am experiencing bush pilot entertainment.

Eventually we fly past a small abandoned town. It looks like a Hollywood set for a Western, one story wood buildings with fake two story fronts and a church at one end. "There it is!" my fiance shouts over the engine noise. "Flat, Alaska, a boom town of 6000 in 1914. Now it has 3 permanent residents. We're getting married in that church."

We fly a few miles past the town and circle a large open pit mine surrounded by huge tailing piles. At one end is a large dredge hoisting material out of the piles and dumping it into a long slush box with flowing water. An enormous bulldozer is pushing the material down into the dredge site. Both operators wave as we fly over.

Further down the stream we circle her family's mining camp, a collection of tired wooden buildings perched on the edge of a river bed, and land on a gravel strip at the stream's edge.

Nowhere during the flight do I see infrastructure. No roads, bridges, not even dirt trails. The interior landscape, past the Alaskan range, consists of unspoiled forests and streams. Everything is flown in, including the dredge and bulldozer. Driving is strictly local.

Upon landing, I discover the forest trees are pigmies, not even six feet tall. It is Nature's bonsai garden. I am told this is a consequence of permafrost. The ground is permanently frozen eighteen inches down, severely limiting root structure, naturally stunting the trees growth. In mid-August, the temperature is in the fifties at mid-day. The sun never sets, but orbits the horizon at a mid-morning, mid-afternoon altitude. I have been warned to bring lots of mosquito repellant. The moist climate supports clouds of these tiny irritants that constantly orbit us everywhere we go.

Conversation at dinner that night has a strange twist to it. My fiance's father and brother have some ancient feud going on, the source of which eludes me now. They stopped talking years ago. Though they work together, they never communicate directly. Necessary communications are conducted through her mother.

"Please tell your husband to pass the potatoes," her uncle mutters.

"Tell my brother we need to start at 7:00 a.m. tomorrow." The reply would come.

It is all done with surface civility and an underlying tension that has gone on for so long it is taken for granted.

The next day I am taken on a tour of the mining operation. The dredge and bulldozer are enormous. It is stunning to me that they could have been flown in to the little gravel landing strip in the riverbed in pieces and assembled there.

Later we drive into town to see the church. A strange incident takes place on the way.

The road is no more than a one lane rutted car trail. We are bouncing along in a pickup when we round a curve and are confronted with a rapidly approaching vehicle just a few feet away. A head-on collision seems inevitable. An intensity takes a hold of me that seems to project an energy out of the center of my chest, accompanied by a powerful emotion that refuses to accept the reality of a head-on collision. Both vehicles lurch in opposite directions and return to the ruts unharmed. No one even seems to notice. Perhaps this is a common occurrence for them.

The church, which is finely crafted like a ship, is tight and intact. Pine boughs and other decorations taken from the surrounding forest are being hung around the room. A portable generator is set up to electrify the building and a stereo system is being installed. I am introduced to a collection of Eskimos and miners, many of whom had been my fiance's childhood friends. It begins to dawn on me that this is the social event of the season in a small community, the members of which are scattered over hundreds of square miles of Alaskan wilderness.

Later that afternoon a Southern Baptist missionary flies in from an Eskimo village on Alaska's west coast. He is another classic type, a large, flamboyant, bearded man who spends his life bringing the word of God to the heathens. We hold a brief rehearsal in the church and have dinner that evening at the camp.

Next morning my fiance and I don our finery, I my tuxedo, she her white gown, and we squeeze into her father's pickup to return to the church. What greets us is the most eclectic group of people I'd ever seen at a wedding. The family's Eskimo friends are all decked out in their colorful cultural costumes. Their miner friends are dressed in new work boots and plaid shirts. As I step out of the pickup in my tuxedo and black patent leather shoes I momentarily feel over dressed. Then I shift into the moment, realizing I and my fiance are the main attraction.

The miners are loud and boisterous mountain men, huge thick chested specimens of humanity with flashy gold nugget jewelry ready to party.

The event goes smoothly, the Baptist minister delivers a touching traditional Christian ceremony that is followed by a hard drinking party. Everybody in this culturally diverse crowd knows and likes each other. They appreciate this opportunity to get together and celebrate our wedding.

The following morning I fly two-hours with my fiance's father to Fairbanks, where he has some business. Small planes are the cars of this wild untamed land and distances of hundreds of miles are the local neighborhood. As with any small community, everyone knows each other and nothing is hidden or sacred.

CHAPTER NINETEEN

The Honeymoon

The next day we began our honeymoon with another wild plane ride. The sky is a rare clear blue and so, with a twinkle in his eye, my wife's brother proposes we take a different route back through the Alaskan Range, one that is not approved by the local aviation authority for its riskiness, so he cannot file a flight plan. The route entails flying into a canyon straight toward a towering peak and making a right turn into another canyon too narrow to reverse direction once entered. The risk is that the narrow canyon could be fog bound and there is no way to see if it is clear until you are in it. The reward for the risk is some of the most magnificent scenery in the world.

I am riding in the front seat as we fly toward what seems to be certain collision with the soaring granite wall in front of us. At the last possible moment, the canyon wall on the right opens to reveal the pass. We bank to find clear sailing. No fog. My prayers were answered.

The canyon narrows even further as we fly into it, rising to meet the watershed of the range, the place where the water begins to flow toward the sea. We emerge from the canyon into a high valley surrounded by jagged icy peaks. Below is an emerald green meadow with a lake in the center. Two wild white swans decorate the water. It is breath taking beyond description. He circles the lake, touring the high valley.

On the far side, a tiny stream trickles out toward the sea down a canyon. It rapidly grows into a raging stream as the canyon widens, dropping steeply down the seaward side. Huge boulders and tall pines dominate the winding canyon. Bald eagles perch on the branches or tend their nests in the canyon walls. The pilot keeps the plane low, inside the canyon, banking and turning to follow its twisting course, giving us a magnificent close up view of the wild life. It is the experience of a lifetime, creating conscious memory.

We round a bend in the canyon and come out above a small plateau just in time to spook a huge grizzly bear standing in the stream. He runs toward the cover of the forest, water flying everywhere. The canyon widens into a valley that sweeps down to the Anchorage airport where he expertly sets his frail craft down. It is an unforgettable experience, definitely the best present I have ever received.

We board a plane bound for Juneau, the state capital, located near the coast of the Alaskan panhandle, arriving late afternoon. It is a town of winding streets built into forested mountainsides next to an inland waterway. We are here to take an overnight cruise the next day into Glacier Bay National Park.

We board a small tour boat holding 50-60 passengers that carries us through the inter-coastal waterways into a bay of Orcas and icebergs. The peak of the trip is an evening at the face of a large glacier, at the head of the bay. We watch huge chunks of ice fall off the face into the freezing waters to become floating islands, icebergs. The trip is punctuated with whale and eagle sightings.

Back at Juneau the next afternoon, we board a historic train for a ride through the Canadian Yukon Territory to Vancouver, British Columbia. From there we take a ferry across the sound to Victoria where we check in at a themed hotel staying in the Queen Victoria suite, complete with four-poster bed. Our objective here is a visit to the world-renowned Butchart Gardens, where we spend the entire next day drinking in the exquisite beauty, verifying the school's theory that beauty is indeed high vibrational food for the mind and the soul.

The following morning we travel to the Seattle airport where we board a plane for San Francisco and drive back to The Retreat.

CHAPTER TWENTY

Settling In

In reflecting on these experiences now, thirty years later, I see that I deconstructed one world only to construct another. All the things I left behind I reinvented. A few months after returning to The Retreat, my new wife and I move into a small housing unit designed and built by a local resident to take advantage of the burgeoning student population.

The owner is a local character that owns and maintains a zoo on his property, the key focus of which is his pet mountain lion. I go there one day on some tenant business, but no one answers my knock on the door. Right across from the door is a small caged in yard with a low shelter. As I turn my attention toward the enclosure, the mountain lion springs out of the shelter onto its roof and strikes a menacing posture, fierce yellow eyes glaring at me. A few strands of dog wire separate us. It is one of those moments of full attention here/now. I have never been this close to a predator that might consider making a meal of me. I stand my ground, glaring back at him, taking in the experience. It is a clear example of presence making an intense memory.

I resume the exhausting routine of daily buying trips to Marysville and Sacramento. Always in the forefront of my awareness is my determination not to let the job burn me out. Returning to the outer world is unthinkable, even though I know there is absolutely no job security. I could be asked to go anywhere at any time. Students come and go in this fashion constantly. My only hope for longevity is to make myself essential.

I endure the mindless routine through presence, disciplining my mind to maintain present-moment focus and find the uniqueness hidden in mundane repetition. While I operate within a repetitive structure, the content of each moment within that pattern is unique and unpredictable. Then there are always the punctuation points, moments of vivid focus and deep learning. One of these appears one afternoon off a freeway ramp in Sacramento. I have a huge heavy load piled on large sheets of steel with the tailgate down. I am in a hurry, at day's end. I come off the ramp too fast, take the turn too hard and the entire load dumps onto the street.

My first thought is denial. "This is not happening!!" I am in the middle lane of four lanes of rush hour traffic. I have no idea how I am going to reload this myself, so my first strategy is to stand there looking helpless in the hope someone will take pity on me and lend a hand.

When that fails, I finally begin to take action myself to clean up my mess. The sheets of steel are banded together. I release the bands and begin wrestling them back onto the truck bed one by one. Within minutes three more sets of hands appear and in the blink of an eye, I am on my way again. The phrase "God helps those who help themselves" springs into mind. I get it. Only when I make the commitment to help myself does help arrive. I see this is true on every level and in every circumstance.

My wife and I settle in to our little apartment where she sets up her jeweler's bench and eventually attracts a steady flow of student clients. We do all the things newlywed couples do. We buy furniture, have friends for dinner, and plant roses in the front yard. Weekends we attend concerts and socialize with visiting students who are my wife's customers.

Her sister, a lawyer in Oakland, is eventually able to achieve a settlement from the accident, which nets enough money to consider buying land in the hills across from the retreat. She purchases ten acres of undeveloped property and we begin the development process.

First we need to find water. We hire the ranch manager. He's an experienced dowser. He walks the property with a forked stick. It plunges down. He marks the spot.

Next comes the drilling rig. We find five gallons per minute at 300 feet. A plumber follows, dropping a pump and pipe down the hole. Then comes another student with a backhoe to dig holes for a cistern and a septic tank. We also clear a portion of the land for an orchard and a building site. Then comes a day when, having had electrical power brought onto the property, we flip the switch and drink the water that flows up out of our well, rooting us deeper into the land and a new way of life. We dream a dream of spending the rest of our days perched in our mountain retreat far away from the chaotic world as it approaches Armageddon.

The school promotes disconnection from the media. There are no television or newspapers and no connection to pop culture. The entire focus is on timeless classical music and art. Dress is conservative, especially for the women. Clothing that emphasizes sexual characteristics, like exposed cleavage, short skirts and pants or jeans, are frowned upon. They call it "infra-sex", meaning artificial, unfulfilling sexuality.

The Teacher gradually introduces family values, first encouraging marriage, even to the point of suggesting certain individuals marry each other. Then couples are encouraged to adopt dogs. It becomes a fad at The Retreat. Dogs pop up everywhere, some of which are gifts from The Teacher. This is, of course, preparation for having children.

There are also name changes. It is suggested people Anglicize their names to avoid discrimination during hard times. A list of potential names is drawn up and distributed. Many change their names, some to reflect their function in the community. The gardener, for instance, changes his last name to Fields. One evening, at home, we are going through a stack of old papers when my college diploma appears. She notices my middle name and comments that it would make a great last name. Since it is not on the list of suggested names, I personally seek out The Teacher at a weekend concert to obtain his permission for the change. I note now how I want his attention, like seeking parental approval.

This is how I become James Westly. This development dovetails with my interest in personal reinvention. My biological father has never been in my life. My mother remarried when I was four to a man with an Italian name. He is a good man who raises me well, but the physical appearance of my English/Irish descent never matches the Italian name. I feel that making the middle name my mother gave me my last name would have a positive karmic consequence.

CHAPTER TWENTY-ONE

A Promotion

One morning, nineteen months into my stay, the purchasing manager calls me into his office to tell me I will be taking over the dispatcher's desk. It is sudden, no warning. I am to trade jobs with the current dispatcher because he has fallen in love with an office accountant and the relationship is interfering with his job performance.

Finally!! I survive the burn out job. It is like passing an initiation. I pass through entry level to the next step. My persistence has enabled me to endure the unendurable, the constant grind of twelve to fourteen hour days. I never give up. By learning to live more and more in the moment, with no thought for anything but taking the literal next step, an unexpected development, a miracle occurs. I become a member of the office staff, opening the door to having a personal life and a little more job security, one step back from the abyss of uncertainty.

My daily life changes from one of hours alone on the road unloading late at night, to involvement in an intensely social situation. The office is a beehive of activity. It coordinates the business activities of an international organization. People seeking funding for their projects meet with the treasurer across the hall, department heads arrive at the purchasing office in the morning to check on the progress of their material requests, and others just drop by to get the latest gossip. Visiting students from all over the planet show up to help out or just to see what is happening. There are a large number of people crammed into a very small space.

My job is to track requisitions, place orders for pick up, develop vendor relationships and maintain acquisition records. I also have to field phone calls from all the people who have placed orders and want to know the status of their requests. Everywhere I go I am met with people's identifications with their stuff, anything from a pair of gloves to a major piece of machinery. I am assaulted on every side with the "where is my's".

In The Work, identification is deemed to be a major obstacle to higher awareness. It is the mind's automatic tendency to attach identity to just about anything. I find myself saying:

"I am **not** your shovel, your gloves, or your backhoe."

The people who constantly approach me are identified with their requests. The identification manifests itself as impatience, irritation and, sometimes, downright arrogance. Pointing out their identification releases me from my own identification with my function, and reminds both of us of the importance of presence.

There are also daily visits from The Retreat's various

department heads, turning the tiny room into a standing room only crowd. They come with their lists, wanting to know the status of their requests, or research items to buy, or just gossip.

The office is gossip central. The Retreat is the smallest of small towns, primarily because we are all linked through our mutual interest in The Work. Everyone practices watching without appearing to watch. This entails attending to one's senses. We listen omni-directionally and watch with peripheral vision. The permanent residents, those "on salary", total anywhere from 125 to 175, depending on the season. Another hundred or so live in the vicinity and work in Marysville. It is a very small community with the political and social dynamics of any small town.

The center of attention, of course, is The Teacher. There is a continuous buzz over where he is, what he is doing and saying. When he is not traveling he will dine most nights with a dozen students in his special dining room on the second floor of The Lodge. Most everyone has a turn to dine there, and serving there is considered a high honor. It is called the Meissen Room after the china service. He uses these dinners as teaching platforms. A scribe records the conversations. Other students then debrief the dinner attendees and the buzz circulates what The Teacher said.

The most powerful phrase in the community is: "The Teacher said." Although there is an established power/ management structure, he will frequently make things interesting for his managers by asking a student not in the management structure to make a request outside regular channels, like going directly to the treasurer with a suggestion or request. This happens frequently in the treasurer's office across the hall where a vineyard worker will appear unannounced and say the magic words followed by a direction to buy or do something completely unplanned for, and at times outrageous. There often are hoots of laughter and amazement after such visits, followed by phone calls to The Teacher to confirm the request. The most extreme example of this occurs when a wise guy student decides to have the auto shop repair his car by using the magic phrase. He marches into the treasurer's office with: "The Teacher said you should have the auto shop repair my car." When called, The Teacher confirms the request, even though it is a lie. Giving his students challenge is part of The Teacher's job.

Each day, after a morning of office intensity, I travel to The Lodge for lunch, served outdoors in good weather on a deck looking down the vineyard slope. Restaurant services are a five star experience, beginning with being seated by the maitre d', the atmosphere of hushed conversation with classical music overlay, punctuated with a poetry reading, not to mention gourmet food. It is life at a high level of refinement, where conscious intention is the watchword and is brought into life at every possible level.

I am now living the life I dreamt, devoting myself to serving a conscious community. It contains all the elements of life; home, marriage, and occupation, all in alignment with our spiritual practice. I enjoy the challenge of community politics. I have five star lunches and dinners, evenings at home with my wife, and weekend concerts, deepening my roots in the community. I vision my life continuing to develop in this fashion endlessly into the future.

CHAPTER TWENTY-TWO

Politics

Working in the school's nerve center in purchasing gives me a unique overview of the community structure. The political system is a monarchy. The Teacher is the king, the top celebrity, the focus of attention wherever he goes, attention that is given through the technique of watching without appearing to watch. He has absolute power which he wields benevolently, for the most part. If he approaches a crowd of students the way parts for him. If you are in visual range of him you are aware of his presence. You feel him.

An example of this happens to me one afternoon as I drive my truck through the vineyard toward the entrance. The Teacher is standing by the roadside speaking to a student. I stop to offer them a ride, a common custom. Both decline. I drive further on still having an awareness of them through the rearview mirror. When I am fifty yards away, The Teacher turns and raises his hand, motioning. I immediately stop and back up. He then insists the student take the ride previously offered. It seems like a test to see if I am watching.

Then there is an heir apparent, the crown prince, a student dubbed by The Teacher to be the next conscious being. He is the president of The School and male center director of The Retreat, another celebrity role. He leads meetings, coordinates the leadership of the worldwide network of teaching houses, counsels residents, travels to the teaching centers and is held in high esteem. What he says is also part of the buzz. There is, of course, a female Retreat center director who performs similar duties to her male counterpart and writes The Journal, a monthly newsletter printed on vellum with hand set type, a beautiful thing to behold.

Then there are the leaders of the various functions: the farm manager; the vineyard manager; winery construction; repair shop; wood shop; pressroom; antique restoration; the artists; housekeeping; maintenance; kitchen; restaurant; office; and purchasing.

Other members of the king's court include a handful of elderly women who helped fund the school in its infancy, and the president of the winery, a middle aged German man who has been wine master for several big name wineries. I marvel at how capable The Teacher is at attracting just the right people to fill the needs of his school. This in itself is a confirmation of The School's connection to something higher. The community organization and power structure grew organically from a handful of originators in 1970 and is tightly held together and operated by the principles of The Fourth Way.

This leads to the other power structure. There is the organizational hierarchy, delineated above, and then there is the Being status structure. Being is a highly regarded word in this community, you might say it is a measure of the soul. It refers to a person's consciousness, or level of vibration or enlightenment.

The Teacher stands at the pinnacle of this pyramid, followed by the prince, the identified "next conscious being". Then there is a loosely defined group of older students who have earned the respect of the group and have helped pioneer The School in any number of ways. The School's teaching structure offers leadership opportunities as well as being an open-ended test tube for personal growth. This group is known as the Inner Circle. It is not a formalized structure, but rather operates on the basis of attraction. People whose Being qualifies them are naturally drawn into relationship with others like themselves.

This is not to say all is Light. Like any community there are tensions, competitions, secrets and interest groups. What makes it different is everyone is dedicated to inner growth and service to The Retreat community. We are deeply connected in a common endeavor, to attain greater degrees of consciousness. This intention alone is a powerful influence on external behavior, tending to soften the typical conflicts that can arise when living in close quarters under intense conditions.

There is an atmosphere of Love that spontaneously arises when individuals are working to set aside obsessive judgmental thinking in order to find inner peace and deep connection to the precious present. An on-going school exercise is the non-expression of negative emotion. This is a group agreement that gives us license to call each other on our negativity, our automatic behavior. The shutter click hand movement of a conversational "photograph" jars everyone's attention more fully into the moment. It is a great way to defuse the tension that arises out of automatic behavior.

School exercises like intentional listening, not interrupting each other when speaking and intentional movement, all coalesce to produce an atmosphere of high vibrational awareness. Two hundred people in a room having private conversations produces a low hum. The goal to make movement intentional turns mundane activities like serving tables into an art form.

There is no coercion or obvious manipulation in the communications between the leaders and those led. We are all volunteers in service to a larger cause. Everyone has the option of saying no to a request, and, in fact, as I discovered in my later years there, learning to say no is an important survival lesson. The political structure is flexible, and subject to frequent change, keeping everyone focused and listening for every emerging nuance.

CHAPTER TWENTY-THREE

I Become a Performance Artist

Shortly after I become a member of the office staff, I hear about a small group of students who are meeting at a private home to read Shakespearean plays. Having always had an interest in drama, especially Shakespeare, I attend one of these meetings, immediately feeling a kinship with the group. They meet once a week. I drag out my copy of Shakespeare's Complete Works, a birthday gift from my mother at age sixteen, and begin attending faithfully. It is the beginning of a long-term friendship with a group of like-minded travelers.

I love speaking beautiful words: the sensation of a sound; the resonance of voice; rhyming and rhythm; the economy of poetry; intricate meanings; deep realities revealed in metaphor. Wednesday evenings we gather in the coziness of the comfortable living room of a woman's home and family.

The Retreat residents are a unique collection of human beings. Simply having made the journey to live at this place qualifies one for the title. Some are more unique than others, and this lady is one of those. She has an olive complexion with long dark tresses and dark brown psychic's eyes. She dresses like a European Gypsy and has a similar mystique. Hers is one of the very few established family households at The Retreat, complete with husband and teenage children. Her living room is a warm welcome place to unwind, have a glass of wine and discuss deep metaphysical issues. Her parties are legendary, a resident's inner circle. You are in if you are invited. Wednesday evenings at her house become one of the great delights of my week.

In two parallel developments, The Teacher decides the next step in The School's cultural development is to form an orchestra and a choir. Two relatively new students will lead these activities, one a professional conductor who joined the school in Australia and the other a Peruvian professional opera singer who joined the school in France. They are due to arrive in the next six months.

In preparation for their arrival, The Teacher asks various students to begin practicing music. He randomly/ intuitively selects individuals to play violins, violas, basses, flutes and clarinets. The early evening vineyard comes alive with the squeaks and squawks of beginning efforts to learn stringed and wind instruments. I begin practicing the trumpet, an instrument I played from the sixth grade through high school. Each day during lunch hour at the office, I go next door to practice, much, I'm sure, to the chagrin and displeasure of the office staff that remain behind during the lunch hour to do extra work. My sour notes are another opportunity to work against my fear of what other people might think.

The school's culture is entering another phase. In ten years The Retreat has gone from six hundred acres of forest with a log cabin and barn to four hundred acres of meticulously terraced hillside vineyard with a sophisticated Lodge building and a meeting center, Town Hall. With this infrastructure in place, The Teacher begins sowing the seeds of a classical culture based on European Renaissance values. Overnight, groups of students begin participating in the formation of an orchestra, a choir and now, a Shakespearean drama company.

The drama group begins spontaneously, without The Teacher's encouragement, in this lady's home. We are the Bohemian element, free thinkers who enjoy reading and discussing dramatic literature. It begins with weekly play readings, first Shakespeare, then others. As the group solidifies, interest in performance arises. Meanwhile, we learn that a professional British actor has joined The School and is planning to move to San Francisco. Within a few months he begins making regular visits and starts weekend drama classes.

Everyone in the reading group and others join the class. We study Method Acting, the technique developed by 19th Century Russian actor/director Constantin Stanislavski. His holistic, psychophysical approach, which explores character and action both from the 'inside out' and the 'outside in', adds to and intensifies our Fourth Way consciousness practices, especially those of awareness and inner self-examination.

Early Sunday mornings find me sitting on the Town Hall steps sipping coffee as the morning sun filters through the windows I glazed three years ago, illuminating a large room with mahogany floors and a wood paneled stage at one end, dominated by an inlaid mahogany Steinway grand piano originally constructed for 19th Century British Royalty. Cleared of seating, the room feels like a sacred creative space, pregnant with potential. This becomes one of the most precious moments of my week.

The people with whom I feel the greatest kinship are gathering to participate in a sacred practice, drama, humanity's oldest art form. We chat, mostly about our enthusiasm over becoming actors and how it is impacting our inner work on consciousness.

Precisely at 9:00 a.m. the acting teacher appears. We assemble and he gives us updates and plans for the day's class. We start with an intensive 30-minute aerobic routine, the difficulty of which escalates each week.

Once sweaty and breathless we begin vocal warm-ups. First we imitate someone chewing gum with exaggerated motion, stretching and distorting our faces to loosen up the jaw muscles, cheeks and lips. Then we rapidly chant "lilly, lally, lilly, lally" for five minutes to limber up the tongue. Next we make an exaggerated "...ing" sound, pressing the back of the tongue up to loosen the soft pallet. For weeks I feel silly and stupid when we do this, discovering I have an ego around looking goofy.

It gets worse as we move onto diaphragmatic voice exercises designed to teach projection and develop vocal power and range. Being heard at the back of the room is not about volume but about projection on the breath. Done effectively, a whisper can fill the room. We take turns with a word or a phrase given by our drama coach, learning to float our verbal expressions on the breath and breathe them into the far corners of the room, which resonates like the sound box on a guitar as we visualize filling the space with our expression.

After a break, we circle the room to work on stagecraft. We take turns rushing into the center of the circle to deliver a line, an action or an emotion. Two of us will occupy the center to improvise a brief scene, or two will start something, then the coach spontaneously instructs someone to run in to deliver a nonsense syllable with an emotion and an action. This part of the class evolves over the weeks and months, developing into scene studies and eventually into play rehearsal.

This is all very confrontive to what we call "the good student act." For four years I have cultivated a set of behaviors that are "intentional", but are also in conformity with the school's culture that includes an unofficial dress and behavior code modeled on unconscious imitation of The Teacher. It is one of those things that just happens. Egos "think" that if they act and speak like the role model it will make them, or at least appear to make them, more conscious. None of this is official or in any way actively encouraged. We are, however, consciously aware of the tendency and call it "the good student act". Obviously, we have some judgment about it. The exercises and activities of the drama class fly in the face of this tendency and are excellent work on witnessing our own versions of this phenomenon.

The drama coach is a type whose quickness, wit, power and dominance, along with his British demeanor, not to mention his Being, directs us with a clear vision and a strong hand. Each week is unique and challenging. I am passionately involved, dedicating every spare moment to the study and implementation of Stanislavski's work.

As the months progress, and the drama group solidifies and intensifies, he begins discussions of putting on a Shakespearean play. It is decided to do As You Like It, a pastoral comedy involving a bad duke who has banished his brother, the good duke. I am cast as the bad duke. For almost a year we rehearse on weekends, struggling, working to bring our acting skills to the level he requires to create a performance. All through the fall, winter, spring and summer the group works hard to shape its first creation as our director keeps pushing back the performance date, finally setting it for the following fall.

Putting on a play involves more than learning lines and blocking out action. We need a theater. Now you might think Town Hall would make a great theater, but this is complicated by community politics. Town Hall has become the domain of the music group, the orchestra and choir, who feel theater is too messy or unrefined. It is one of those cases of "where ever you go there you are." Just because we are working to be a conscious community does not mean we have completely lost our egos, or as The Work calls it, False Personality. We all have them. We acknowledge them and we work to observe them. However, observation does not necessarily lead to change. There definitely is a pecking order and the music people seem to have the upper hand. So we have to create a stage somewhere else.

We decide to build an outdoor stage around the base of a huge oak tree in the middle of a field next to the house of the woman who hosts the readings. Student carpenters and architects come together in their spare time and construct a platform that embraces the thirty foot trunk of this sprawling giant on the side of a gentle slope, forming a natural amphitheater.

Our hostess is, among her many talents, a gifted seamstress who has experience in costume design. She creates beautiful Elizabethan designs that so capture the essence of our characters that one of my friends did not recognize me on stage.

As the summer progresses toward an early fall performance deadline, life becomes a swirl of activity, all with the delight that comes with exploring and creating new territory. Costume fittings, stage building, and rehearsals consume most of my spare time.

CHAPTER TWENTY-FOUR

Our First Performance

While this is going on, the reading group continues to meet Wednesday evenings. One spring evening, a group member brings in copies of an English farce, a fast moving comedy about a 19th Century sea captain and his first mate. We read it through that evening and love it. One of the group decides to direct, and assigns roles. I am cast as the first mate.

It is an instant hit with the group and we read it again the following week. I adopt a voice for my character, a salty obnoxious sailor with an English accent and a pirate's inflections who is his captain's caretaker.

The following week we read it again. By the fourth week our self appointed director decides to block out the action, turning one end of the living room into a stage area, and using the hallway on one side and the entry door on the other as stage entrances. Now we are no longer sitting around reading, we're standing, moving, emoting, gesturing, entering and exiting. Each week another layer of complexity is added. Lessons learned in acting class are applied. The director begins doing scene work with the actors to develop their characters.

Every day, during lunch, I give up going to The Lodge and spend the time in the woods behind the office doing voice exercises, orating to the trees and memorizing my lines. When I project my voice powerfully enough, it comes back to me, bouncing off the trees. Each time we rehearse, I come closer to having the entire script internalized, enabling me to put more effort and attention into character development. The group starts meeting two and three evenings a week, going late into the night. We decide to stage a dramatic reading at the house the beginning of summer. Rehearsal begins in earnest.

Finally, one Friday evening in June, I stand in the hallway behind a curtain waiting to start the show. This is my green room moment. All preparation is complete, there is nothing left to do, just wait. It is the most difficult task of all, to maintain presence, not look ahead, just stand in your shoes. The final minutes to performance tick away, and very long minutes they are. I am costumed in black jeans, a red and black striped tee shirt with a navy blue seaman's cap cocked to one side. I hear the room filling up outside the curtain. Present moment focus is critical. Allowing the mind to think into the future will be disastrous. I feel exhilarated, alive. My heart is pounding, but I feel actively calm as I diligently apply every practice I know to keep focus. There is no fear, just creative expectation.

After what seems like an eternity, the room outside quiets down and is filled with a palpable sense of expectancy.

Finally I am given the sign. Taking a deep breath, I burst through the curtain and rush onto the stage.

"Fine cruising this, without flip or biscuit!" complains my character.

He is sarcastic, cynical and obnoxious. He strides to the front of the stage and addresses the audience as a narrator, setting the scene for the story to come. He will do this through out the play. My witness Self scans the room impartially as my character speaks, seeming to have a life of his own.

The attention of the audience is electric. In class we discussed using audience energy to elevate consciousness, but discussion does not in any way approach experience. All art forms are presence practices because they are challenging, and, require concentration. This is what makes them so intense and joyful. It is like entering another dimension. I open to and embraced something larger, allowing it to operate through my instrument, my human incarnation.

The performance unfolds smoothly, effortlessly. No one misses a cue and the audience adores us. We perform again twice that weekend, and twice every weekend for a month. Many people come to see us more than once. We continue rehearsing one evening a week, making it even better. Eventually everyone learns their lines and our reading turns into a full-blown play.

CHAPTER TWENTY-FIVE

I Become a Singer

Sometime during the spring of that same year the conductor arrives, a short, wiry type with dark hair, a brilliant smile and a quick wit. His intention is not only to start an orchestra, a seemingly impossible task given the rag tag bunch of squeakers and squawkers that first assemble, but also to create a choir.

I am determined to squeeze everything I can from my Retreat experience. It is like a microcosm of life, you never know when it will end or how much of it you get, compelling you to seize as much of it as you can get before it ends. The opportunities it offers would each take an entire lifetime to fulfill in the outer world, but in this tiny community life is compressed and condensed, making more possible in less time and space.

I sign up for the choir, even though I am intensely involved in drama, and, am practicing the trumpet. My dance card is getting full. I rise at 5:00 a.m., work full time, seven to five, six days a week. Monday evening it is my turn to man the evening switchboard at the office from five to ten o'clock, something required of each male office worker. It is like pulling guard duty in the military. Tuesday is choir rehearsal night, Wednesday evening is the reading group, Thursday evening I wash dishes at The Lodge (a turn we all take) and Sunday morning is devoted to drama class. In addition, I begin taking singing lessons with the new conductor one afternoon a week.

If acting is exciting, singing is ecstatic. That first Tuesday evening about forty people gather on the stage in Town Hall. The Conductor gives us basic instruction. He is small and wiry in stature, with dark wavy hair, bright eyes, a brilliant smile, an Australian accent and brilliant repartee, a natural entertainer.

Finally the moment comes, he raises the baton, we focus, and sing as one voice. From the very beginning the experience is one of total presence. I believe I can honestly say that, once I moved to The Retreat, I never wanted to be somewhere else, one of the primary obstacles to present-moment awareness. In the outer world it is common for people to want to be somewhere else. License plate holders proclaim, "I'd rather be _____", filling the blank with words like fishing, golfing, sailing...etc. The simple experience of wanting to be where you are is elusive in the modern world where most are rushing to be anywhere other than where they are, rarely experiencing the Now. (I capitalize Now because it is a sacred place)

Singing in this setting is transcendent ecstasy, an indescribable experience of intensified positive awareness that gets better each time the choir meets. The group is talented, so we move through the formative stages rapidly. People working on consciousness tend to learn faster since most or all of their attention is focused into the moment. The average person in the outer world is multitasking their attention significantly away from the moment. Ask someone what percentage of their attention is here/now. The ordinary answer is 40-50%, meaning anywhere from 50-60% of their attention is directed elsewhere, fragmenting their consciousness and leaving their programmed mind (auto pilot) to automatically do the work of the moment. This tends to make it more challenging to learn something new.

Before long we are working on a chorale piece to present to the community. While it is tedious hard work at times to construct a complex piece of music, the ecstasy of singing remains and intensifies with practice, making Tuesday evening a treasured event.

CHAPTER TWENTY-SIX

A Performance Disaster

In spite of play and choir rehearsals, I continue practicing the trumpet. I progress to the point where I am working on a Bach piece with piano accompaniment, an over ambitious project doomed to failure. I manage to squeeze in an hour a week rehearsing with a pianist to attain some level of competence and I continue daily practice. The Conductor calls on each person practicing an instrument to prepare something for a student recital, an event to be attended only by the musicians themselves. Not all moments of presence are magical, uplifting or traumatic, many arise out of humiliation and failure. This is one of those.

The afternoon of the performance I appear at Town Hall, nervous and shaky. Of all the talents I am attempting to develop, trumpet playing is the one in which I have the least confidence. When I am nervous, I am the worst klutz in the world.

I take the stage and place my sheet music on an antique wooden music stand, feigning a confident attitude. The stand is too low. As I grab the stand forcefully to raise it, it lifts right out of its base. I reinsert the stand, turning a ring in the base to tighten it, but it does not tighten. It keeps sliding down. Finally, a student in the front row reaches down on the floor and retrieves a small wooden wedge.

"This might be what you are looking for," he wryly remarks. I smile slightly, struggling between the desire to be elsewhere and the urge to laugh out loud.

Part of student presence practice is being emotionally non-reactive, remaining in a state of dis-identification or detachment. When taken to a dysfunctional extreme it produces non-reaction in the face of emergency. A workman once fell screaming off the roof of a two story-teaching house right past a dining room full of students. No one moved! They were "working against identification". You might say they were identified with being not identified. An "older" student jumped up and went out to help the injured man. She was applying another work principle, scale and relativity, which is to say some things have more importance than others.

A present person calmly accepts whatever the moment produces. Put into practice, this eliminates extreme emotional reactions, including laughing out loud in the face of a comedy of errors. As I struggle with the music stand, the room is perfectly still, full of straight-faced poker masks, all non-judgmentally watching me make a fool of myself.

Shaken by this catastrophic beginning, I take a deep breath, pause to focus, and start playing. Five notes in, the sheet music slides off the stand. Stopping, I glance up and notice they are maintaining their conscious cool, though many eyes are starting to twinkle, including mine. I accept the now inevitable disaster and am even amused by it, remembering that as a process starts, so it goes.

I reset the music and begin again. The music remains in place a little longer this time, but eventually begins to slowly slither south. This time I keep going, holding the horn to my lips with my right hand while adjusting the music with my left when needed. In this fashion I stumble my way through to completion. My concentration at this point is severely challenged as my mind battles with thoughts that want to rewrite recent history. My standard of excellence becomes getting through. I make every mistake I ever made in practice. It is my worst ever performance. The best part of it is my persistence. I do not give up. Bowing slightly to polite applause, I creep off the stage as my face burns with humor and humiliation. Not once did any one chuckle, or even smile.

At the tea party that follows, my friend who picked up the wedge from the floor observes that each time something went awry my eyes got bigger. I am given several positive observations for persistence and grace under fire, but no one says anything at all about my playing. Needless to say, I never play another note. To my relief! I am overbooked, overextended, and overworked. I decide to devote my energy to acting and singing.

CHAPTER TWENTY-SEVEN

As You Like It

Throughout the spring and summer that year work on our first Shakespearean production intensifies. I am cast as Duke Frederick, the usurping bad guy in this comedy filled with beautiful words about the nature of human existence. Unfortunately, my character speaks none of them, but mostly has vitriolic, mean things to say. My ego resents being cast in this obnoxious role, though I eventually see the wisdom of the director's decision. My adrenal body type is well suited to play an angry character that finds redemption. I am forced to confront my imaginary self-picture, my illusory self, another humiliation (opportunity for greater awareness).

Duke Frederick is the bad guy who disenfranchises his older brother, the good Duke, who is now living in exile in the forest. He is a positive, expansive man who extols the simple life and seems to have no upset over having his birthright stolen by his brother. It is an uplifting comedic tale that in the end demonstrates how love triumphs over evil. The bad Duke sees the error of his ways and joins a monastery.

Everyone in the drama group is cast into this caldron of self-development, this struggle to free our creative selves, bonding us together. I am not the only one undergoing self-realization/humiliation. Doing drama in a conscious school is like living in an ongoing awareness training. As the work of creation intensifies, we each witness the others' unfolding process. It becomes part of the buzz, our shared daily interaction with Self-discovery, breaking down ego to penetrate the character while having moments of intense self-awareness.

Improv sessions are staged where our characters are given hypothetical situations not in the script and asked to improvise their reaction. Using vocal intonation and body language we feel our way into sensing the character's thoughts, expressing them in spontaneous word and action.

It is hard work that requires a willingness to actively confront our self-imposed limitations. It is also the most joyous of experiences. We are on an adventure into the unknown, entirely focused on the experience unfolding in this very special moment. The gray upset of yesterday, and worry about tomorrow vanishes, leaving the brilliant rainbow light of Now. You see the beauty of things as they are, rather than how you "think" they are. We are learning to shed our fear of what others think of us, the inhibitory factor that limits or entirely stifles the flow of creativity.

The other side of fear is intense exhilaration. Releasing this fundamental human emotion and emerging into triumphant self-love, the other fundamental human emotion, is an unimaginable high, a huge release of energy. I walk out of these Sunday morning sessions fully immersed in spiritual awareness. I stroll up the hill tasting the air, drinking in the beauty of the hillside, through the terraced vineyard to The Lodge, in appreciation of everything my senses encounter.

Other exercises delve into our character's back-story, the psychological dynamics that bring each to his or her point of action. We use our creative imagination to add in details of our character's history.

Duke Frederick seems to be the classic jealous younger brother wanting to steal what is not his birthright. Once he has it, his actions force him to push away everything else of value, like his relationship to his daughter. Eventually he encounters a holy man on the road to wage war against his brother who brings him to the light and he retires to a monastery.

He has a seed of goodness in him that eventually triumphs. I can see some of my own story in his. I find the character within, which shapes the emotional truth I deliver when I speak the lines. The Fourth Way studies the mechanics of human behavior, so does Shakespeare. Finding The Fourth Way in Shakespearean parallels helps develop character expression and deepens our self-knowledge, bringing greater degrees of awareness to our performance. Through this we find the character within and learn to express it on stage.

CHAPTER TWENTY-EIGHT

The Other Side

Now, you might think that, at this point, I have the best of all possible worlds. I am a dreamer who seeks participation in a conscious community, self-realization, and connection to a greater reality. My intense desire for this draws it to me like a magnet draws iron filings. The Fourth Way calls this a 'magnetic center', an inner drive to find and practice the transcendent in life, refusing to settle for surface reality. It teaches that friction is a requirement, a payment. It is the heat that will ignite the flame of consciousness. Friction can be defined as challenge or difficulty, a resistant something encountered that creates the opportunity to go beyond one's self imposed limitations.

You might say I am driven. Once I discover and join The School, every beat of my heart is dedicated to becoming a permanent member of this community. Nothing can stand in my way. My challenge (friction), in large part, is the long-term consequence of the head injury sustained in the accident mere weeks before coming to live at The Retreat. An "accident" (there are no accidents) perpetrated by Mr. Wright, a murderer fleeing the scene of his crime.

The synchronicity is stunning. I am given the gift of friction for my journey to Now. I suffer from traumatic brain injury (TBI) that includes the dislocation of my skull off of my first cervical vertebrate. In plain language, my head is no longer on straight. You may rest assured there are some people who will make this the reason for my deciding to move to The Retreat.

TBI is frequently not noticed or diagnosed immediately. Symptoms may take days or weeks to emerge. The diagnosis itself may not even have been in the diagnostic lexicon at the time of my injury. The onset can be so subtle it is not noticed by the victim, but is seen first by those around them. So it is with me. I just think my pace is making me tired and emotionally flat. The first attempts of my wife, the only one who notices, are met with impassioned denial. The symptoms, extreme fatigue, severe short-term memory loss, headaches, sleep loss, and depression, I attribute to long hours and hard work.

This is my deeper friction, this resistance. My desire for evolution is the driving force that meets the daily challenge of my symptoms with an equally deep determination to succeed no matter what the risk or difficulty. Every day I reach through my suffering to touch the miraculous, in a community where it is concentrated and occurs daily. I AM irreconcilably resolved to staying open to the challenge of living at The Retreat, no matter what the cost. I AM RESOLUTE!!

Every day I experience the miracles in some way, small or large. The walkway to the Lodge kitchen from the parking lot has five or six rose bushes. I stop to inhale their nectar every time I pass. On the same path I pause, turn and look down the vineyard slope, drinking in the beauty of the vista that sweeps down the mountain to the fog shrouded Sacramento valley, reminding me I live above the fog line, in a place of greater clarity. These experiences, and many like them, saturate my brain with serotonin, endorphins and other pleasure producing, energizing, natural pharmaceuticals created from the ingestion of beauty and work on presence, nature's antidepressants. The brain is a pharmacy. The chemicals it produces are determined by the content of thought. When I keep my focus on the Now and look for and ingest beauty where ever I can, I am at peace with what is, including my friction.

The fatigue I initially attribute to the grueling pace, the hours of driving, late nights unloading, six-day workweeks, but it continues once I am taken off the road. I continue to fight an exhaustion from which I never seem to recover.

The depression is subtle, outside my awareness. At the highest emotional level, I am in ecstasy over my life situation. I have attained a cherished goal, climbed a mountain and made a life in paradise. My exhaustion, however, flattens my affect and de-energizes my thought process, leaving me a pretty dull guy. Dinner parties with my wife at The Lodge find me present but not terribly interesting. Often I am struggling to stay awake, to maintain an existence, a façade of wellness. At a concert in Town Hall, I am standing behind The Teacher attempting to consciously hear the music as my body is shutting off, leaving me standing dead asleep.

The memory loss is the worst part of it. I am fine as long as I am focused on a task, when all my attention is present-moment. This makes a critical difference. Anything less than total presence, however, results in memory deficits. My long-term memory is untouched, and is in fact strengthened by the memorization exercises I have been practicing.

My short-term memory, however, is at times non-existent. Ask me to do something routine, like empty the trash. Ask me again five minutes later did I empty the trash and I do not remember being asked. This is less of a problem at work, where my tasks are list and pattern driven and I am generally more focused, than at home, where I am less vigilant and tend to be defensive when my competency is challenged. Here the memory loss is an irritant, a source of conflict. My only defense against it is presence, making the effort to anchor my full attention into the contents of Now for even the most mundane of interactions. Transactions that used to be performed automatically must now be performed consciously or they simply do not occur.

Imagine the emotional friction this produces. While my wife tries to be compassionate and sympathetic, the disruption this causes to ordinary daily interactions begins to take a toll on our relationship. My automatic short-term memory is rapidly vanishing while all my physical energy is concentrated on taking the literal next step through a veil of exhaustion. I feel, at times, on the point of break down.

My wife, who has her own chiropractic challenges from the accident (a broken back), finds an unusual chiropractor in a nearby town that specializes in upper cervical adjustments, the first seven vertebrae, a rare breed according to him. His adjustments prove to be effective for her. Encouraged by her success, I drive the ninety minutes through the foothills to visit him in his backyard office in Paradise, California. This where I find out my head is not on straight.

He x-rays my neck. Develops them and makes several precise calculations where he shows me where the blow that tore off my ear caused a dislocation of my skull on my first cervical. He then places me on a low padded table fitted with head and neck clamps, positioning my skull very precisely to locate an exact spot he marks with a scrape of tissue. Then, standing poised over my exposed neck, he summons energy through an intense breathing procedure, lays two fingers on the spot marked on the neck and delivers an intense jolt. The impact feels electric. Following this comes another x-ray to check results and a half-hour nap on his waiting room couch to allow the adjustment to settle.

Upon awakening, he tells me I am in alignment. I drive back to The Retreat feeling spacey, altered and emotionally energized. I start seeing him every week. Each intervening seven days I fall out of adjustment and have to be fixed. Then, it begins to hold. Slowly my brightness returns, my emotional responsiveness, and my memory gradually improves, but not quickly enough to save my marriage.

My wife keeps saying to me, in the ramp up to our wedding, how marriage has never been her vision of adulthood. She is a creative independent spirit who adventures alone in the world. I can say now, from this distance, that we had a significant friendship, but not a romance. We are a Retreat couple, closely matched in body type. We are of similar appearance, bookends some say, and are considered a model couple.

Internally, however, we never merge, but operate more as sexually involved roommates, independent individuals. She makes material decisions without consulting me, decisions creating commitments requiring my involvement. Most notably, she plants fruit trees on the property before we acquire a water source, making it necessary to carry water up the mountain daily. Another day I come home to a buzzing, shoebox size, wood and wire mesh box filled with thousands of bees. She has decided to become a beekeeper without consulting me.

We do not operate as a partnership, nor do we work to nurture the relationship. On the good days we co-exist, on the bad ones we fight. I am wrapped up in the developmental opportunities The Retreat offers. This consumes most of my time and energy. She gets what is left, which, given my medical situation, is very little. She, more than any other person than my self, receives the brunt of my exhaustion, depression and memory loss, while I give The Retreat the best of me. I guess you can call me a spiritual workaholic. While my memory and energy improves, in my estimation, she has pretty much had it with the friction generated by the challenges of my brain injury.

In early fall the British farce is briefly resurrected to go on tour to the San Francisco Bay Area teaching houses. It is a celebration of the group's achievement, but bittersweet for me. She and I have agreed to separate upon my return, a growing ache that gnaws away at my solar plexus. I hope up until the last minute for a reprieve, but that Sunday I move into a large room I have to share with two single men who are strangers to me.

CHAPTER TWENTY-NINE

On To Performance

I immerse myself in our theatrical production in order to be distracted from the pain of my loss. We work diligently to bring all the elements of a theatrical presentation into being. Our costume designer is busy making fitting appointments for each actor, designing Elizabethan costumes. My character is dressed in a gold trimmed black tunic with puffy period sleeves, a flamboyant black hat and black tights. I start wearing the hat to rehearsals, verifying the theory that "clothes make the man" as my character begins to take shape.

As purchasing agent, I use my vendor connections to arrange for the delivery of all the building materials necessary for the construction of the stage. With the help of school architects and carpenters, the drama group builds the theater. I spend what spare hours I have swinging a hammer, helping to create a platform for our performances. Soon drama class moves out of Town Hall to the new stage.

We "take the stage" and walk the boards for the first time, exploring. I stand at the front, confronting an imaginary audience. The dream is becoming reality. The Sunday morning session begins with an intense aerobic workout followed by vocal exercises. Then the cast assembles center stage. We sit cross-legged on the floor in a circle and have a read through performance.

Most of us have memorized our lines by now. Some are more zealous than others in doing our homework, and there are, of course, those who lag behind, or have trouble being responsible. I must confess to being one of the most zealous and find a great deal of irritation (judgment) with those who are less committed. They are my friction, as I am theirs.

Now we have the stage and are free of the schedule constraints and politics of Town Hall. We rehearse all day Saturday and Sunday every weekend. Entries and exits are blocked out. Scenes are worked on intensely, minutely, line by line, detail by detail. Each part is refined and intensified, then put together into an ever evolving whole that flows naturally from scene to scene to finale.

The build up of emotional energy around the project develops toward the crescendo of performance. The cast is a family now, with all the relational nuances, intricate relationships and hierarchies. The commitment of time and energy intensifies, straining relationships outside the group, like marriage partners. My marriage is the first of many to be sacrificed on this alter of creativity.

Administrative details are worked out. A performance date is set in late September and published in The Vine, a monthly newsletter sent out to all the Teaching Houses. It contains announcements of all sorts, including new exercises, new rules, or the release of old rules or exercises. It links the Teaching Houses to developments occurring at The Retreat, the heart of The School.

Now we are in the home stretch, and that is how it feels, a nine month long race to the finish, requiring every ounce of vitality you can muster, forcing us to find and utilize inner resources heretofore unknown. We are pulling the vision of the unborn creation from the future. It really has a life of its own now, a gathering momentum that propels us forward to completion. The final touches are put on the stage: paint, lighting, back drop curtains to create a backstage. The field surrounding the stage is mowed and benches are constructed to seat the audience. A million last minute details are completed by dozens of students all endeavoring to bring high levels of intentionality to every task they perform. The director takes a vacation from work for the final two weeks and rehearsals intensify, culminating in a full dress rehearsal the night before our first performance, which is set for a Friday evening, to followed by performances Saturday afternoon and Sunday evening, all to be repeated the following weekend.

Friday evening the cast gathers in a small orchard beside the costume designer's house, donning costumes and make up. The energy is intense. Actors are wandering around warming up their voices. Across the field in the deepening dusk our first audience is assembling underneath the magically illuminated giant oak, parking in the field and filling the seats. Friends of the drama group set up a concession stand and are selling various homemade refreshments to the crowd.

Standing in a circle, we breathe deep in a meditative ritual, uniting our energies. We cross the field to the backstage area, take our places and the play unfolds, igniting an evening of philosophical comedy, rich in poetry, dance, music and high drama. A peak moment for me is in the third act.

My character, the evil duke, angrily enters to confront his niece, the good duke's daughter, banishing her from his court. His own daughter begs him to be merciful with her cousin, breaking into tears as her father rages, demonstrating to all his ruthless, power hungry arrogance. An emotional crescendo is reached here that transcends acting and becomes real feeling, a method acting epiphany. In the end the forces of love and light triumph over the forces of darkness, the bad duke repents and order and harmony are restored to a standing ovation, something that would never happen on The Retreat grounds.

CHAPTER THIRTY

Post Performance Blues

The play is a huge success. Six performances later we are spent, basking in the afterglow. Nine months of build and two weeks of climatic performance are followed by a six-hour drive north past Mount Shasta through fall colors to the Shakespeare Festival in Ashland, Oregon.

The trip is intended to soften the let down, the post-partum depression that naturally follows such an intense effort. We are well pleased with the results of our effort, but now our calendar is empty and we must return to our routine living patterns.

In the months leading up to performance, the hole in my life formed by the loss of my intimate relationship is filled by play preparation and the camaraderie and closeness that naturally arises between actors in a play. My wounded heart is vulnerable and secretly aching. It begins to form an infatuation for the Irish actress who co-leads our drama group. I go so far as to buy her tickets to the Shakespeare Festival.

The predawn Monday morning after our final performance she, myself and another friend drive up the Sacramento Valley into the crisp fall landscape in my ex-wife's vintage Mercedes. For five days we immerse ourselves in Shakespeare and wine, celebrating our theatrical triumph and speculating on our next project. I take a back stage tour and walk the boards of a real theater, standing at the edge, projecting a sound into the space. The days fly by and we are soon cruising down the late Friday night highway back to the lives we left.

CHAPTER THIRTY-ONE

Dark Night of the Soul

With the dissolution of my theatrical family, I am alone, more alone than I have ever been. I have no personal life. As You Like It is over. The reading group continues to meet Wednesday nights, but not with the same enthusiasm of self-discovery. I work in the office, attend weekly choir rehearsals, have switchboard duty weekly and wash dishes at The Lodge.

Now the choices that led me to living at The Retreat feel empty. I have moments of desolation and regret over those decisions, bouts of self-doubt and recrimination. I feel overwhelmed by the empty feeling in my gut. The room I share with two young men is cold and empty of belonging. They remain strangers to me, probably due to my own withdrawal.

In these moments of darkness I deepen my inner work. There is literally no place to hide. Even my most private moments, my sleep time, are shared with students. I begin living the life of a monk. My involvement with work, my commitments to choir and drama, switchboard duty and dish washing fill my time. As long as I focus my attention on the task at hand, I am well. When I don't, I slip into a self-pitying psychosis.

Presence is, again, the quality of existence that saves me from despair. In this state I AM at peace with What Is, the past and the future have no hold on me. I AM simply Here/Now. The yawning chasm of self-pity thoughts becomes a great motivator, a cognitive pattern to be avoided at all costs.

Every morning I rise early to maintain my membership in the breakfast club where I begin my day with study. This winter I am reading and applying The Enchiridion, a handbook for conscious living penned by Epictetus (AD 55—135), a Greek stoic philosopher who was born a Roman slave. Philosophy, he taught, is a way of life and not just a theoretical discipline. To him, all external events are determined by fate and are thus beyond our control, but we can accept whatever happens calmly and dispassionately. Individuals, however, are responsible for their own actions, which they can examine and control through rigorous self-discipline. Suffering arises from trying to control what is uncontrollable, or from neglecting what is within our power. Another expression of Gurdjeiff's dictum: "Man cannot 'Do', everything happens." Deciphering what is within my power and what is not has become my daily challenge. How many times do I butt heads with what is not in my power, including the course taken by my marriage.

In my introspective moments I come to see the

marriage as the manifestation of an immature fantasy, an interpretation, a theoretical meaning attached to an event, the accident. I felt brushed by the wings of Death and my mind took this to mean our marriage was the intention of higher forces. I was even told by The Retreat centre director that I did not have to marry her. This is one of those moments burned in my memory, a message from above I choose to ignore, thinking I know better. Perhaps my intransigence is driven by some lesser, more human, motivation, like the need for belonging.

Each day the most difficult moments come at the end when I have to retire in a cold room with strangers. This is when the monsters of the deep emerge from my subconscious to torture me. I resort to my old Transcendental Meditation mantra to hold the mind parasites at bay.

Initially I make sporadic efforts to resuscitate the marriage. One evening my ex and I go to dinner at a restaurant in Marysville where the bartender is her friend. We became quite intoxicated there and have a screaming fight on the way back. Another time I take a Sunday morning to wash her car, hoping to please her. She takes it when it is done and drives off. The sense of abandonment and separation from reality plunge me into a disconnected state I spend the day fighting off. Finally, just before spring, I surrender, accepting the situation. I release my resistance and embrace the reality of it, feeling at peace for the first time in months.

As if on cue, a furnished bedroom becomes available in the main house where I stay. The room belongs to my old center director from Philadelphia, the physician, who stays there on the weekends he visits. I sleep on the floor when he comes. This small change makes a huge difference internally. As the trees begin to show new growth, my soul emerges from its dark night. I begin to appreciate and flourish in a new freedom. My personal decisions are no longer subject to the opinion of another. I am free to be me myself, having only to deal with the direct consequences of my personal choices.

CHAPTER THIRTY-TWO

Realizations

Once again I come full circle. The restless wanderer within me departs one world with its characteristic structure of marriage, occupation, and material striving only to recreate its mirror image in this microcosm. The only difference is the speed with which it develops. In three years I go from nothing to everything to nothing. Now, I am again starting over.

There is a repeating pattern, like a symphonic theme and variation on a singular, simple set of sounds. Beethoven's Fifth Symphony is built on the first four notes. Viewed superficially it seems linear, that is it appears to proceed in a straight line. Seen from a greater perspective, it is more circular, or perhaps spiral. The pattern is the same or similar each time, but each repetition takes less time to complete and each cycle takes on a higher vibration, is an ascending process. I experience the same lesson, meet the same life challenge, over and over, each time in a different way, at a higher level of vibration. I am evolving, my life is quickening, and, I come up against the same wall each time, painted a different color.

My ego is disappointed. It "thought" (this goes to the uselessness of most "thinking") spiritual growth would resolve or make disappear, the inner obstacles that originally brought me to The Work. Once more I encounter "where ever you go, there you are." The core challenge is the same dressed up in different clothes, playing different roles. The growth comes in seeing it. This is friction. Rarely does what I see about myself conform to what I imagine. So the seeing can be painful and confirms again Gurdjieff's proposition that: "Man cannot do, everything happens". Ouspensky says: "We imagine ourselves, really!"

After all my efforting, all my inner work, I still feel I do not belong, that I am an outsider, even when, to all appearances, I am the exact opposite. I am living in the heart of The School, about as inside as you can get physically, culturally. Yet I still do not belong. My ego still has some version of the old identity in place. There is still someone in me who is a stranger where ever he goes, an outsider.

Traditionally I have buffered this feeling with intimate relationship, one person who is my best friend, with whom I dream a dream. This is where my ego builds its identity. My dream with my ex was to spend the rest of my life at The Retreat, living in our home on the hill above the fog. Now, after another marriage, I am again alone. The pain of this becomes a spur for presence. When I AM truly and completely Here/Now, my consciousness is disengaged from my mind, where my ego lives. When I AM present

I no longer feel the pain of the outsider. This time I plan to focus entirely on my evolution, to give my all to the community and develop my talents, to forego a personal life. I work to surrender to and make friends with who I think I am, this loner, to accept it as is, without question or judgment. This comprises my daily internal struggle between yes and no. Do I say yes to what is, or do I resist and negate?

CHAPTER THIRTY-THREE

My Day Job

My careers in business have always been ones in which I have access to overview of business operations, giving me privy to an enterprise's larger picture. Such was the case in my corporate insurance career where I would underwrite business liability policies on the basis of an assessment of the risk in their operations, and so it is in purchasing. Having the task of filling the community's material needs, I am given day-to-day access to and involvement in most of the activities, except food. The kitchen does its own shopping.

During my eighteen-month stint as driver, I make acquaintances and friends with the people who are leaders of the various departments and activities. More than anything else, The Retreat residents are a collection of extraordinary, unique souls. It is my joy, each day, to participate in the construction and development of a young conscious community. It was nine years old when I arrived. Land is still being cleared and terraced. We periodically have huge evening bonfires to incinerate the piles of brush accumulated from this process. We drink wine and enjoy the late evening blaze.

New structures are constantly being constructed. Once Town Hall is completed, work begins on The Goethe Academy, a single story mansion that eventually replaces the Blake Cottage as The Teacher's residence, and contains a magnificent library, ballroom, formal dining room and world class kitchen where meals are prepared by a student who is a five-star chef. The School has an extraordinary ability to attract excellence. Everything is constructed by student labor. I spent a weekend before moving to San Francisco helping to pour the foundation for this edifice. Eventually the Blake Cottage is jacked up off its foundation and transported to another part of the property to be used for some other purpose.

Three large industrial metal buildings housing the auto shop, the wood shop and the metal shop eventually replace the old barn, originally the heartthrob of vineyard operations. On a sunny spring morning we gather on this spot of ground that has been the crossroads of the community, and watch as our D-8 (bulldozer) knocks it down. After all the rubble is cleared, I walk the foundation. The barn housed the auto shop, a wood shop, a metal shop, an antiques restoration area and probably a few other things I cannot remember. Yet, when the walls are gone and all the partitions taken away, it is almost impossible to conceive how it all took place in such a tiny space. The next day the D-8 begins digging a pond on the barn site that eventually becomes the home to several swan couples, improving the view from The Lodge.

The biggest building project is the winery being constructed on a prominent knoll overlooking the property. The architect's model resembles a circular Greco Roman structure. The early temporary structure is a huge white inflated plastic dome dominating the crest of the knoll attached to a circular concrete foundation. Just below the dome aging cellars are being excavated.

The rhythm and pace of daily life is focused around planting and nurturing the vineyard. In the winter, the vines are trimmed back. During the spring new growth is trimmed again to shape the plant's carefully planned development. Drip irrigation is installed and maintained. As spring moves into summer, weeds are cut back to minimize pest damage and control fire danger.

In the fall it is harvest time. Students arrive almost daily from all over the world to participate in this celebration. The entire community drops everything and gathers in the chilly late September dawn armed with clippers and picking bags. Lug boxes filled to the brim with rich warm colors are loaded on flat bed trucks and taken to the winery knoll to be crushed within minutes of being picked.

Every few weeks I visit each project to maintain my relationships with the department leaders and the progress being made. It is one of the most rewarding experiences of my work, these relationships. I feel blessed to know and work with such high quality individuals. Someone once joked this place is a school for geniuses. Working intensely to bring all of your attention to bear in the moment does have the effect of bringing forth a person's inner Einstein, their personal uniqueness and talents.

Living in a conscious community is like being plugged into a larger light socket. Everything is amped up. The membership is working to unify its consciousness and bring focused awareness to every detail of living. Inner qualities are revered over external accomplishments and external accomplishments arrive at greater and greater levels of excellence through focused awareness. As a result of this process, everything is accelerated.

Do not think for a moment this results in a "perfect" society. Just because most members are intending to be more conscious does not always mean they have attained that goal. Also, the bigger light socket accelerates the emergence and intensified awareness of our internal obstacles. Since living at The Retreat is a 24/7/365 awareness training, everyone here is experiencing this emergence, and their behavior, at times, is driven by the external manifestations of these internal obstacles, creating drama.

CHAPTER THIRTY-FOUR

Office Politics

There are many levels of perception to any situation. There is the black and white level, the story of right and wrong. Up one step is the psychological level, where events are seen to be the manifestation of childhood, cultural conditioning and cognitive/behavioral habits. Right and wrong is replaced by functional verses dysfunctional. The logic remains dualistic.

Next is the mystical level where everything that happens, positive or negative, is seen in a holistic, developmental context. Everything contributes to the development of consciousness and spiritual growth, even when the events are perceived to be wrong or bad at the dualistic levels. This entails telling the story from an overview perspective, leaving out the details of what happened and focusing more on what those experiences birthed in my inner world. I have no desire to cast aspersions on anyone with whom I had drama, and am grateful to every person with whom I have had interaction, no matter the nature of that interaction. It all has created growth in me in ways I am still discovering over three decades later.

The Fourth Way values friction, as I have mentioned several times already. It is the something we avoid or reject in life prior to entering The Work. The mystic's approach is in seeing the evolutionary value of adversity and challenge, setting aside our complaints about life's pain and suffering, or getting lost in the story. I have verified over and over in my own life, and in the lives of others, how adversity and challenge are principle factors in personal development.

Cramming four people into a tiny room eight to ten hours a day is a formula for friction. My naïve self started out thinking that life in a conscious community would be free from conflict, would be harmonious, and indeed, in some ways this is true. The School's exercise in the none-expression of negative feelings, and the avoidance of extreme emotions does have a civilizing influence on external behavior, and, the students the School attracts do tend to be more advanced individuals. But the pressures of accelerated development also tend to bring inner divisions to the surface for resolution. So it is for me working in the office. Every day I am given the opportunity to work on strengthening my internal shortcomings and discovering my true Self at ever deepening levels.

My day job at The Retreat is the purchasing department. I begin as the runner, graduate to dispatcher and eventually am the manager. These are the external events, the skeletal framework for my inner work. I work intensively with many people along the way, some of whom are dear friends, and some of whom are natural enemies. It takes me awhile, but eventually I come to realize having enemies is a part of nature. My friends support my inner growth, but really the most valuable relationships are with the people who dislike me. It is the friction of this enmity that facilitates the strengthening of my inner weaknesses and creates many moments of presence, the bottom line intention of inner work.

We have all met people we instinctively dislike, for no particular reason. Maybe we just find their mannerisms irritable. Maybe their body type dynamics clash with our own. We have also met or had to work with people who instinctively dislike us. There is just something about us they find irritating, and, try as we may to rescue ourselves from their disregard, they continue to behave badly toward us. These are our petty tyrants, the people we have *contracted with* to help us awaken. (There is a significant idea contained in the italicized words. It implies we are spiritual beings having a human experience for a purpose, and, we have made agreements with other beings to play the roles they play. To learn more about this, read Sacred Contracts, by Caroline Myss.)

The huge idea behind this is that personal evolution is the reason for our physical existence. Personal growth and development is the answer to the philosophy 101 question: "Why do I exist?" For me, and for perennial philosophy, of which The Fourth Way is an expression, the answer is that we are having a human experience for a developmental, evolutionary, purpose. We are here to develop consciousness. The idea of a contract implies that we are living out a prearranged scripted drama in which all the players have agreed to play their roles, agreed prior to emerging on the physical plane. The game is to become aware of this as the drama unfolds and not become lost in or identify with the play. Omar Khayyam, in his Rubaiyat epic poem alludes to this idea with these words:

Tis' all a checkerboard of nights and days,
Where Destiny with men for pieces plays,
Hither and thither moves and mates and slays,
And one by one back in the closet lays.

What I said before about life in a conscious school being amped up, applies particularly to friction. In ordinary life adversity is considered irritating, frustrating or confrontational, something most attempt to avoid or minimize, mainly through attempting to please others. In the school we are trained to value and apply friction to facilitate inner evolution. It is often apparent that different cosmic rules are in operation.

My enemies provide the friction necessary to see myself. Challenge and adversity are considered to be sacred qualities. To alleviate my resistance, I internally express my gratitude for the opportunities they offer. Thoughts have enormous power. They shape perception. The body responds to them with emotion. My body's internal response to gratitude is acceptance. I stop resisting and taking things personally each time my brain acknowledges gratitude. This is the beginning of transformation of negative emotion into present moment awareness.

Having said all this, doing it is at times challenging. I am not always able to maintain an objective awareness of the play as it unfolds. When I lose this perspective, I take the drama personally and react accordingly. The Work teaches that all negativity is the consequence of restricted awareness. When we are negative, we are not present, and our behavior is driven by our mind's programming, by habitual thought. What is also driven by habitual thought is my reaction.

Thus, there are times when I am forced to deal with restrictive requirements of fellow students who I answer to, and find ways to do so outside the range of my automatic responses. Sometimes it involves my reporting their behavior to the next higher authority for resolution. Another time, I write an individual a letter identifying them as my enemy, along with a dissertation on how we all have natural enemies and thanking them for playing that role for me. This strategy was especially effective as it brought matters to a higher level of awareness, rising above the story to glimpse the bigger picture.

All this matures me as each episode reveals more of my shortcomings. I look at these experiences now and wonder why I just didn't confront them directly, realizing the fear I had around such situations, fear of failing perhaps, battling inner considering over how I would appear to others, not wanting to cause a scene or look stupid. One thing about living in a tight community working on consciousness is that everyone is witnessing, is practicing the art of watching without appearing to watch.

In this community, and especially at the office (gossip central), everyone knows everything, and we are all trying to be, or at least appear to be, conscious. All of which are different levels of ego. It is interesting to note that the mind will form an identity around anything, including, of course, the idea of becoming conscious. There it is! What we call "the good student act". We all have an idea in our minds around what constitutes conscious behavior, and are judging others and ourselves according to that subjective standard.

Sometime in my third year of working in the purchasing department, the student who was managing was sent by The School to support a European center, leaving me to run the show. We had been working understaffed for some months prior to his departure, and the resulting slowdown in the flow of materials had begun to aggravate the department leaders, all of whom met at the wine master's home each week. The week following my unofficial ascendancy into management, the wine master himself summons me to this meeting. I discover when I arrive that I am the subject of the meeting.

Across the creek in the draw leading to the main property nestles an architecturally modern mountain cottage decorated with lush greenery. It is my first visit to this inner circle, an initiation. A trial by fire, as it turns out. The wine master opens the meeting, acknowledges my arrival, and then proceeds to list his grievances with the purchasing department. Each of the ten other leaders then follow suit. I listen carefully, respectfully, to each and every detail, affirming nonverbally my attentiveness, internally resisting each knee-jerk defensive response, working diligently to say yes to every attack, surrendering, accepting, in attentive silence. After an hour, they run out of things to say. Silence falls as all eyes turn in my direction.

Using the stagecraft I learned in drama, I root my attention in my body, take a deep breath and slowly gaze around the circle, making eye contact with each person as I listen internally. I AM HERE NOW, in that mystical place, that fertile void of expectancy where you have no idea what you will say or do until it is said and done, giving up your little will to the Will of something greater, allowing it to operate through you. I marvel at what comes forth.

Words flow from me intuitively taking the exact necessary direction needed. They outline the reasonableness of the circumstances under which purchasing is operating, and offer solutions and time lines in a way that opens the door to cooperation without making excuses or justifications, but is empowered and effective. Everyone begins offering suggestions to support the plan offered and there is a complete release of tension. It is a great piece of improvisational drama. I leave the meeting intensely present with a new sense of freedom never felt before Now. I truly feel the Truth, Power and Simplicity of meeting the needs of the moment through Presence.

CHAPTER THIRTY-FIVE

The Winter of My Discontent

"**N**ow is the winter of our discontent..." This is the opening line of Shakespeare's The Tragedy of Richard III and the theme of my first winter as a single man. Bereft of an intimate relationship, I plunge into my work in purchasing and my creative life. I take singing lessons to improve the quality of my voice. Our theater director moves to The Retreat and our group of actors begins meeting one evening a week, as well as on Sunday mornings.

If I feel at home anywhere, it is with this group of creative individuals, many of whom become good friends. Every Wednesday evening we meet in Town Hall where The Director never fails to offer new challenges, vocal exercises and improvisational workouts. He has a great talent for pushing our envelopes deeper into experiential connection with that force within that craves expression.

I live the life of a monk, entirely devoted to my conscious evolution. I rise before dawn, make my way up the hill through the tongues of predawn fog that lap at the shores of this paradise, past the vineyard to The Lodge with its welcoming fireplace. There I warm my bones by the fire and study a text I put into practice each day. As mentioned earlier, I am fond of the work of Epictetus, especially The Enchiridion, his manual for living, fifty-three paragraphs, each a practical instruction for living an aware life. Number seventeen, for instance, instructs:

> "Remember that you are an actor in a play, and
> the Playwright chooses the manner of it: if he
> wants it short, it is short; if long, it is long. If he
> wants you to act a poor man you must act the
> part with all your powers; and so if your part
> be a cripple or a magistrate or a plain man. For
> your business is to act the character that is
> given you and act it well; the choice of the cast is
> Another's."

Be a conscious actor on the stage of life he instructs. I go forth into the day determined to play my role with grace and awareness. Each day I inch my way deeper within, realizing moment to moment I am not the role I play, removing my sense of identity from my actions, striving to listen for each line I speak, each gesture I make. With this effort more and more of my attention is focused into the only reality, Now, the portal to a greater, co-existing, reality, an idea that is saturated with meaning beyond my comprehension, is beyond description except through metaphor and memory.

My roles are many. During the day the role is purchasing, The School's face to the outside world. Monday evenings I am the night switchboard operator, Tuesday evenings a member of the choir, Wednesdays an actor in training, Thursdays a dishwasher at The Lodge. Fridays are my night off.

Most lunch hours I spend on the ridge behind the office doing voice exercises and reciting speeches. I project my voice down the hill into the forest until it bounces off the tree trunks and echoes back to me. After work I practice the weekly singing lesson I have recorded before going to the evening's rehearsal. I strive to make the most of every moment as a developmental opportunity. The time I spend at The Retreat is precious, and can vanish in a heartbeat.

In the fall and winter after the As You Like It performances the choir approaches readiness to perform. Forty voices come together under the expert guidance of the Music Director who molds us into a single entity. It culminates in a Friday night concert for the community shortly after the New Year.

We squeeze into the Town Hall green room on the appointed evening. Now I know why I purchased a tuxedo. These are the toughest moments of the performance process, the final moments of waiting. Finally we file on stage to greet a room filled to capacity, standing room only. The music director raises his baton. The pianist sounds the opening chords. We open our collective mouths as a never before felt energy moves through us to create a new level of sound. The energy of the audience propels us into another dimension. Now I know how performers become hooked on performance. The ecstasy of singing during rehearsal is entirely superseded by a performance that roots the entire room into the moment.

In the weeks that follow two new performance groups are formed, one from the drama class, the other from the choir. The intention is to put on a show at the Goethe Academy for The Teacher and guests where the actors read Shakespearian Sonnets and a chamber choir sings Elizabethan madrigals. I really want to be one of the sonnet readers, having memorized several of them during my long hours alone on the road.

I petition The Director to be chosen a reader but, for reasons that escape me now, I am rebuffed, a severe disappointment. Looking at this event hindsight, I wonder if I failed to directly ask for what I wanted. One of my internal failings in life has been a reticence to ask for what I want, waiting to be invited. I have clear memory of demonstrating to The Director my proficiency in the memorization and performance of sonnets, spontaneously auditioning at one point. What I have no memory of is directly asking him to be a part of the reading group. It seems so simple in retrospect, just ask! It's like standing at the door without knocking, then wondering why you are not invited to enter.

In retaliation I ask, even persuade, the music director to include me in the chamber choir. He agrees, making me one of two bass singers, committing me to another evening rehearsal. It replaces my Thursday evening dishwashing job. It turns out that singing in the chamber choir is even more ecstatic and challenging than the main choir, and, a more rewarding experience than reading. My actor friends complement me for being so talented, yet, inside, I feel left out. I am struck now by how my ego's attitude can diminish an experience. I am beginning to learn the value of acceptance, or surrender to what is, by seeing that everything contains a blessing, unveils a purpose.

Two months of rehearsal later, on a Friday evening, my tuxedo and me stand in the elegant ballroom of The Academy in front of The Teacher and a selection of resident students. The eight-voice choir is an acapella masterpiece of Elizabethan madrigals. Our voices blend together in an intricate dance that delights the ear and sooths the soul, off setting the serious impact of Shakespeare's deepest thoughts. The chamber choir is such a success that the music director decides to take it to the next level and we begin rehearsing Latin masses.

Now I am running flat out. Every weekday evening is taken. Most evenings I retire around midnight and rise at 5:00 a.m. to resume the cycle of incremental efforts, keeping balance through presence. I have moments where the next step is the only action I have the energy to accomplish, making the thought of anything else overwhelming. The value of holding attention in the Now is no longer theoretical. It is profoundly practical, no longer an option, but a necessity, the one thing holding my sanity together.

Rehearsal evenings are followed by late dinners at The Lodge where friendships blossom. The evenings after drama class are especially vivid. It is this group that pushes the envelope of consciousness.

Four of us adapt Gurdjieff's "stop!" exercise. During his meetings, when his group was taking a break and socializing, Gurdjieff would suddenly, without warning, shout the word "Stop!" At this signal, every person in the room would freeze, remaining motionless until he shouts, "resume".

One of our group has an alarm wristwatch. He sets the alarm to go off sometime during our dinner. Each of us at the table freezes when this occurs, counts internally to sixty, and then resumes. In a crowded dining room it is performance art, creating an elevated state of awareness in both the performers and the witnesses.

One evening the alarm goes off just as our server approaches the table. We all freeze, right down to the cessation of eye movement. It is like stepping off the stage of existence. For sixty seconds we stop participating in life. I am a witness to the drama, a prop on the stage. The server dances around the table, trying to make eye contact. No one breaks concentration. We are a pool of stillness midst the swirl of life. The experience is transcendent.

The choir begins rehearsing Faure's Requiem, in Latin. The theme of the piece takes the joy of singing to another level. The phrase "Libera mea domine" (liberate me lord) stimulates an intense emotional surge every time I sing it. The emotion is so intense I weep at times. I feel the plea in the very root of my being. I pray for liberation. It is the entire objective of The Work, transcendence.

A complex piece, it requires months of preparation. Every week my soul soars with the music. I come to rehearsal each time thirsting for the moment these words appear, my heart bursting over and over. There is nothing, no past, no future, no 'situation', nothing but these words to the heavens floating on my voice. In these moments I AM LIBERATED!

CHAPTER THIRTY-SIX

Transcendence in Rehearsal

The following spring, healing from the loss of my marriage, I surrender to my aloneness and begin to enjoy my freedom. My work and cultural pursuits leave little time for a private life. The seeds buried in my inner world have germinated and are beginning to blossom, creating new transcendent experiences.

One of those occurs during rehearsals for the next round of poetry reading. The drama group decides to stage a reading of American poets. Ten of us each choose a poet. I chose Bob Dylan, my favorite Sixties culture hero. One of the presenters, the one who is working with Walt Whitman, is unable to attend a weeknight rehearsal, so I stand in for him. A lady student playing classical guitar accompanies. The title of the poem is: "One Hour to Madness and Joy".

I begin to read as she begins to play. We did not

practice at all prior to rehearsal, we just spontaneously connect. It is a first run through. We do not know if the reading will match the music in mood or length. I am immediately caught in the emotion of the poetry, which is itself transcendent. The first line is:

"One hour to madness and joy! O furious! O
confine me not!"

My heart and voice soar on these words, as does the music, a perfect match of tonality and feeling, deepening my emotional reaction. They are an exquisite expression of the life I am living. It touches me to the core of my being. I stand on the podium in the cavern of the empty Town Hall, a few actors the only audience. A column of light glowing from within illuminates me. I am riveted, transported. The words tell it all.

One hour to madness and joy! O furious! O confine
me not!
(What is it that frees me so in storms?
What do my shouts amid lightnings and raging
winds mean?)
O to drink the mystic deliria deeper than any
other man!
O savage and tender achings! (I bequeath them to
you, my children,
I tell them to you, for reasons, O bridegroom and
bride.)
O to be yielded to you whoever who are, and you
to be yielded
to me in defiance of the world!
O to return to Paradise! O bashful and feminine!

O to draw you to me, to plant on you for the first time the lips of a determin'd man.
O the puzzle, the thrice-tied knot, the deep and dark pool, all untied and illumin'd!
O to speed where there is space enough and air enough at last!
To be absolv'd from previous ties and conventions, I from mine, and you from yours!
To find a new unthought-of nonchalance with the best of Nature!
To have the gag remov'd from one's mouth!
To have the feeling today or any day I am sufficient as I am.
O something unprov'd! Something in a trance!
To escape utterly from others' anchors and holds!
To drive free! To love free! To dash reckless and dangerous!
To court destruction with taunts, with invitations!
To ascend, to leap to the heavens of the love indicated to me!
To rise thither with my inebriate soul!
To feed the remainder of life with one hour of fullness and freedom!
With one brief hour of madness and joy.

The music comes to a climax as the poem ends. It moves with my feelings, as if it was written for this moment. The intensity is magical, profound. I am so moved I cannot speak. I look around me, emerging from a journey to another dimension. The stillness in the room is deep, rarely felt. The performance resonates in the ethers. The poem's words are mine. It is my cry to the universe, the sounding of my determination to live passionately now.

We perform the show the following week. I read Dylan's song "The Times Are A Changin'" as a poem. It is powerful, filled with presence, but nothing, no other moment on stage, ever comes close to that night in rehearsal when I AM Whitman's words.

CHAPTER THIRTY-SEVEN

Erasure of Personal History

As the spring unfolds and I become more immersed in the life I dreamed into being, the path that brought me to this place fades into the remote recesses of my consciousness. My personal history disappears bit by bit each day as I endeavor to more intensely focus my attention into Here/Now reality. It is one of the intentions of inner work to not be ruled by the past, nor expect what happened yesterday to occur again tomorrow, to completely die to your history in order to create, not replicate.

It is not that I forget my past, but I give it less and less attention, over writing the files on my hard drive with present moment experiences. In the idealization of this principle, one would become a pure instrument of the unseen world and lose all awareness of what happened before now.

Even if some memory is associatively evoked, it feels like it belongs to someone else. It is not quite real, and is completely separate from my current reality. I discipline my mind to focus entirely on the tasks in front of me, avoiding conversations about my origins as much as possible. In order to do this I release my attachment to disappointments, frustrations, regrets, angers, feelings of injustice, grudges, all the negative connections my mind has formed around my history.

Forgiveness clearly is the key here. Release is impossible without it. It comes naturally with the realization that yesterday's events are inevitable, a confluence of influences the consequence of which have brought me to this place in my life. Gurdjieff says "Man does not do, everything happens". Shakespeare, in "As You Like It", gives these words to the melancholy Jaques:

"All the world's a stage,
And all the men and women merely players;
They have their exits and their entrances;
And one man in his time plays many parts."

Johann Goethe hints at the existence of a life script in his novel about self-realization, Wihelm Meister's Apprenticeship. Epictetus points in a similar direction. The more I get it, the more I become aware of the simplicity of it. My task is simply to live consciously, Here/Now, being here for the drama to unfold. All I have to "do" is show up completely: mentally, emotionally, physically, and spiritually. The rest is out of my hands. I am making the choice-less choice. "To Be, or Not To Be" is always the question, the moment-to-moment decision. How often am

I choosing not To Be through some form of resistance or denial, wishing the moment to be different?

In the four months of separation from my wife I reinvent myself. I miss having a life partner. However, I am free from the concerns and compromises required by marriage. My personal decisions are completely my own. I need to be alone at this time in my evolution. When she approaches me around this time asking: "Do you want to come back to the marriage?" I breathe deep, pausing, listening. A resounding "No" comes back from my intuition, my inner guidance. Through this act I release the last vestiges of regret and loss, peeling away yet another layer of the ego onion, revealing the next challenge.

I dedicate my life to The School and The Work. I participate in work on myself, work with others, and work for The School. I am not completely selfless. I have ambition to awaken in this lifetime. The Teacher has declared his school will produce seven conscious beings. I want to be one of them. Yet, I still have that nagging little worm in my subconscious that feels it does not quite belong, or sets itself apart in some indefinable way.

I stop having thoughts and memories about anyone outside the community. My entire attention is focused on the Here/Now of my life. Once I am taken off the road, I rarely leave. When I do, it is only to go to a teaching house in the Bay Area, or a Teacher's meeting in the Oakland hills. We are completely cut off from mainstream media including politics. I have no contact with daily headlines, with trends in culture and music or anything else that is going on in the world outside The Retreat.

This disconnect from societal programming is profound and freeing. I am off the grid. No more daily upgrades from the media. If life is a dream then I have stepped outside the dream, or am dreaming a dream within the dream. The distinction between what I see and experience outside The Retreat and within it is vivid, like the difference between black and white and full color vision.

I am also free from the need to forage for a living or find a career identity. Materially I zero summed out my life when I resigned from AIG and drove off to the mountains in a borrowed car. I took a few thousand dollars with me to fill in the gaps, but my possessions amount to clothing, a few books and two cameras. By life standards I am homeless and penniless. Yet I feel rich beyond imagining. The strange thing is that I am completely comfortable with the situation. I know that, if or when it becomes necessary to manifest a material life again I will work it out. "It all works out" has been a mantra of mine for years. It clearly is a part of my belief system and it has served me well. The mind has a problem with this philosophy of living because it wants to know how it will work out. The answers it wants are provided moment-to-moment, which is when and where it gets worked out.

CHAPTER THIRTY-EIGHT

The Duino Elgies Reading

The Town Hall stage darkens as eight actors file on stage. Outside it is an early spring Sunday afternoon. A leaf green haze of new growth floats over the vineyard. Dressed in black, they take evenly spaced positions on stage with their backs to the gathering as the lights dim. There is a tension-building pause as the viewers sit wondering what the crazy actors are up to now. The lights come back up and the center stage actor turns, engaging the audience with a longing expression and questioning eyes.

"Who", he resonates. Immediately another actor turns.

"If I cried" she intones, as another turns,

"Would hear me," he resolutely declares, and another,

"Among the Angelic orders?" she queries.

It continues in this fashion, voices rising up in the spiritual longing so eloquently expressed in this poet's masterwork.

"And even if one were to suddenly
Take me to its heart, I would vanish into its
Stronger existence. For beauty is nothing but
The beginning of terror, that we are still able to
bear,
And we revere it so, because it calmly disdains
To destroy us. Every Angel is terror.
And so I hold myself back and swallow the cry
Of a darkened sobbing."

This performance is the culmination of the drama group's spring project. The Irish actress, our co-leader, designs, directs and performs in a dramatic reading of Rainer Maria Rilke's masterwork, The Duino Elegies, a ten stanza emotionally charged epic poem of the seeker's cry in the wilderness, "Who, if I cried, would hear me???" Rilke is declared to be a conscious being by The Teacher. Nowhere is this poet's level of Being more clear than in this colossus of a poem that was ten years in gestation.

Rilke had been visiting Princess Marie von Thurn und Taxis in the Duino castle near Trieste in January 1912 and, according to his own recounting, had taken a stroll near the castle, atop the steep cliffs that dropped down to the beach. Rilke said later he had heard a voice calling to him as he walked near the cliffs, and he had used its words as the opening line.

Once again profound poetry deeply moves my soul as we prepare this complex performance. Rilke's expression of the soul's passage through life and beyond turns my "winter of discontent" bittersweet. The deep emotion of the work and the sheer joy of creating performance art from it add fire to my infatuation for the Irish actress.

What had been a smoldering coal last year is fanned into a roaring blaze by working with her on The Elegies. It soon is raging out of control, bombarding my inner world with obsessive thoughts that I fight off daily using presence practice tools.

Nothing like this has ever happened to me. Every time I am near her I am intently watching without appearing to watch. When not with her, my mind constantly attempts to usurp the moment with obsessive fantasies. The attraction is more emotional than sexual, being connected to the deep emotions the poetry arouses in us all as we work on becoming the words. I look for any hint of reciprocation; although it instinctively seems to me my feelings are not returned. In fact, I feel we are not a match. Yet even when I tell myself that, the obsession will still not leave. It becomes more apparent every day that I must do something external to break this spell/curse. I must shatter my fear of being rejected or ridiculed, and directly confront the situation.

Finally one evening I invite her to dinner at The Lodge. We have wine and talk about the Elegies project throughout the meal. After dessert and coffee I bring forth my confession. She does not seem to be terribly shocked, but rather goes reflective, muttering mostly to herself how she is, in fact, in love with someone else. I am released from my obsession.

CHAPTER THIRTY-NINE

Mountain Retreat

Monday morning after the Elegies presentation I pack my bag and head out in my grandmother's old Chevy for my family's Sierra cabin. This is the first time in years I am alone. I head down the Sacramento Valley, turn east toward the town of Sonora and head up into the mountains. Just past the 5000-altitude marker, a few miles before the town of Pinecrest, I turn off onto Snow White Ridge Drive, down a hill and left to the base of a slope. My family's cabin sits atop the slope facing south down the Sierra range.

Once I am settled, I head into town and stock up on food and wine, then on to take a look at the lake. This was where I spent my childhood summers, playing on the beach and in the icy waters of this alpine pond surrounded by granite peaks. It looks foreign and familiar simultaneously, a formula for surrealism. I have never been so deep into myself, so disconnected from almost all obligation. Alone with no one to talk with, it feels my body is a space ship I am traveling in to visit a distant world. I peer out of the portals of my eyes at the beautiful scenes, content to be alone with them.

I take my supplies back to the house, open a bottle of wine and enjoy the sunset. After a delicious dinner, I build a fire, play Bach's grandiose organ recital Toccata and Fugue in D Minor, and open Rilke's only novel, The Notebooks of Malte Laurids Brigge . It addresses existential themes— the quest for individuality, the significance of death, and reflection on the experience of time as death approaches, all written in the existential style best described as being and nothingness. The fugue's dark overtones suit the theme of Rilke's story. My mind soars with the music as the fire blazes and I ponder my own life in the context of the tale. Eventually I succumb to the external warmth of the fire and the internal warmth of the wine, dozing off to awaken in the early a.m. with a mouth full of cotton and crawl into bed.

The next morning I take my coffee out on the deck to carpe diem(seize the day) just in time to glimpse a mountain lion disappearing into the forest below the house. I glance over into the trees on the right and remember a special moment when, visiting with my family who built the get away, I chain sawed a perfect round off a huge log, drawing the blade around the cut so perfectly that it precisely lined up with the beginning of the cut on the other side, cleanly dropping off.

Underneath the deck is a garage containing my father's favorite toy, an old open-air jeep powered by a Chevy V-8. Tied to the roof rack is the beautiful mahogany dingy my father and I built together when I was a teen. I fire up the jeep, put a book of Walt Whitman poetry into a backpack with some drinks and food and head for the lake. Once at the water's edge, I lower the boat into the water, place the oars in their locks, load up, and row two miles across the lake to the far side where the river enters.

The river flows into the lake at the bottom of a box canyon down a series of falls. I tie up the boat and head upstream, coming into a grassy meadow sheltered on either side by groves of Ponderosa Pine. The water looks so inviting I strip down and take a plunge, lying on the grass later to air-dry.

On to the base of the falls, I climb up the side until the lake is a glimmering mirror hundreds of feet below, the entire San Joaquin Valley falling away beyond and below it. I find a flat rock, take out my refreshments and book, have a meal and read Whitman aloud to the angels. I have not seen another soul since crossing the lake.

It is all unspeakably beautiful, sheer delight, but there is an edge. I have led such a busy life for so long my body is still responding to the pattern of "doing" I left at The Retreat. Though I have nothing to do and nowhere to go, I cannot quite relax into the moment. My mind says "Chill!!" but my body does not know how. I am sitting on this rock, high above the world, contemplating the path that brought me here, bringing it all to bear on this moment, my entire Being, contemplating my nothingness, my no-thing-ness.

When I have had all I can tolerate of this, I pack up, climb down the falls and walk back down the canyon to the lake's edge where the dinghy awaits. After a leisurely row back to the dock, I load the boat and return to the cabin for another robust meal with Bach and Rilke.

On day three I drive down to the lake and hike the shoreline, enjoying the crisp, cool alpine air as I revisit the sites of childhood and adolescent joys. Memories bombard me as I pass the sites of various early adventures. The first time I swam across the lake, a two-mile effort; or when I first tried SCUBA diving after borrowing a tank from a fellow I met on the trail. Days of fishing the deep waters in the hopes of catching the legendary giant trout the old timers talk about at the tackle shop.

I realize now in recalling these experiences how, joyful as they were, they had a deep tinge of loneliness to them. It feels good to get away from my fast paced busy life, but I really am not having a good time alone, without someone to share the experience. I know being single is necessary to allow me the freedom to experience all the cultural opportunities of The Retreat, but it is all bittersweet when tinged with aloneness.

That evening it really gets to me. I struggle to be where I am, but my mind keeps replaying recent social events. Since his arrival, our music director has patiently labored to create an orchestra. Two months ago they had a debut performance. More recently, it was decided to stage a ball at which the orchestra would play Viennese waltzes. Tuxedos and ball gowns appeared and we all spun around the floor. I had a particularly good time dancing with a woman from the San Francisco centre. We whirled the night away. Now, as I sit gazing down the slope into the woods, I imagine closeness to her.

After three days without human interaction, and half a bottle of wine, a desperation arises in me that must have gratification. Picking up the phone, I reach out. She answers and for the next thirty minutes I share the contents of my vacation with her, telling her that, after three days alone, she is the one I think to call. I feel and ignore the strain of credulity in her voice as she tolerates the release of my pent up need to communicate. The following morning, after a leisurely breakfast on the deck, I close up the cabin and return to The Retreat.

CHAPTER FORTY

My Life Blossoms

I t is spring. The sap is rising. Everything is blooming. I settle back into the rigors and demands of my practice routines: voice lessons, drama class, and choir rehearsals, periodically punctuated by performances. The chamber choir is doing Gregorian masses in Latin (finally I realize the benefit of studying Latin in high school). We again combine with the sonnet readers for another evening of ecstasy at the Goethe Academy. The choir stages another performance at Town Hall, and the drama group begins rehearsing Romeo and Juliet on Sunday mornings.

In the Wednesday evening drama class we are given an interesting exercise. Each person is given a word and instructed to create a skit using it. My word was "conductor". I took it to mean orchestra conductor rather than train conductor. I interviewed the music director for clues and he told me the story of a conductor who was so dictatorial and cold that the entire orchestra walked out on him. He lent me his baton to use as a prop.

The following week, having conceived a general outline and direction for my performance, I take the stage in front of the class, walk up to a music stand and begin abusively addressing an imaginary orchestra, not even calling them by name, but by the instrument they play. I castigate them for an excellent but flawed performance the previous evening and tell them we will have to work all weekend to make it better. As my rant gathers momentum my abuses escalate, until one by one they rise and leave as I run after them apologizing, begging them to return, calling to them for the first time by their names.

This year our second drama season is developing much faster than the first, we know a little more about what we are doing. In addition to all my other commitments, I am also the production manager for Romeo and Juliet. The stage in the field is being remodeled and upgraded, requiring me to coordinate the acquisition and delivery of building materials. A stairway is built up the backstage side of the enormous oak tree, becoming Juliet's balcony, with a sweeping ramp that swoops down one side to the stage. Three sides of the stage are ramped, allowing entries and exits to be made through the audience.

This year we are seasoned actors who learn our lines quickly. I am cast as Lord Capulet, father of Juliet, who has been feuding with the family of Lord Montague, father of Romeo, who comes uninvited to a banquet thrown by the Capulet's where he is smitten by the beauty and charm of Juliet. The drama ends in the tragic suicide death of the two lovers.

This project requires the actors to learn fencing and

has several fight scenes, the first of which opens the play and is between the fathers, Capulet and Montague. The play also contains a masked ball with a choreographed dance sequence. The costumes are flowing capes for the men and ornate dresses for the ladies.

Since our director is now a Retreat resident we have more frequent rehearsals and the production comes together in much less time than As You Like It. We are ready for performance by the beginning of summer. This year our production values are at a much higher level in every respect: the costumes; the acting; the staging, lighting and music all have become more sophisticated and we all have more a sense of knowing what we are doing. The performance series, four shows in two weeks, is well attended by the community, and we once again head off to Ashland to celebrate.

CHAPTER FORTY-ONE

My Fourth Year

It is 1983. I have been living at The Retreat now for four years, becoming more and more deeply enmeshed in this community. Needless to say, I never want to leave. I am determined to live the rest of my life here. I have made a place for myself, proven my worth and it just keeps getting better. The outer world I came from, the larger context within which this community exists, has faded into a black and white dream I give no attention. It has ceased to have meaning and hardly ever enters my thoughts. I almost have it all, though the part of me that needs to love remains unfulfilled, is an empty ache in my heart. I fill it during the day with the richness of the life I have created here, but at night I am alone with the ache.

This is not to say that everything is easy. The Work is all about effort. I continue to run my life flat out, pedal to the metal. I exist on an average of five hours sleep. I am still a member of the breakfast club. My day starts at 5:00 a.m. and goes until midnight most evenings. I still sing in two choirs that have periodic performances. I even am a lunchtime server at The Lodge once a week and still spend Monday evenings working the switchboard until ten o'clock.

I have a moment one of those Monday evenings. It is a new moon phase. The road out of the office is a quarter mile dirt track up a hill. With no moon to light the way I cannot even see the ground at my feet, having left my flashlight home. I am walking slowly by my memory of the path and the feel of my feet on the ground. This is one of those times where I am so exhausted that life is reduced to literally taking the next step. Then I hear something on the path ahead, stimulating an adrenaline surge. I freeze, listening. Perhaps it is the hooves of a deer. It passes and I feel my way, step by step out to the road. This is the quintessence of inner work, ones entire life brought to focus in an ordinary moment, a focus so intense it remains clear in my memory to this day.

The Teacher remains a peripheral figure to me. I attend occasional dinners with him in the Meissen Room where he teaches. Conversations in this venue generally focus around him. Students generally do not have side conversations in his presence. One evening he begins talking about a major tool he uses to keep focus. He refers to it off and on throughout the evening, creating a build. We eagerly await the revelation; feeling like some great secret is about to be given. He has our focused attention. Finally it comes.

"I keep my feet parallel when seated."

My first reaction is disappointment. My mind expected

something of greater consequence, some new piece of deep knowledge. Years later, as a teacher myself, I tell this story to my students as an example of how the small effort of connecting to the sensation of your feet on the ground can bring one's attention into the moment. When I try it, I find the relaxed, natural position of the feet when seated is a "V" configuration. It is actually uncomfortable to keep the feet parallel. It takes focused effort to hold them in that position.

I have other incidental interactions with him. He has occasion to place calls in the evening when I am on the switchboard. I have had brief encounters with him throughout my time here, and his movements and actions continue to be the central focus of The Retreat culture, but he remains enigmatic, an iconic figure, an impenetrable mystery. I am deeply grateful to him for having created this community, but the person behind the role remains elusive, unknowable.

CHAPTER FORTY-TWO

The Cherry Orchard

I receive a call one early fall morning. A buzz has been circulating the past few weeks about an older student (a former center director). She lives near the retreat and wants to stage Anton Chekhov's play The Cherry Orchard in Town Hall. This in itself is a radical idea, since, up to this point, Town Hall has been off limits to theatrical productions. The play takes place in post revolutionary Russia and is an existential drama about an aristocratic family losing their ancestral orchard to debt and decline.

"Hello James. I am calling to ask you to be the stage manager for my production of The Cherry Orchard?"

A pit of disappointment begins pooling in my solar plexus. "Hi. My interest is in acting in your production. I have no interest in missing an opportunity to play Chekhov. Ask someone else."

"Well James, I can understand your position, but you

are the most reliable person in the drama group. I cannot imagine pulling this off without your support. In fact, I will not do this without you. If you turn me down, I will cancel it."

I try to bargain. "OK. I will do it if I can have a role too. Playing a non-creative part is unthinkable!"

"No James. I need your complete commitment to the production side. Halfway measures are not an option."

The conversation goes around and around this point a few times until I finally cave in and agree. This is the last thing I want. I have a passion for acting and am already fantasizing about the role I want to play. To have no creative involvement is difficult. It brings up my old emotions around being left out, the same feelings I had when I was not asked to be a sonnet reader.

At the first cast meeting I sit beside the director taking notes and being given directions, action items that need follow-up. She is an active type with an emotionally volatile, aggressive personality. Immediately she begins using me as emotional backup. The same emotional drive that fuels her creativity is also her source of doubt and insecurity. It becomes my job to transform these feelings when they come up through support and reassurance. I become the can-do guy who has to bring her creative ideas into manifestation. It is my job to take the heat, giving her creative space. Mostly the heat I have to take comes from her emotional volatility, intensive interactions requiring me to be the emotional rock, unmoved by the storms of her fearful reactivity.

"James. I know myself well enough to be aware that I am going to go through an emotional rollercoaster to pull this off. I need you to be my anchor of rationality and reasonability, to absorb my fear and doubt so I can give unconditional love to the actors."

As stage manager I am responsible for having every material need met for each rehearsal, be it props, furniture, or backdrops. I arrive early and get everything ready. I arrange and announce rehearsal schedules, locate, acquire and store all the materials needed, inform the cast of what the director requires, and coordinate with set designers and artists to meet production demands.

My actor friends watch in amazement as I consistently handle her volatility, absorbing, deflecting and managing every emotional outburst without taking a single thing personally. It is one of the greatest growth trials of my life in The Work. Internally I fight the feelings of regret over not being one of the actors, feeling left out. The Work never fails to force confrontation with my internal weaknesses. She treats the actors like lovers, me like a husband with whom she has a constant irritation.

Not only is there rehearsal, there is set design. My best friend in the acting group is the lead, and also the set designer. His day job at The Retreat is landscape architecture. He, the director and I work together to turn Town Hall into a community theater in the round. Using the choir risers we create a tiered audience on two sides of the main room, hanging a hand painted mural representing the orchard across the musical stage. One of The Retreat's artists in residence paints the mural on a huge canvas, barely making production deadline, another cause for stress and upset.

There are also political obstacles to be overcome. First, there is our relationship with the music department and with the lady who manages Town Hall. She became manager when she began offering The Teacher complaints about how the facility was being managed, or how there was no management. In a typical Gurdjieffian move, he gave her the job. Also, there are prohibitions in the school against smoking and guns. (There is a $2,500 fine for being caught smoking.) The plot requires one of the actors to be smoking a cigar. It falls to me to get a dispensation from the school president for this to happen, great material for my inner work, to ask permission to break the rules. Word of this gets out and becomes part of The Retreat buzz, adding to the drama group's reputation for pushing the envelope.

Two months into the build, and one month to performance, at a Saturday afternoon rehearsal, she invites two visitors from the drama department of a local college to observe our process. All goes extremely well until the end when I am addressing the group concerning the date and time of our next meeting. In the middle of this she intercedes, contradicting the information I have just given. When I politely indicate she is misinformed, she heatedly argues with me in front of the visitors and the actors. I get embarrassed and feel humiliated.

I say nothing, merely acceding to her revision, but feeling hurt and offended over her treatment of me. For me she has become disrespectful. An obsessive part of my brain I had not seen in some time emerges and stews over the whole affair for the next two days. All the pent up unresolved emotion I have over her treatment of me boils to the surface, feelings I "thought" I had managed. Apparently I have not been completely honest with myself and have some pride over being cool and controlled. She is standing behind me when she intervenes. It is like getting shot in the back. All my defenses are down. At brunch on Sunday, I am sitting with a friend venting about this when the music director comes over to me to speak about the same scheduling issue.

"You must be special." My friend says. I look questioningly at him. "You are receiving a lot of attention." He points upward, a slight smile, almost a smirk, lighting up his face.

Back in the office Monday morning I call her to straighten out the situation. Again she argues. A huge surge of adrenaline shoots up my spine and explodes in my brain. I began screaming into the phone.

"I QUIT!!. You do the play yourself. I am out of it. DONE!!" I shout, slamming the phone into its cradle repeatedly in an out-of-control rage fit. My two co-workers sit beside me straight faced, eyes bulging. They continue to watch without watching, looks of frozen calm on their faces. I go outside and walk around the building, recomposing, then return and resume the day's activities. Not a word is spoken about what had just happened.

Now my struggle is with an inner demon, a mind trying to run wild while my consciousness fights back with every tool I know. It is the simple struggle to attain and maintain presence, full attention into the moment. No past, no future, just NOW. I struggle to immerse my awareness into this singular reality, using the pain of the event to ignite consciousness, turning ordinary moments into high drama. Externally all is calm and placid, save my eyes are more intense than usual. Internally the ego rages, alternating between anger with self for losing its cool, obsessive self-justification and countless "shoulda, woulda, coulda" scenarios, a battle royal between the forces of light and dark in me.

Every step I take, I feel my heel land, foot roll forward to launch the next step fluidly from the toes. I smell every rose on the path, taste the air driving through the vineyard, feel the sun on my face, give every person I encounter my loving full attention, taste my food, recite Shakespearian Sonnets in my head, focus on the mantra learned from Transcendental Meditation, in two words, Remember MySelf, the reason I AM Here.

When not doing some or all of the above my mind attacks with feelings of self-loathing, frustration and rage. During the day I am more successful maintaining focus, the evenings are more difficult. The unoccupied mind is more vulnerable to the dangers of random association. There is truth in the old saying: "An idle mind is the devil's workshop."

I stay away from rehearsals Monday and Wednesday nights, checking in with my best friend to find out what is happening in my absence. My inner child wants to know if I am missed. I hear how she has to struggle doing my job too. This information pleases the vindictive part of me. Friday evening, a sit down read through of the play is scheduled. The cast sits in a circle and reads the entire play. I show up, but talk to no one, sitting off in a corner. The rehearsal continues for two hours, concludes and all the cast leave but her. She makes every attempt to ignore me. I finally walk up to her and blurt out,

"I just want to make this play happen!" and burst into tears.

She begins crying too and we embrace. Neither one of us apologizes, nor do we ever speak of the inciting issue again.

The project proceeds to performance without any

further disruption. I am vulnerable and sensitive throughout the process. My ego feels embarrassment and shame, at times, for having failed at not taking her personally. It turns out I do have a role to play. During the performance I operate the sound track, a series of environmental sounds, such as birds twittering, contributing to the mood of the scenes. The long awaited painting arrives days before we open, covering the music stage with an impressionistic orchard vista. The three performances go off smoothly and we gather at a cast member's house that Sunday evening to celebrate.

CHAPTER FORTY-THREE

Traveling With The Teacher

I t is December, 1983. I am working late one night at the office when in comes The Teacher's scribe, the person he designates to follow him around writing down his important thoughts. He met the school in New York City where he had been a cab driver. When he first arrived at The Retreat he was assigned to work on the construction team at the winery knoll. While there he contracted a rare disease that hospitalized him. He barely survived. During his recovery he had a seemingly chance encounter with The Teacher the outcome of which was the creation of his job as The Teacher's secretary.

I meet him while washing Meissen China and we become friends. He comes to the office this evening to inform me The Teacher is leaving the next day on a car trip for several days to view the King Tut exhibit in San Francisco and I am invited to go with them. It is not uncommon for students to travel with The Teacher and is, of course, considered a great privilege. My dilemma is, I cannot, in good conscience, just drop what I am doing and go without arranging for someone to cover my job. As much as he tries to persuade me to leave with them the next morning, I feel it would be irresponsible of me to do so and send my regrets. I see The Teacher the next week while serving his table at lunch, he tells me he will invite me again with lead-time.

One evening in January I receive a call.

"Hello James," says a soft but powerful voice. There is always a pause, an in breath, when he speaks, like a gathering of intention.

"We are making a journey to southern California in two weeks. Would you be able to come? Is this sufficient warning?"

I agree. In two weeks I find and train another student to cover my work. This is it. I finally get to experience him close up and personal. Maybe I will glimpse the person inside the role.

On a Monday morning I arrive at the Goethe Academy with my suitcase. There are five of us; The Teacher, the scribe, another male student from The Retreat, and a young woman who is a television actress and lives in Los Angeles. She has a rental car she must return and I am asked to drive it. The other student is asked to keep me company. The Teacher, the actress and the scribe will ride in his Mercedes. I am, of course, disappointed, having envisioned my departure in the Mercedes. Instead I am driving a compact rental.

We head down the mountain toward Sacramento. Two hours later we are on the freeway loop that circles the city when the Mercedes pulls over. My student companion goes to the car and is instructed to ask me to lead our little caravan to a certain restaurant where we lunch. Then we head down the San Joaquin valley to Bakersfield where we dine and spend the night in a motel. On the drive back to the motel from dinner I am riding in the back seat with the actress. We became friendly during the meal, me being curious about the details of professional acting.

The next day we cross the coastal mountains heading for Ojai. We stop for lunch in San Luis Obispo. The scribe is driving and, as personal assistant to The Teacher, he carries a satchel that contains The Teacher's valuables. I have been teasing him about being more intentional with the money. In the restaurant he lays it down and goes to the restroom, leaving it unattended. I take it and hide it, letting him fuss for a while about losing it, then give it back to him. Oddly enough, on departure he puts it on the roof of the Mercedes and forgets it until the force of the car's movement causes it to slide into the open moon roof, hitting him on the head.

We arrive in Ojai, shop a little, and then head to a fancy restaurant for dinner. While waiting to be seated, a waiter passes by with a tray of full water glasses. As he passes he trips, spilling the water onto The Teacher's lap. There is an intake of breath, his eyes enlarge, but he does not lose his composure or react negatively toward the waiter, who is, of course, falling over himself apologizing. He looks at us:

"It is cold in here!" he calmly says, almost like he is referring to his inner world.

At dinner I find myself seated with the actress. We

engage in a discussion of acting techniques, enjoying each other's company. On the way back to the hotel that evening we all are riding in the Mercedes. I am in the back seat with her when she starts shivering from the chill of the evening. I sit behind her and wrap my arms around her, projecting my body heat into her.

The next morning at breakfast I find myself in a discussion with her about poetry reading. My contention is that poetry should not just be recited but acted, giving the words emotional values, as if they were being spoken in passionate conversation.

"I remember attending a reading in college by the Russian poet Yevtushenko. His presentation was so passionately expressive it transcended the language barrier. Consider Shakespeare's sonnet number six:

Then let not winter's ragged hand deface
In Thee thy summer, ere thou be distill'd:
Make sweet some vial, treasure thou some place
With beauty's treasure, ere it be self-kill'd.
That use is not forbidden usury,
Which happys those that pay the willing loan;
That's for thyself to breed another thee,
Or ten times happier, be it ten for one.
Ten times thyself were happier than thou art,
If ten of thine ten times refigured thee:
Then what could death do, if thou shouldst depart,
Leaving thee living in posterity?
Be not self will'd, for thou art much too fair
To be death's conquest, and make worms thine
heir.

"For me, this poem is all about how we internally store up the finer substance acquired through Self-Remembering (presence), creating a being ('another thee') that transcends physical existence, a consciousness that goes beyond the third dimension. 'Winter's ragged hand' is our fear of death which, when given in to, distills us, self-kills us."

After breakfast the actress leaves in her car. The rest of us pile into the Mercedes and head for Los Angeles. We enter through a luxurious Hollywood neighborhood. The Teacher instructs the scribe to drive through the best part of town so that we might feast on the finer substance of beauty. It is particularly striking given my total material disconnection from the outer world. It feels like I am passing through an alien world. We stare out the window, getting lost in the wonder of it all when The Teacher shouts:

"REMEMBER YOURSELF!! This is all illusion."

It is a penetrating moment. Simple and direct, shocking us into deep presence.

Fifteen minutes later we arrive at a restaurant where we are meeting the Los Angeles Centre directors for lunch. They are a delightful couple that I know from my time in Santa Barbara. He is the man who sold me my ex-wife's Mercedes, an embassy car he imported from France.

There is light conversation between the couple and The Teacher. Somewhere in the flow I manage to contribute my experience of our moment of presence on the way there and how it was similar to the "Stop!" exercise we performed in the drama group.

"James is a native Californian." The Teacher says. (This had come up in last evening's conversation.)

"San Francisco." I include, feeling a strange discomfort.

I smile and feel my feet on the floor. The conversation moves on.

Later that afternoon we arrive at the teaching house, up a twisting mountain road, perched on the edge of Topanga Canyon. It is a magnificent property with a separate carriage house where The Teacher stays. We pull into a broad driveway overlooking the canyon. The Teacher and the two other students leave the car, climbing the stairs to the carriage house. After a moment of indecision, I follow them.

The hesitation arises from a conflict between my intuitive self and my mind. My "work on myself" mind has set the aim to ask for what I want. My wanting on this trip is to have as much face time with The Teacher as possible. My intuition says: "This is not for you." My mind asks for what it wants, following them up the stairs into The Teacher's suite, risking rejection. In the process of pulling a chair into the circle, I am asked to visit with other students in the main house.

This request makes me aware of my responsibility as a Retreat resident. I remember being intensely interested in the people who lived there. Now I am the object of that same scrutiny from the Los Angeles students. I walk back down the stairs, drinking in the vista, and cross the courtyard to the kitchen where I soon am the center of a small group, being peppered by questions about life at The Retreat, the story of my journey, what happened with my wife, what is happening at the property, what it is like to travel with The Teacher and so on, for hours. I am now officially an "older student".

I sit practicing presence. I feel my feet on the floor. Most importantly, I listen. I am listening externally to the conversation and simultaneously internally to my intuition (inner guidance). I am in a new circumstance and have a new role to play, all of which adds power to my practice.

My intuition takes over my conversation, producing responses I find astonishingly beautiful and wise. This new role has a script that emerges in my awareness moment-to-moment. I must work at being a conscious actor to meet the demands of the script. The result is sheer delight! I tell my stories, using them to relate or illuminate Work ideas, much of it coming from my drama experience. A few hours into this scene, the scribe comes down from the carriage house and pulls me aside. "Do you mind taking the car to pick up Kentucky Fried Chicken?" he asks.

"No, of course not." I ask a student who knows the way to come with me and we head down the canyon in The Teacher's Mercedes looking for KFC. It is a gorgeous evening in an equally beautiful place. I am endorphin intoxicated from all the aware moments with the students. Life feels fabulous. I see now, in writing this, how the teacher in me emerged that afternoon.

The following morning we head out to the LA County Art Museum, then go shopping on Rodeo Drive, one of the ritziest shopping districts in the world. I go from celebrity status older student to penniless monk cruising through a candy store. The resulting discomfort makes me feel raw and out of place. It does, however, help me focus, forcing me to intensify my efforts to be where I Am.

We lunch late in an empty restaurant where we make a celebrity sighting. The man is dining alone with a furtive look on his face that says "leave me be!" Afterward we pick up the actress at her home and drive off to Palm Springs. She becomes my backseat conversational partner again. I enjoy her company as we speed off into the desert.

That evening after dinner, The Teacher retires early. The scribe, myself and the other student take the car cruising and end up at a nightclub where we have a drink and watch people dancing. During my four years living in isolation at The Retreat, the world of music and fashion has moved on, giving the scene a surrealistic feel. The only dancing we do in the school is waltzing. A young woman approaches and asks me to dance. I decline, feeling uncomfortable with breaking the school's customs. Later, back at the hotel, I take a midnight swim in the pool alone.

After checking out the next morning, we head to the base of a thousand foot high cliff where we ride a cable tram to the top and have lunch. The rest of the afternoon is spent searching for just the right accommodation to spend Super Bowl Sunday. We stop at a half dozen hotels. The Teacher checks the rooms, looking for the right feeling. Eventually we find a luxurious suite and settle in for the night.

The next day, as we prepare to watch the game, the actress indicates she will spend the afternoon sun bathing at the pool, hinting she would enjoy my company there. I am still waiting for something profound to happen, some special something that will come through spending time with The Teacher. I decline the invitation, and spend a boring afternoon watching a game that holds no interest for me, feeling like a fool for having passed on her invitation. At some level I know she has been invited to Palm Springs for my benefit. The Teacher is known for playing matchmaker. While I enjoy her company, pursuing a relationship with her does not feel right. There is something missing. There is no zing, no magnetism.

The following day we return to Los Angeles long enough to drop her off and head back to The Retreat, making the trip in one day. My fabled vacation with The Teacher is over. I enjoy the break from my routine. I am closer to The Teacher, having a social connection with him, but no closer to discovering the man behind the role. I realize the impossibility of that now, having had my own experience of being a group leader. In the presence of students you are compelled to be what they expect you to be. It cannot be otherwise.

CHAPTER FORTY-FOUR

Looking For The One

Upon my return, I find the week of travel with The Teacher has changed my status in subtle ways. I begin receiving more attention from him, which is, of course, noticed by my associates. This comes mostly in phone calls asking me to do things for him, things mostly concerned with my purchasing function. Students ask me about the trip, wanting to know what I learned, what I observed, feeding an addictive curiosity we all have about him, trying to penetrate the mystery of his being, believing this will somehow bring us closer to consciousness. The mystique is the thought he has something we do not have, something we may or may not attain in this lifetime. My best story of the trip is the incident with the spilling of the water glasses in the restaurant, how he maintained his composure.

It is year five of "being there". I am the manager of my department, and seem to have made myself somewhat indispensable. I feel that it is less likely I will be sent away. My life is rich in cultural involvement. I continue to sing in two choirs and act in poetry readings and plays. Occasionally I am asked to do poetry readings at dinners, including one for a Teacher's dinner where I read Rumi. I have it all, except a partner. My life is full and empty at the same time.

In the months leading up to the trip, I begin having the feeling that someone is coming. All I need to make my life in Shangri La complete is a life partner, a soul mate to share this sweet life. I explore various opportunities, go on dates (dinner at The Lodge), but nothing gels.

One evening I am invited to a dinner party at the home of the female centre director who divorced the same time I did. When I arrive I discover I am one of twelve eligible men invited. The only woman there is the hostess. It is like a group job interview. We sit around a formal dining table competing for attention from her.

She is an interesting woman, witty, wise, intelligent, and, a school celebrity. We find each other interesting. One evening I meet her at The Lodge for dinner, where she proceeds to get highly intoxicated and has to be escorted home by a friend. I try meeting her for Sunday brunch, but find myself waiting for her to finish a board meeting. I realize then that I would be a celebrity husband, something that has no appeal. I enjoy her company but feel no chemistry.

I conduct other experiments, dating a few other women, but still nothing. Finally I surrender, realizing the futility of trying to make something happen. All I ever have to "do" is show up for what is already scripted to come my way. Anything else is madness.

CHAPTER FORTY-FIVE

A Fated Meeting

I t is a spring Saturday evening, March 24th, 1984. I dress for the evening's concert. The Retreat orchestra is performing. I call ahead to Town Hall to have a seat reserved. This evening in particular, I feel at peace. My life is in an exceptionally good place. All is well. The first half of the performance is a delight, as I note how far the orchestra has progressed. Three years has taken them from a bunch of squeakers and squawkers practicing in the vineyard, to a cohesive organism capable of creating musical beauty.

During the halftime break I leave my seat, walking to the back to find refreshment. The flash of someone across the room catches my eye. A beautiful woman rivets my attention. She glows. It is like she is standing in a spot light. All else is in shadow. She is not exactly dressed in the school fashion (conservative and covered up), causing me to wonder if she is a student or a visiting "life" person. Curiosity aroused, I maneuver through the crowd toward her, practicing watching without appearing to watch. As I circle, feigning disinterest, she turns suddenly, looks me dead in the eye and says,

"Have I seen you before?"

"Perhaps you have seen me in a play." I reply.

We introduce ourselves. I ask her if she is a student. She seems shocked.

"I was not sure whether you are a student or a life person. You do not quite fit the mold."

She laughs infectiously. What a beautiful sound!

"I do not wear the student uniform." She flashes a dazzling smile. "I am not so good at following rules."

"What do you do?" I ask.

"I am an artist," she replies.

"Really!" I respond skeptically. "Now, tell me your day job."

"No. Really, I paint for a living."

"I am impressed. You paint paintings and sell them. Nothing else?"

"Yes."

"Wow. I once did free-lance photography and struggled."

We start talking like two old acquaintances, catching up. When the intermission is over I offer her my seat. She takes it. I stand on one side of the audience.

My eyes never leave her the entire concert. I am boring holes in the back of her head. My mind floods with speculation. Is she the one I have been waiting for? There is an extraordinary familiarity. Though she is a beautiful woman, it is not her beauty that draws me. It is something else, something indefinable and infinitely more powerful.

When the performance ends, I walk over to her and offer her a ride to The Lodge. She smiles politely, "I already have one." Hmmm. Maybe I am mistaken. She seems different now, remote.

I make my way to The Lodge and buy a glass of wine. She is hanging out on the mezzanine talking to a group of students. I walk by and she turns, greeting me with another brilliant smile. We begin talking again with that same energy, that familiarity. She has an amazing knowledge of The Work. The conversation turns deep almost immediately and we again become engrossed.

She is very popular, greeting many students as they walk by, pausing to chat with her. Each time this happens I turn away thinking: "Well, that is over." But she does not let me go more than a step, always turning to include me.

Eventually people stop interrupting us. Students, who are practicing watching without watching, surround us. I discover the next workday that they are all fascinated with what is unfolding between us. We are leaning against a post sharing our lives, discussing The Work, intensely engaged. Everyone around us in this crowded space fades into a background blur.

No one else exists for us. Our minds click like clockwork. She fascinates me. I fascinate her. I have found a conversational partner like no other. She inspires me to the expression of awesome truths, and then adds her own twist, causing me to soar into another dimension. We are drunk on each other. The world is spinning past and we are standing still in amazement.

Hours pass like a movie on fast forward. We are still while everything around us is in motion. Before we know it the building is empty and a server is asking us if we want dinner before the kitchen closes. He escorts us into the now empty dining room that is cleared of all tables save one. The server is a friend of mine, a carpenter during the day. He has this sweet subtle smile plastered on his face and is not at all disturbed that we have kept him up.

We are alone and everyone is watching. I feel it. It is like the whole world is standing still, holding its breath. We have stepped into an alternate reality. It is high drama. Each of us is fully focused on the other. There is no time. All is Now. The spell is broken at the end of the meal when the server trips while bringing coffee, spilling it down the back of my suit. He apologizes profusely while I remain unruffled, remembering how The Teacher interacted with the water glasses on my trip with him.

After dinner we stroll down the hill to the parking lot under a dazzling canopy of stars. The altitude is eighteen hundred feet. The air is clear. There is no light pollution. I feel I am floating on air. I drive her to where she is staying. Standing at the door, I invite her to brunch and a tour of the property the following day. She agrees.

Ten o'clock the next morning I pick her up for brunch. As we walk through the mezzanine toward the dining room a male student greets her from across the room.

"Still deadly at fifty paces!" he grins.

I look at her puzzled. She smiles subtly, a twinkle in her eye. "I will tell you later."

After brunch I stop by the kitchen to assemble a picnic, then we head out to explore the property. An hour or so later finds us standing midst the winery construction. I am telling her the school's vision, how we are building a new civilization, one based on consciousness, how it is the seed of a new world that will emerge out of the coming chaos.

"This is it!" She exclaims passionately. "The Valley of the Blue Moon!"

She grabs my face and plants a kiss on my lips. Shocked, I return it with equal passion. Standing in the middle of the construction site, a barrier drops, flood gates open, trumpets sound, a choir of angels sings halleluiah, rocking my world, changing it forever.

We drive to an orchard tucked away in a hollow beneath the crest of the hill, behind a line of Ponderosa pines, the same place where I made a resolution to live here when on my first visit. The grass is deep and lush. The fruit trees are in blossom. A blanket is thrown on the grass beneath the trees. We fall to the ground embracing, intoxicated with each other. We cannot stop kissing.

"I have to tell you something." She says when we come up for air. " My whole life is up in the air. Three days ago I returned from a two-week tour of Europe with the person I had gone there to marry, my partner from before I met the school. I left a marriage in Marin and was planning a glorious life with him. When I got there the shock was we no longer had chemistry. I refused to go forward with our plans. He was devastated, as was I. He showed me Paris, then sent me home.

Yesterday I resolved to live my life as a single person. I spent the entire day alone, on a date with myself. I went shopping, then to the movies. I was weary of relationship disasters. I kept moving away from you last night because I was still in that mindset."

"Wow!" I exclaim. "So, you let go. You released all expectation, all identification with an outcome, clearing the deck, making space for the unknown. Then, when it showed up, your identification with your resolution held you back. What changed back there on the Winery Knoll?"

"The realization of a dream, a fantasy I had after reading Lost Horizon, a story about a conscious utopian society called Valley of the Blue Moon. Your story about the vision and purpose of The Retreat triggered the memory of that fantasy with the realization I was living it."

We spend the afternoon beneath the flowering fruit trees, bathed by gentle breezes, alternating between tasting each others lips and talking excitedly about what we each felt unfolding, beginning already, within twenty-four hours of meeting, to plan a life together. Time stands still. We are floating on a flowering island in a sea of lush green grass, hidden away in a nook beneath the hilltop, pausing, at times, to just lie there and take in the puffy clouds floating above.

As the sun begins to approach the horizon, she suddenly sits up. "What time is it? My ride to San Francisco is leaving soon!"

"Do you need to leave?" I ask.

"No. I have nothing I need to do, nowhere I need to be."

"Why not stay here awhile?"

"OK!" she grins.

We go to The Lodge, find her ride and arrange for her to stay at a different house (the woman she stayed with last evening is my ex-wife's friend).

My reality is completely altered. Everything I considered important turns into backdrop. It exists on the edge of my peripheral vision, but is completely cast in shadow by the brilliant light of our emerging love.

That night we dine again at The Lodge. The Irish actress who co-leads the drama group reads Shakespeare's sonnet number 116:

Let me not to the marriage of true minds
Admit impediments. Love is not love
Which alters when it alteration finds,
Or bends with the remover to remove:
O, no! It is an ever-fixed mark
That looks on tempests and is never shaken;
It is the star to every wand'ring bark,
Whose worth's unknown, although his height be
taken.
Love's not Time's fool, though rosy lips and cheeks
Within his bending sickle's compass come;
Love alters not with his brief hours and weeks,
But bears it out even to the edge of doom.
If this be error and upon me proved,
I never writ, nor no man ever loved.

I sit looking into her deep brown eyes, living the words. I realize that, despite having been married and loved before, I have never been "in love" nor had a clue as to what that meant. I felt that love at first sight was a romantic myth, yet now I am experiencing it. The energy bubble surrounding us is so brilliant it outshines all else. Nothing matters but that I nurture this burgeoning love, allowing it to unfold in its own way.

We talk into the night, consuming each other like wanderers in the desert finding an oasis. There is a sense of relationship that transcends time and space, has existed, and does exist over many lifetimes. She is from Philadelphia, met the school there one year after me. We share a great affection for the City of Brotherly Love. The energy of the conversation rises and falls, to rise again, epiphany after epiphany, like the waves of passion between two lovers. It is a love of the mind, heart, and spirit.

When The Lodge closes, we stroll under the moonlit starry sky, down the hill through the vineyard, inhaling the sweet spring air. We drive up the slope to a spot overlooking the property, park, and make out like teenagers, getting high on the nectar of each others lips until we are exhausted. I take her to where she is staying and we say a passionate goodnight, planning to meet for lunch the following day.

Monday morning at the office, staffed mostly by women, I am greeted with little smiles and sweet eyes. The world loves lovers. Each person I encounter interviews me. I approach the treasurer whose company car is a sedan and ask if he will swap vehicles with me the next weekend, sharing my intention to have a getaway with my new love. He agrees. The morning flies by as I rearrange my duties and obligations (including all my rehearsals), freeing the afternoon and the week. I pull up to her house just in time to see her on the porch stretching up to smell a pink-red rose, dressed in a jogging suit the same color, a vision of delight.

While dinning on the deck over the vineyard, I am called to the phone. I leave the table to respond. When I return a young man known to be a womanizer is cozied up to her eating off her plate. Strangely, I feel no competition. The bond between us is already so strong it feels bulletproof. I smile at his antics and send him on his way. We joke about his immature intrusion and continue our conversation, firmly implanted in and protected by the bubble that has formed around us.

The afternoon continues pleasantly as we hang out on

the patio having coffee. I have never felt so comfortable with anyone. We totally enjoy each other's company, not for a second tiring of the intense interaction, being energized by it.

That evening we again dine at The Lodge then head to a secluded spot for another heated make out session. I keep expressing puritanical thoughts about not consummating our relationship until we are married, trying to hold back the rush of passion. She smiles sweetly, a twinkle in her eye, saying nothing. Tuesday's activities are a repetition of Monday, intensified. The evening ends even more passionately in her driveway, the windows steaming up from our heat. We realize then that waiting until marriage is absurdly idealistic and plan to consummate the following day.

Wednesday after lunch we return to her house. It is empty. Everyone is at work. In her room we struggle to maintain a semblance of intentionality, to make our consuming passion a conscious act. Failing this, we surrender to an overwhelming force that sweeps us into an undiscovered world of shear ecstasy, another dimension, a deeper Now. We revel there for hours, transcending time, place, ego and history, immersed in an all consuming, Eternal NOW. It is an archetypical merging of epic proportions, a scene lifted from Greek mythology, complete with lightning bolts and screams of passion. We reluctantly re-emerge into linear time/space reality as the sun is setting, just in time to greet the arrival of her roommate.

Now we are really in a bubble. We drive to The Lodge for dinner in a glow of amazement. We were talking intensely before, but now our consummation has unleashed a sizzling, high voltage, energetic hookup. We are radiant. At dinner I know we are the subjects of a lot of subtle attention. This a close, loving, conscious community. New relationships are always of interest. I can almost hear them thinking: "Oh yes. They have done it. It is clearly visible."

The voltage crackling between us is beyond intoxication and unfathomable, saturated with meaning beyond our comprehension, a highly elevated state of awareness, like tripping, but without drugs. This new energy is moving through the neural pathways created by The Work, profoundly amping up our awareness. To say we are amazed would be an understatement. The intense attention we receive in public deepens and intensifies the energy bubble surrounding us. It is true public solitude (a drama exercise).

We have wine, eat delicious food and bask in the afterglow, always talking, sharing, having ah-hah moments. For every story one of us tells, the other has a corollary in both kind and chronology. We discover we have been living parallel lives, going through the same life stages simultaneously.

Does it get any better than this? At the top of my game, I am: private counsel to The Teacher; an executive with privileges; experiencing artistic fulfillment through music and drama, and Now, the absolute love of my life has just fallen passionately into my arms. She is an artist. She can paint anywhere. With a little luck, I will persuade her to move to The Retreat where we will live "happily ever after". This is my "plan". Take note.

CHAPTER FORTY-SIX

Living the Dream

Thursday I work in the morning, getting lots of nosey questions and raised eyebrows. At noon I go to her cottage to find her wearing a tight fitting blue dress borrowed from her roommate. It is French looking and tight in the bodice, not quite containing her voluptious bosom. Later that afternoon she keeps the dress on, enhancing our passion.

Friday morning I give instructions to my staff and swap cars with the treasurer. I am on vacation. I pick her up, we go the lunch, pack up her stuff, take care of a few last minute chores, then head out for the Palo Alto teaching house where she is temporarily staying.

We arrive at the Palo Alto mansion late in the evening. The house appears empty. She is staying in the library off the large living room. I am hanging out there waiting for her when the male center director appears from upstairs, surprised, of course, to see me, who he knows from The Retreat. I tell him whom I am with, saying we are just stopping by for a few minutes on our way to Santa Cruz.

I can see him struggling to control his facial expression. He excuses himself, hurrying off to the library where I catch overtones of a heated discussion. It sounds like he is confronting her on her decision on something, probably me. She settles him down and we drive off.

Arriving late in Santa Cruz we find a motel and fall into passionate embrace. Unlimited by time constraints and interruptions, we fall asleep entangled, to awaken early and begin again. Finally, a late breakfast, stroll to the beach, shop on the boardwalk, lunch in a restaurant, afternoon love, late evening dinner, stroll on the beach and midnight passion.

Sunday morning we laze late, breakfast, stroll the beach, then reluctantly set out for Mountain View where she has acquired a room in a teaching house. She needs to check it out before returning to Palo Alto to retrieve her car. We arrive late afternoon, she accepts the room, it has a bed, and then begins stressing over the logistics of the move. I tell her I will stay one more day to help out. We sleep in her new room that night, already a couple. I help her move the next day, then return to The Retreat.

Now, we are not only lovers, I am involved in her life, helping her with guy stuff. You know, lifting, hauling, carrying, and using The Work to cope with life's speed bumps. I am making room in my life, already compromising, the essence of relationship. She has become more important than anything else in my life. Not my job, The School, The Retreat community, my art, nothing will be a higher priority than nurturing, maintaining and growing this relationship, and all will be tested. We agree to meet again in two weeks. She will drive to The Retreat.

Back home I resume my duties, my schedule. I call her morning, afternoon and late evening every day. We talk for hours late into the night. She is struggling to clean up her Marin marriage, retrieve possessions and legally end the relationship. I refer her to a lawyer friend.

She needs to find work. I am beginning to realize how much on the edge she lives. One of the benefits of The School is that it provides a support system for this type of experimentation. You are living on the edge with others who are there too. We are all edge dwellers here.

The School is a version of Mount Analogue, a book by Rene Daumal, a French Gurdjieffian student, who describes a mystical island that can only be found at a certain latitude/longitude one hour before sunset. It appears only to those who are ready to see it. At the base of the mountain is a village that supports the people who have sought and found this place, and prepares them to climb the mountain. The Retreat is that village, appropriately positioned in the high foothills of the grand Sierra Madre, looming in the near distance. I am part of the support system that prepares people to climb Mount Analogue.

One day she calls me very upset. She is down to her last twenty-five dollars and cannot see ahead. "I am terrified James! What can I do! Like you would know, sitting up there in your ivory tower."

I stay calm, listening internally.

"Take your last twenty-five dollars and spend it on yourself. Buy something special."

"What??!! Are you crazy?!"

"It is an act of faith in your connection to the Universe.

We are in a conscious school. I have had all sorts of crazy stuff happen. You have to take this risk!"

"Are you going to bale me out when I go broke?"

"Take a deep breath. Find your focus. This is coming through me. I know you need to do this. Trust. You have trusted so many times before. It always works out."

"All right! I can feel what you are saying."

"Do your favorite thing. Go shopping and call me when you come home."

I go about my day. Around four she calls.

"You will not believe this!?" She screams.

"What?"

"I went to Macy's and looked around for hours. I kept coming back to a particular skirt on a sale rack. I really loved it, its style, color and cut. There were several of them. Finally I came back to it and brought it home. I tried it on in front of the mirror and as I am modeling it, I thrust my hands into the pockets. I feel something, like folded paper. I pull it out. You won't believe this!! It is money, two tens and a five. The exact amount I paid for the item. The money is new, kind of stuck together."

"WOW!!"

"Thank you James for helping me remember how the Universe always takes care of me when I engage it with courage and Being, when I do not turn away in fear. I will never forget this lesson! I am so present the whole time I am there, shopping. Who is present shopping? I keep vacillating between boldness and obsessive terror. One moment I am totally into it, the next moment my mind is calling me an idiot for listening to you."

She drives up the next weekend, alone. This is something new for her, I discover. She is directionally challenged.

Someone who knows the way usually accompanies her. Undertaking the complex journey from the tangle of the San Francisco Bay Area, through Marysville and beyond, alone, is a major challenge. I give her driving instructions but fail to include a turn in Marysville I take for granted. She calls me from a phone booth lost and upset with me for my omission. I calm her down, trying to determine where she is, when she says in a calm, tense voice, "There's a bee in the phone booth. I'm allergic to bees."

The way she delivers the line cracks me up. I try hard not to laugh out loud. She opens the door and asks the bee to leave. It complies. I calm her down, find out where she is, and adjust her directions.

She arrives in time for lunch, but we decide to go to the nearby town of Grass Valley to a movie, a very out of patterns thing to do for students of The Work. The school is not friendly toward the media.

It is Friday afternoon. We arrive at the theater and buy tickets for Romancing the Stone, a Michael Douglas romance/adventure. The theater is completely empty. We are the only audience. It is like we are having a private viewing. The movie is a fun ride, a rare treat for two people from a media exempt culture.

We stroll through the town's shopping district afterward and run into my ex-wife. They eye each other politely and make courteous remarks. It is strange for me. I feel like the elephant in the room everyone is aware of but no one acknowledges.

This is the weekend I begin working to integrate my new relationship into the fabric of my life at The Retreat. Saturday morning I work at the office and spend the afternoon with my love. Sunday morning I attend drama class then meet her for brunch at The Lodge. We spend the afternoon and evening together before she returns to the San Francisco Bay Area. We have no place to be alone together. We share stolen moments of passion on the bed of the person she stays with, but have no real privacy. I stay in a tiny bedroom in a crowded house. It is too small to be an option. She understands about the time I spend away from her going to class, but there is a rising sense of irritation from the interference this causes in the flow of our growing friendship.

My relationship to everything I hold dear before meeting her is rapidly changing. She is more important than all of it. This causes some internal conflict for me, but withdrawing from my involvements becomes more and more the choice-less choice. Growing a new relationship requires time and energy. It is my entire focus. I live for her visits.

Weekend evenings are classical music concerts followed by late evening dinners with friends. We are The Retreat buzz, a new couple every one is covertly watching, even The Teacher. She and I are driving off the property one afternoon when I see the vineyard manager driving toward us. He signals me to stop. The Teacher is sitting beside him. He smiles his brilliant Cheshire cat smile. The smile becomes the only thing visible. In that moment all movement ceases.

A few weeks later we are invited to dinner at the Goethe Academy on a Monday night. My close friend from the drama group is also invited. The three of us convene in the Academy kitchen early to hang out with the chef, her close friend, and then we enter the ornate, elaborately decorated, formal dinning room. There are twelve people at the table, all dressed in their finest. She is wearing the high collared wedding gown from her last marriage.

There is a poetry reading, a student serves wine, and The Teacher offers a toast,

"To Self-Remembering!"

He looks around the table, smiling, "Tonight is family night." (Meaning all at the table are residents) His eyes land on her. She says,

"I have waited a long time to meet you."

It is rare for a student to initiate conversation.

"And I also have waited a long time to meet you" his smile broadening.

We know he has heard stories.

"I was in an earthquake last week," she offers.

"Yes, I felt it here."

"It was very strong in the Bay Area. The floor rippled like liquid."

"Oh my. Were you frightened?"

"Yes and no. It altered my state, made memory."

"Mr. Gurdjieff said, 'we always make a profit.'"

The Teacher turns and asks the chief carpenter about his progress on a project.

More wine, appetizers, and a sumptuous main course, are followed by an exquisite desert and after dinner wine. The conversation is light, mostly concerned with various Retreat projects. At one point, The Teacher turns toward my love and says:

"Elizabeth, how is the art business?"

She looks up, "My name is Lynne. Not Elizabeth," she asserts in measured tone.

What she does not know is that there is a student sitting in the corner behind her who is acting as scribe for the dinner conversation. She too is an artist. I whisper the mistake to her. She startles, apologizing.

After dinner we return to the kitchen and party with our friends. I take her back to where she's staying. Her roommate has not returned from work yet so we take advantage of the privacy, then I go home to my monk's cell.

After several weeks of stolen moments, she suggests we spend a Saturday night at a hotel in Nevada City.

"I have a surprise for you" she coyly intimates upon arrival, mischief in her eyes. She turns around taking something from her purse, holding it up, showing it to me.

"That looks like a joint!"

"It is. How do you feel about doing it with me?"

She is watching me attentively. I know immediately this is a test, a pass/fail watershed.

"You know The School does not approve of this. We will be thrown out if found out."

"And you know I am a rule breaker." She grins, more charming and seductive than ever.

I shrug. "OK. I used to love the stuff. It has been seven years. I stopped indulging when I met The School."

She smiles. "This is my medicine. It helps me stay sane."

We light the joint and smoke it halfway down. I immediately feel the cannabis invading my cerebral cortex, putting my critical mind to sleep, releasing endorphins. She puts her arms around me. I feel her heart beating against my chest, engulfed by its expansive warmth. Its energy is enormous. Slowly we undress until our embrace is skin to skin. We sink down onto the hotel room waterbed, completely taken by the rhythms of passion.

Later, lazing in the afterglow, she mentions: "The

woman I stay with is moving out. She offered me her room. Why not take it. You can live there during the week and we will have a private space on the weekends. No more running off to cheap motels to be with each other."

"Sounds great! Make the deal."

CHAPTER FORTY-SEVEN

Settling In, Again

This brings us closer to my dream of living together at The Retreat. We return the next day, make all the arrangements and move in the following weekend. Now we have a love nest, the room where we first consummated our passion. It is the upstairs bedroom/bathroom master suite in a French country style cottage set on a hilltop gazing at the Sierra range. Our huge bathroom window looks out on the towering peaks a few miles away. This immediately becomes part of my "living happily ever after" vision.

I move in the following Monday. After almost five years, a move for me still consists of a backseat full of clothes and books. I am still a penniless seeker, living on the edge. My love returns the following weekend and we settle into a pattern of weekends together, passionate afternoon interludes, laced with elegant meals, classical music concerts, and Sunday brunches at The Lodge. It is a rich life, culturally and socially.

Now, on the surface, things are looking good. Yet the surface does not tell all. She is not the rugged type. She describes herself as a hothouse rose. As cultured and sophisticated as The Retreat is spiritually, it is also a small community carved out of the wilderness. We dress up for dinner and concerts but have to wade through the mud wearing goulashes, carrying our dress shoes in a bag, finding our way without lights under the stars. This is semi-acceptable for a while, but it gives her friction.

There are other glitches. The beautiful room we occupy has no auditory privacy. One wall of the room has two shuttered windows that overlook the living room, making everything that happens in our bedroom audible, turning our passionate encounters into performance art for anyone listening below.

Every time I open a conversation about her moving to The Retreat, saying she can paint anywhere, she counters:

"There is no place to sell my work here. Yes, I can paint anywhere, but who will buy the paintings? There are students in the Bay Area who buy my work. I also get involved in shows there. What do you expect me to do, go on salary as a housekeeper or a flower arranger?"

Living at the retreat is compelling when it is also your day job. If you are not working in the vineyard or engaged in some occupation that fills the needs of The School, you are an outsider. There is a clear distinction between those who are "on salary" and those who are not. This has implications on many levels. Being "on salary" is a private club, and, as the weeks and months unfold, this distinction becomes a sticking point in our relationship, especially on the social level.

She feels like an outsider. The social entrée to The Retreat inner social circle I take for granted, intimidates her. For example, there is a voice recital one afternoon, a performance opportunity for those studying singing. I have been working on two Schubert lieder for months, since before we met. The recital is for music students and their friends. It is not open to the public. First she does not like my song choices (sung in German), and then when the recital is over she refuses to attend the tea service for the performers, feeling uncomfortable. I feel pulled between two worlds, the delicate balance of my carefully constructed life of service to the school, and pursuance of my art, is being overturned by this extraordinary force, love, something I have never known before now. I am upset over her opinion of my singing, and, I love her beyond reason (a phrase we use to this day).

This "unreasonableness" is disturbing. It upsets my delicate balance. It is like having two sets of conflicting values, two passions, two loves. For five years my passion, the great love I have for The Retreat community, has been an irreconcilable force that easily defeats all resistance, all competition, leading me to a life solely dedicated to The Work and the community.

Every day, in every way, I strive to enfold her into this level of commitment, but the irritating little details of life here keep interfering with the goal I have of "living happily ever after" in the community. It is like the Quantum concept: change one thing, everything changes. The performance events I so enthusiastically immersed myself in before, are now impediments, roadblocks to our relationship. They take precious time away from the "us" we are forming, the bonds we are establishing, raising doubts in our minds as to its long-term viability.

One Saturday afternoon I take her to a lake where we swim, leaving her there to attend a rehearsal. She is very gregarious and gorgeous, attracting male attention wherever she goes. Putting her in public, in a bathing suit, exacerbates this tendency. I feel confident in our connection and am not a jealous person, but she tells me what happens and lets me know I am not watering the garden of our love. Another afternoon I am away rehearsing and she remains at the house. I return later to find her with one of our roommates who is a hunky guy. I feel some tension. She eventually tells me something "almost" happened.

One of the dynamics of a passionate relationship is the dark side of that passion. We are both intense people. When that intensity turns negative, our fights are equally intense. We blow up, scream and yell, then intensely make up. In the beginning we do not understand this and believe each time it happens that we are done with each other. But then the thought of being apart is unbearable. It reconnects us each time. Eventually we get it. This is the way we are, this is what we do.

It all comes to a head one hot August Saturday afternoon. The owners of the cottage are entertaining guests. All the doors and windows are flung open to allow air circulation (there is no air conditioning), and the house has no screens. She goes down to the kitchen to get a snack and returns completely astounded by something.

"Come quick!! You have to see this! It is unbelievable!"

Puzzled, I follow her down to the kitchen. The walls

and ceiling are completely covered by every etymological specimen of the region. They are pulsating with bugs, large bugs. Not a space is unoccupied. Thousands of bug eyes stare back at us. The walls and ceiling are pulsating with their aliveness. I have never seen anything like it. It is supernatural, bizarre.

"That's it. You know how I feel about bugs. Why are there no screens? The heat, the dust, and now this!! I am done. I am too sensitive for this life. It is not for me! I will not be returning!"

She is so adamant I do not even attempt to argue or resist. The next day we go to the voice recital I mentioned earlier. Afterward, she finds herself a ride back to the Bay Area. I attend a post recital meeting that evening where performance critique is given, but it means nothing to me. My mind is completely a buzz. Presence and Inner Peace are nowhere to be found as my two loves are now at mortal war. It appears I am being forced to choose between them.

CHAPTER FORTY-EIGHT

The Most Difficult Decision of My Life

I continue to function. I participate in the critique meeting, but my heart is not in it. I am going through the motions of external events while my inner world is in shock. Everything outside my skin seems dim, vague, and inconsequential. I am permanently changed, a change that began that fateful evening when I saw her across a crowded room. It would be a cliché were it not so saturated with truth. Something heretofore unknown was unleashed in me that night and I have not been the same since.

The next day I go to the office and perform my duties, but all my activities are merely background to my internal dialogue. My house of cards has collapsed. All day Monday and Tuesday I keep myself busy while internally processing, struggling to find a workable compromise, some something that would fix the situation.

Re-entering the world seems unthinkable. I have been away from it for so long I have forgotten the skills I used to sustain myself there. In addition, I have been operating my life at such a pace since joining The School that I am continually exhausted. It is an exhaustion that cannot be fixed by a good night's sleep. Part of living in-the-moment for me has become a focus, each moment, to find the energy to continue to the next moment. It is literally taking the next step, putting one foot in front of the other using every ounce of energy I can summon. The thought of leaving The Retreat to begin a new life is unthinkable.

By Wednesday morning I have a decision. Late that afternoon I climb into my grandmother's old Chevy and head for her house in the San Francisco Bay Area. There is to be a big meeting this evening in San Francisco, but I intuitively feel that she will not be attending. I plan on arriving unannounced. It is dark when I get there. I stop along the way to buy roses from a street vendor.

My three hours of intense focus reach a crescendo as I stand at the front door, flowers in hand, heart pounding. I knock. The door is opened by her roommate, who gasps upon seeing me.

"Oh my god!" she screams.

My love is standing behind her wrapped in a bath towel.

"We were just talking about you. I told her just this moment we were over, that you would never leave The Retreat, not even for me." she gasps.

I thrust the roses into her hands, kissing her.

"You are more important to me than anything else, even The Retreat. I'm your man!!"

She throws her arms around me in a sweet embrace.

I stay the rest of the week. We vacation in Santa Cruz

and visit friends, all the while discussing our next steps. As difficult as it is for me to look at, I know intuitively, especially since receiving the bug message, that I have to consider re-entering society. It is clear to both of us that something larger than ourselves has intervened to shake me loose from my attachment to The Retreat.

Part of the discussion is the condition of my health. I am running on empty, and some School physician even decided I might be experiencing a disease process. I have no interest in labeling myself in some scary way, and decide to take the holistic route, which she encouraged.

She does some research and finds a two-week health retreat that specializes in fasting/detox work and reprogramming diet. The cost is $1,000, which neither one of us can afford. I call my mother and persuade her to loan me the money. It is scheduled for the first two weeks of September. With her enthusiastic support, I agree to reemerge back into life. The plan is to wrap up my affairs at The Retreat and move to her house in Mountain View by the beginning of October.

LEAVING THERE

CHAPTER FORTY-NINE

Preparing to Depart

I drive back to The Retreat Sunday afternoon. North of Sacramento, crossing the rice paddies in my grandmother's car, again, I flash on the first time I crossed this landscape. I am a new student anxious to meet my Shangri-La, crossing the endless paddies, dreaming dreams of living out my days in this sacred community. That was my "plan". Remember reader, I told you to take note back then.

Obvious to me now is the existence of greater intentions which I occasionally glimpse, like Mr. Wright, the skirt story, and the especially the recent bug incident. If I had resisted the unexpected, and ignored the miraculous, I would have missed out on the great love of my life, the partner with whom I am destined to climb Mount Analogue. My lifetime at The Retreat is coming to an end. It is time to close it up and take the next step on my journey to Now.

I have lived in the village at its base for five years, preparing to make the climb, all the while believing that living in the village that prepares others to make the climb is making the climb. The power of Love brings all this into crystal clarity. What is called for now is yet another, more profound, empty handed leap into the void. When I left the world five years ago I knew where I was going. This time I have no clue. I must reenter the world at the age of forty-one with nothing more than The Work and my wits.

Monday morning, back in the office, I pave the way for my eventual departure. First step is the health retreat. I arrange for someone to cover my job. I say nothing about my plans for leaving, but make my health the issue. It is time to rest, regenerate and purify the body I have made work so hard these past seven years.

I meet with my choirmaster and drama director putting all my activities on hold. I cease rehearsing and singing, and begin drawing my energy inward, withdrawing from Retreat life. All my passion for these activities has disappeared, redirected toward building and strengthening my new partnership. I finish work at five each evening and go to The Lodge for dinner, savoring my last moments, tasting them like you taste fine wine, and retire early to my now empty love nest.

My love and I talk daily. We are two birds hanging out on a branch, twin souls adventuring through life. Each conversation adds details that continue to deepen the understanding of our connection. She remembers seeing me cross a street in Philadelphia during my dropout days, describing how I looked then and what I wore. We have a synergy that enhances us, minds that merge and meld in spiritual experience and realization. We talk about

The Work for hours, constantly applying it to our in-the-moment experience, making connections, verifications.

I drive down to see her the following weekend. Her visiting The Retreat is no longer an option. We visit a couple that are her friends. He photographs us in joyful embrace, capturing the essence of our passion. Twenty-seven years later, during the writing of this book, I discover it posted on a website devoted to School graduates. It clearly captures the magic between us.

I return to The Retreat and have another week of endings. I struggle with my mind's fear of the unknown. What will happen when I leave? How will I find my way back into "normal" society? Will I find work? I have forgotten how to operate in that world.

I am burned out, exhausted. It feels good to just relax and enjoy. I give up striving, becoming, and focus on Being. I Remember My-Self, the deepest, highest part of me that never changes, is Eternal. I remember I do not have to "figure it out", that is not my job. I just need to show up, to watch, listen (internally and externally), keep my all attention where I am, and trust the universe will support me.

CHAPTER FIFTY

A Healing Retreat

Early the following Saturday afternoon, I arrive at a hilltop private property in the hills above St. Helena, California, a town in the Napa Valley wine country. It is a large rambling private residence, old, and a bit funky. The owners are a Seventh Day Adventist couple. She is an alternative-healing guru, who leads, while her husband plays a supportive role and administers colonics. A colonic is like an advanced enema. Water is forcefully circulated into the colon to wash away impacted fecal matter and toxic substances.

About a dozen people gather in the living room. We are given an outline of the activities for the next two weeks. The first week is to be devoted entirely to fasting and colonics. This is where the toxins in our cells are released back into the bloodstream and are washed away by daily colon irrigations. We are told it takes three days for the body's food processing factory to shut down. This will be the most difficult part of the journey, fighting the body's craving for food, and enduring the discomfort arising from having all those stored toxins reintroduced into our blood. We are told that once the factory shuts down a peaceful calm will emerge.

The second week will be devoted to gradually restarting the factory and reprogramming the diet to what is now known as a Vegan regimen. All animal products are to be eliminated. We are educated into a new philosophy of eating which they claim is more holistic and healthy.

After the lecture on diet there is a talk on the science of iridology, the analysis of the iris of the eye, as a diagnostic tool. She says you can actually read a person's iris and learn about their state of health. Each person is then taken aside and the iris of the left eye is photographed with a Polaroid camera and an appointment is made with her to discuss what she learns from the photographs.

Room assignments are then made and we all retire to settle in. I am one of the few single people there and am given an RV camper as a room. It is pretty cool, actually. They take me outside to check it out and tell me I can park it anywhere I want on the property. I drive it down to a shady nook at one end of the building. We then reconvene in the dining room for a light vegetarian meal. The fast will begin in the morning.

Early the next day we receive instructions for the fast which consists of a large glass of water containing a small amount of apple juice and psyllium husks, along with a fistful of herbs meant to facilitate the cleanse. We are allowed to drink herbal tea anytime throughout the day. The drink and herbs are taken three times a day at normal mealtimes. Each one of us is put on the daily colonic schedule, and we each have a conference with her where the results of our iridology examination are discussed. Mealtimes are preceded with prayer meetings conducted by the leader and her husband, and there is a daily lecture in the afternoon on topics related to the purification process.

We are left to our own devices for the balance of our day. My RV accommodation is like a small apartment I retreat to each morning to contemplate. I have brought several books with me. One is A Fourth Way book by a student of Ouspensky's named Rodney Collin, titled The Theory of Eternal Life. It examines the nature of the life process in the context of the body's inevitable death. It draws upon ancient texts like The Tibetan Book of the Dead in an effort to give the reader a larger perspective on the deeper realities of the life process and what is beyond it. Reading it creates, at times, the experience of being an entity existing outside the boundaries of space/time.

I write my love each day, expressing my inner process. Even when we are not together, I am conversing with her. All my attention is on the journey ahead. I am astonished now, writing this 30 years later, how readily I released my attachment to life at The Retreat. It is almost as if there is something within me that has an awareness of the master plan for my life. I was as attached to my life in Philadelphia. Yet, when the time came to release it, I let it go with no clinging or regret. She tells me years later how precious these letters are to her. It is a time of quiet introspection as I prepare to "graduate" from The Retreat.

The letters reflect my inner process in approaching this monumental move. Here are some excerpts.

June 17, 1984: "You know the biggest difficulty I have about our future life together is imagination. That is, negative imagination. I will not go into detail because I know it is all Maya, but it does produce fear in me at times that I have to work with. I feel strongly that, with continued efforts, the play will have its way and a new, un-thought of means will present itself."

June 18, 1984: "The end of the first day. Was very difficult in a passive way, a headache and no activity. None! It's enough to drive an active type bonkers! All ascending processes contain payment and reward. This was my payment day. Externally all is well. My fellow patients are mostly Seventh Day Adventists. They work with the non-expression of negative emotion at some level, although, apparently not directly, not specifically. They work with the idea of a play in the form of "God's Will." This probably is a play for me to see that other humans than students are evolving in their own ways."

June 20, 1984: "The director taught a three hour class last night on the evils of modern dietary practices. The big lesson is that modern man is killing himself with the use of what is called "free fat", or "free oil", or grease. Her research is thorough and well documented. I'm beginning to have a sense for the importance of conforming to the laws of nature. Otherwise one comes under other laws, the law of cancer, diabetes...etc. One can begin to see that disease is a form of unnecessary suffering brought about by mankind's continued effort to find the easy way of doing things."

"Do you realize that I was in a contented niche at The Retreat before I met you? That I made a full life for myself? And how empty it was without you? I had resigned myself to this "disease". I might have deteriorated and died without your efforts. We have given each other so much. I have learned so much from you. My life has become so much more interesting and full."

June 21, 1984: "It is strange to be reminded once more that, to grow, to advance, we must be continually taking leave of our past, favorite activities and endeavors, maybe to return to them in another form, maybe not. It is essential for evolution.

And so, I sit here in another monk's cell, this little motor home, listening to Vivaldi, writing these notes to my true love."

June 21, 1984 (evening): "I finished reading Steppenwolf today, a remarkable book, very metaphysical. He is a character who has highly developed certain sides of himself, the more esthetic, intellectual sides, and not developed other sides, the sensual parts generally, at all. Having reached the pits of despair, he meets a young woman who opens another side of life for him. Although not entirely parallel, it reminded me strongly of our relationship and how we are a balance for each other."

"I'm beginning to realize how tired I am. I've been functioning on shear nervous energy (probably sex energy) for a long time. It is not a negative, however. I feel I've developed a great deal of Will during these years that will benefit me in my trails to come. We lead lives of trial you know."

"Walt Whitman wrote in "Songs of the Open Road":

'Now understand me well. It is provided in the essence of things that from any fruition of success, no matter what, shall come forth something to make a greater struggle necessary.'

It is good to remember this and not be lulled to sleep by our success.

This is followed by:

'My call is the call of battle,
I nourish active rebellion,
He going with me must go well arm'd,
He going with me goes often with spare diet,
Poverty, angry enemies, desertions.'

Such is the life of an adventurer on The Way. The last lines of the poem are:

'Camerado, I give you my hand!
I give you my love more precious than money,
I give you myself before preaching or law;
Will you give me yourself?
Will you come travel with me?
Shall we stick by each other as long as we live?'

I say this to you my love, and you have said it to me! What a beautiful, soul stirring pledge.

A line from Steppenwolf:

'In eternity there is no time, eternity is a mere moment, just long enough for a joke.'

A reminder to take nothing seriously, except one's aim to Awaken."

June 25, 1984: "I called my father last night, and that huge negative barrier that arose last time was still there. Actually, it's probably there with my mother too, but she's afraid of me.

In The Fourth Way this morning I read the following:

'..., strange tendencies appear in children, quite

opposed to their surrounding circumstances, quite foreign to the people among whom they live. Sometimes they are very strong tendencies that change their life and make them go in totally unexpected ways, when there is nothing in heredity to produce that. This is why it happens in most cases that parents do not understand their children and children do not understand their parents.'

My parents have never understood me, nor have I expected their understanding. That is why I have kept most of my life isolated from them, not wishing to stir them up.

"My mother has never understood me, but accepts it, at least externally, when relating to me. She probably expresses her confusion to my father (step) however, who, at times, becomes angered by the pain I have caused her, the woman he loves. Not being his son, he does not relate to me in the same way. I think he likes me, even loves me, but during times when I've produced extreme friction, he reverts to being the angry lover. He even attacked me once, when I was a teenager, though still holding himself back so that the fists he swung at me did not connect. This perhaps lies beneath my feelings of alienation from his family. The true feelings that can exist between a father and a son, and that probably exist between him and my half-brothers, probably didn't exist at all, or as much had he really been my father. I don't resemble him in any way, neither psychologically, spiritually nor physically.

"I feel I am growing spiritually through this experience here, as well as being healed physically. The experience with strange 'life' people who have an intense religious orientation is an indication to me that other people on the planet are growing and evolving too, not just students. It is a verification that student vanity about being students is just vanity, with all that implies."

June 27, 1984: "This day marks my last full day here. We will be together again before this letter reaches you. How precious you are to me, how appealing it is to consider that we may spend the balance of our lives connected to each other through our love for each other.

"Ouspensky feels that we recur into the same life each time, but that through evolutionary events within, that life may change, through Self-Remembering. If this Be the case, then we're old friends, you and me, not just new acquaintances. This would explain our ability to reach such a deep level of intimacy so quickly.

"Remember, all is connected all the time. Each time your heart beats, it is felt by every cell in your body. Each time you speak, your utterance is perceived in more places and by more beings than you realize. The same is true with one's level of being. It is perceived by, and it affects all the beings and things around it. Do not grieve that you are receiving friction from your friend. Embrace gratefully the opportunity you have been granted to rise higher. If you were loved by all, you would be kept sound asleep. We pray to be Awakened, then are irritated when the gods send someone to awaken us.

"We are also given positive reinforcement at times, like the twenty five dollars in the pocket of your skirt. The Work is not all pain, not all friction. It is:

'joy and woe. And when this you rightly know, through the world you safely go.' (William Blake)

"Much has happened here for me internally. This cleansing of my machine (body) has opened new pathways in my being which I am just beginning to explore. One of them is this form, letter writing. Another is being a student of The Fourth Way surrounded by life. The living situation here is as intense as a teaching house instinctively and has given me the opportunity to study myself and others in a new way. Many of the people here are couples. It has been interesting to see how roles are defined, how feminine dominance plays such a large role.

"Many of the people here are in the process of forming magnetic centres (inner search for meaning). They are groping about, questioning their lives, searching for little pieces of the truth, trying to find a way to God. It has been useful for me to fortify my valuation for our school. The tools we have to work with are so infinitely more precise, more accurate, more objective. We have been given such incredible knowledge. We are so very lucky. We, each of us, needs to be the best example he can of The Work. We cannot just wait to be with students to not be identified. Being put into solitary circumstances is a test for this. You have been my only physical or psychological connection with The School for this entire period. This place has been a wonderful sounding board for my internal resilience, to be an invisible example of a student for all these people."

Each afternoon after "lunch" I drive five miles to a small convenience store. There, I use a pay telephone to call her at a prearranged time. I call collect, give her the number of the payphone, and she calls back. It is a pleasant time of suspended animation. I bring my life to a full stop, and purify and regenerate in preparation for another leap into the unknown. The uncertainty of it all teaches me to focus my attention solely on the next step in the journey. Anything else is a fall into a terrifying abyss of uncertainty. If I were to condense my personal wisdom down to a single sentence, it would be: live each moment, looking forward solely to the next step.

The purification process is uncomfortable. I have a low-grade headache everyday that first week. I miss the beauty of The Retreat and feel alone and withdrawn. I am not able nor inclined to reach out to my fellow participants, keeping to myself. The solitude is soothing to my soul. I spend an afternoon helping our leader load herbs into gelatin capsules in the large farmhouse kitchen. An ambulance arrives unexpectedly containing a very sick woman requesting a colonic. Her husband attempts to treat the woman, then, realizing the impossibility of her situation, they send her away, fearing she will pass while on their property. An hour later a police car arrives asking questions about her, saying she died two miles down the road.

As the days pass the food factory shuts down, creating a peculiar inner stillness. I feel I am in a twilight zone between two worlds. I have almost no thoughts of my Retreat life, no replayed memories, and fewer thoughts about my "future". The moment a stray thought dares to look ahead, anxiety arises in the pit of my stomach. It is an abyss I dare not look into knowing it will swallow me whole. The mind is way to prone to fearful speculation left untended. I am still too burned out, exhausted, to have the strength to conjure up positive fantasies. I must content myself and be complete with this Now moment. I had no idea then of the life I would be living now as I am writing this story.

The weekend arrives. We are to break the fast on Sunday morning. I remember a week six months ago where I fasted at The Retreat, and how I pigged out on my first meal. It made me so sick. This time is much gentler. We begin the day with a light breakfast of fruit, a lunch slightly more substantial and a light dinner. The five days that follow are escalations of this process, accompanied with intensive education on the values, benefits and details of a Vegan diet. It all culminates Friday afternoon with a celebratory meal and a closing ceremony.

I call my sweetheart that afternoon and she suggests I come see her for a few days. I agree and in hours I am in my love's welcoming embrace. I spend the weekend with her. We plan our next move. I am ready, ready to take the plunge, to jump off the high board. I am not scared, but am a little anxious. I keep reminding myself, "It all works out." I release my fantasy of "living happily ever after" in The Retreat community, but there is nothing to replace it. The way ahead is completely unknown and unknowable. Perhaps this is always true, but there are moments in life where it is more obvious, and this is one them. The future is a tabula rasa, a blank slate. I have no clue. I can only keep my mind still, wait and watch.

CHAPTER FIFTY-ONE

Final Days

Monday morning finds me once again crossing the rice paddies in my grandmother's old Chevy. The plan is to spend the next two weeks letting go of all my attachments at The Retreat. First stop is the office where I give two weeks notice to the Treasurer; beginning the process of communicating my intentions to all the people I have worked with and had friendship with over the past five years. I share meals with my drama director, music director, best drama friend and many others. I meet with the old German wine master one more time. He asks me about the value of colonics. He has health issues of his own.

It is a sweet relaxing time of letting go, continuing to slow the pace. I have not truly rested in five years. The two-week health retreat was just the beginning. I drive around the property visiting all the worksites one last time. I reflect on the vast growth that has occurred since I arrived and feel proud to have participated. My old purchasing friend, the dispatcher when I started, is brought back to take my position. He arrives the following Monday and I spend a few days handing over the work to him.

In what seems like a heartbeat my final Friday evening arrives. The office staff arranges a going away party on the upper deck of The Lodge where each person at the table honors me. I am given gifts. I tell them how honored I feel to have known and worked with such high quality people. One of my enemies, the one to whom I wrote a letter, gives me a gift. It is a book of poetry with a letter. As it turns out, she has the last word. I smile, amused.

When the dinner is over, the last hug hugged, the last toast toasted, the last goodbye spoken, I stand on the edge of the deck surveying the vineyard, the patio filled with students below, the Milky Way floating luminously overhead, the illuminated white winery dome, the cool air, the stillness and above all the beauty everywhere I look.

I will be back, but it will not be the same. I know this. I have no regrets. I feel no loss, only great love for what this era, this lifetime, has given me. The gifts of this experience are a resource that will continue to serve me throughout this life and beyond. At this writing, thirty years out, this remains true.

I wander slowly downstairs, past the glass door to
the Meissen Dining Room.
I walk down the iron spiral stairs.
I pause at the main dining room, with its
massive fireplace. Late diners are having quiet
conversation.

I walk past the library, where some students are watching a Shakespeare video.

I step out onto the Mezzanine.

The wine bar is still open. I buy a glass of my favorite cabernet.

I walk slowly out onto the patio into the cool autumn air.

I lean against the flagstone retaining wall, feeling the warmth of the noonday sun radiating from the stone.

I drink the wine slowly, swirling the ruby velvet over my taste buds.

I breathe in the flavor.

I have a few more sweet farewell conversations.

Eventually it all gets quiet.

Everyone leaves or finds a place to sleep on The Lodge floor.

The lights go out.

I am bathed in starlight.

I soak it up.

I AM momentarily One with All.

Eventually, the trance breaks.

Human thought intrudes.

This my final moment as a Retreat resident.

I take the rose lined path to the kitchen back door.

I leave my wine glass for the dishwasher.

I go to the service line and pour a cup of steaming black coffee.

I take it out onto the back deck and once more drink in the starlight.

I return the cup.

I walk back up the rose lined path to the small
parking lot where the old Chevy awaits me.
I back slowly out.
I drive as slow as I can down the hill.
I pass the swan pond below The Lodge (where the
barn used to be).
I pass the parking lot.
I pass the shops.
I pass Town Hall whose windows I glazed.
I pass the Poseidon statue at the entrance to
Court of the Caravans.
I pass the lawns, gardens and magnificent
structure of The Goethe Academy whose
foundation I helped pour.
I drive out the front gate.
I drop down through wormhole draw.
I pass the wine masters house.
I pass the general store.
I pass the post office.
I wind down the mountain.
It is done.
I have departed.
I drive off into the deep night to greet my destiny.

CHAPTER FIFTY-TWO

ReBirth

It is 3:00a.m. I am on a causeway crossing South San Francisco Bay. No one is on the road. It is a lonely ten-mile stretch on landfill. The car's temperature gauge has been slowly rising over the past hour. Now it is boiling.

There is no place to get water. I am a half hour from my new home. There seems nothing else to do but push on holding successful arrival in my mind's eye. I finally show up at her house in a cloud of smoke and steam. The engine is dieseling. The last half hour was an act of will. The long late night drive is the birth canal to my new life, and just like any other birth, there is pain, mess and confusion. I crawl out of my smoking, clanking old heap and fall into my love's arms.

We awaken late morning. She has plans. We are going with a group of students to tour Filoli Gardens, the beautiful formal estate used as backdrop for the Dynasty

TV series. I dig out my old Leica camera, resurrecting my photography hobby, and off we go to experience beauty. Afterward, we go to an afternoon reception at the other major Palo Alto teaching house owned by a student who is a psychiatrist. By this time I am so tired I can barely stay awake. Deep exhaustion is creeping into my bones.

Sunday we rest. I unpack my car. I must look for work, a thought that is overwhelming to my exhausted psyche. I move in, put away and arrange my belongings, and begin organizing my thoughts. I am just beginning to understand the extent of my burnout. It is a welcome relief to come to a full stop. I focus my energy, find my old address book and begin to formulate plans for re-entering the work force.

CHAPTER FIFTY-THREE

A New Set of Challenges

Monday, my sweatheart sits me down with a serious face.

"There is something I did not tell you. I have almost no money and no idea when or how that situation is going to change."

"Wow! You told me you earned your living selling paintings."

"I do, but it is not exactly what you would call a reliable, consistent business. Right now I have no clients and no commissions. You need to do something to start earning money as soon as possible. You were a business executive, right?"

"That was five years and a head injury ago. I am completely out of the loop with the insurance business, though I do have a few contacts, including the young man who used to work for me. I will contact them right away."

"OK. I am going to meditate on this as well. We will see

what comes up. I am going to go to a special place I have to seek inspiration. I will return in a little while."

"Great! Remember the skirt story. It is important that we not be in fear, but maintain focused presence. Remember, it all works out. It is essential we have faith and trust!"

She drives off to do her magic, leaving me to ponder my situation. The first thing that comes up for me is my resistance to returning to the insurance business. I was thoroughly convinced, when I drove off to The Retreat five years ago, I would never have to confront this situation again. So much for plans and intentions.

I search for and find my old address book and call my former employee. I manage to connect with him and we agree to meet next week. She returns from her search with an inspiration, full of excitement.

"I have an idea. The daughter of an old client of mine, a wealthy man from New York, is having a baby. I am going to call him and suggest he buy a painting from me for his grandchild's bedroom."

She makes the call. He expresses interest and asks her to send him a sketch of her idea. She draws a swan with a child riding in its back on a lake surrounded by mountains. We send it express mail to arrive the next day. She calls to follow up and a deal is struck for several thousand dollars. He agrees to overnight a 50% deposit. The check arrives the next day and we drive off to Monterey to vacation before she begins working on the piece.

"How did you do that?" I ask incredulously.

"I have a special tree in a parking lot. I feel a connection with it. It resembles two lovers entwined. I went there and said the Lord's Prayer twenty-one times. Before I was finished, this idea pops into my mind."

The following week I meet with my old employee. He informs me that the business is in a recession and almost no one is hiring.

"There is one possibility. Your old friend at Marsh McLennan is looking for a West Coast casualty manager."

"What would that be?" I wonder. I have been out of the loop for five years. Can I possibly pull off being an expert in a field I have been away from for such a long time?

I call and find myself seated across from him the following week.

"We need someone to oversee the liability insurance programs we have in place for our large corporate clients. You would also consult with the account managers and answer their technical questions. For instance, what is the malpractice liability exposure for a real estate broker?"

My left-brain fails me at this point. I am still in the exhaustion recovery mode.

"That's a good question." I lamely reply, realizing I would last about two seconds in this job.

When he asks me what I would require for compensation I give him a number based on my five year old perception of economic conditions. It is way too low. Needless to say that was the last I heard from him.

A week of calling the industry produced the same result, which is to say, no result. At this point I revert to a daily search of the want ads looking for anything at all.

Meanwhile, my partner is busy painting her commission. Each day we contemplate the image emerging on the canvas. Her work is fluid and brilliant. She is a master of color and composition. Her medium is oil on canvas. The work is impressionistic and delightful. She uses our roommate's ten-year old daughter as a model.

Watching her work reminds me of an ancient yearning in my psyche to do art. During my hippie days, I surrounded myself with visual artists, envying their capacity to create images on paper using pencil and paints. I study and practice darkroom photography to fill this yearning, but I still long to draw.

In my conversations with my partner I discover she is not only a talented artist but she also teaches art. I accompany her to the Palo Alto teaching house where she has a weekly children's art class. She is magic for those kids. She claims she can teach art to anyone having the desire to express themself through the medium. She has a following as an art teacher.

I ask her if she would be willing to teach me to paint. She agrees and gives me an assignment.

"Find an image you like and copy it using charcoal on paper."

She gives me several art books to look through. I open a book of William Blake paintings and am almost immediately struck by a small black and white drawing of an old man with a long flowing beard crouched on a huge book, transcribing what he reads onto smaller books with both hands simultaneously.

Before I begin, an intuitive thought enters my awareness. It says:

"You were forced in first grade to write with you right hand even though you are left handed. This stifled your creative nature. If you are going to take up art, do it with your left hand."

It is awkward and clumsy, like doing the mirror image of an activity. Yet, there is something there, something that begins slowly emerging from a deep place. I study the image, wondering where to begin. Finally, I throw caution to the wind, let go, and make a mark on the page. I feel a connection. It has an energy of its own that begins flowing through me.

The more deeply I focus my attention into the Moment, letting go of the need for an outcome, the more a momentum builds. The experience is ecstatic. I am truly stunned by the result. She is no less amazed than I. She says it is a sign of talent.

She gives me directions whenever I get stuck. I work on the piece a few hours a day for a week, bringing it to completion. I still have it. It is dated October 1, 1984. I realize now, as I am posting the image to the manuscript, that the work is the visualization of my life to come. To translate the wisdom of The Work I studied deeply, from the big book of my School experience through my instrument, my mind/body/spirit, to fit the needs of the moment. This book itself is a manifestation of that intention.

Two weeks after beginning, her painting is finished. She waits a week for it to begin drying before shipping it to her patron. Finally, we package it and send it off using overnight shipping. She calls her customer the day after it is received. He expresses pleasure with the work and overnights her check.

The release of the pressure of the project relaxes her into a quasi non-responsive state, an apparent illness the symptoms of which are extreme lethargy, almost like the flu, but with no other flu-like symptoms. She tells me later she suspects it is the oil paints she uses that make her ill. Many of them contain heavy metals and other toxic chemicals. I feel she needs a rest and suggest a visit to my parent's Sierra cabin.

We head across the Central Valley to Sonora and up the mountain to Pinecrest where she is so listless we can do little else but enjoy the mountain air on the deck and take a few short hikes around the lake. It is upsetting to me to see what a toll her art takes on her. We talk about her switching mediums. She says she has always had an interest in watercolor, having done some work in it many years earlier.

Back in Mountain View the following week, I give in to having to find any work at all at any level. Everyday I scour the want ads for possibilities and finally find work as a telemarketer in San Jose. I am selling plastic trash bags for the VFW.

I find myself in a boiler room operation mostly populated by recently released convicts. I realize we have something in common. They have been away from the world. So have I. They have lived in a challenging environment that took all their wits and strength to survive. So have I. While a conscious community may not seem to have anything in common with a prison community, both are dangerous in their own way. At The Retreat there is no place to hide. If you are not prepared to confront your inner demons and bear the scrutiny of a community that is scrupulously watching, you are in danger of losing your grip on "reality". I feel an odd kinship with my fellow "inmates".

My sweetheart, ever the idea person, comes up with a closing line that is stunningly successful. It is: "Are you willing to help someone less fortunate than yourself?" It is the truth. That person who is less fortunate is me. A guilt trip for sure, it either results in a sale or a hang up. Finally, I am contributing to our partnership, beginning to have a paycheck.

One weekend we take a ride to the coast south of San Francisco. Along the way we spot a seashell store. "Let's stop at that store," she says. "I love shells. Can we go look?"

After half an hour looking around, she finds a beautiful shell. "Oh! I really love that one, I wish we could afford it." We discuss making the purchase for several minutes, finally deciding to give ourselves a treat. I buy her the item out of my first paycheck. It cost a whopping ten dollars. The shell remains in our possession to this day, a symbol of our new beginning.

CHAPTER FIFTY-FOUR

Living in the Suburbs

We are still members of The School. We attend weekly meetings and make teaching payments. The School remains our social support network. We continue to be part of the village at the base of Mt Analogue, but we have moved to the suburbs. We are not yet on the mountain. We have become 'older' students (remember my judgmental remarks about them expressed earlier?). We have integrated The School into our lives. When I first joined I was told that, in the beginning, you fit The Work into your life. Later, as you mature, you fit your life into The Work. I am not sure what that means right now.

When I was a Retreat resident wannabe, I looked in judgment on those who had settled into a middle class existence, becoming part of The School's supporting population. I felt superior to them. I was too dedicated to The Work to ever make such a compromise. I vowed to never allow this to happen, an obviously judgmental attitude. It brings to mind the Biblical imperative: "Judge not, least ye be judged." What this means experientially is that you eventually become what you judge. I find this to be true in my life repeatedly. Everything I thought I would never do or be, I eventually did or became.

Now I am struggling to make a living, to keep up my teaching payments while feeling once again at the bottom of some new ladder. I have shame when asked by friends what I am doing with myself. It is the material hierarchy all over again. Once again I find my ego reinventing itself to match the circumstances. It thought it was hot stuff when a Retreat resident working directly for The Teacher. Now it is a peon efforting to stay alive on the fringes of the village. My Observer or Witness Self sees both situations as nothing more than present moment challenges, exercises in loving what is.

I settle in, attend meetings, discuss The Work, go to an occasional concert, and visit with student couples, while feeling my life to be empty of meaning. I am back to striving to exist, for what, I am not sure. It is the same feeling I had way back in Philadelphia before meeting the school. I really get it when the Buddhists say:

"Before enlightenment, chop wood, carry water. After enlightenment, chop wood carry water."

I am still living in a human body, with its survival issues, struggle and effort. For what?

During Christmas week we visit The Retreat for the first time since my departure, staying in a private home. The drama group puts on a play in Town Hall called: Rosencrantz and Guildenstern Are Dead, an existential tragicomedy that expands upon the exploits of two minor characters from Shakespeare's Hamlet. I sit in the audience watching my old friends perform, feeling depressed, left out. More and more I have thoughts doubting the path I have chosen. I was clearly guided to make this transition, but for what? If there is meaning and purpose in my life, what is it? Where does it lead? My sweetheart is still the love of my life, but our romance is frequently overshadowed by the material question, the daily grind of survival.

CHAPTER FIFTY-FIVE

A Faustian Adventure

After the holidays I return to the San Jose boiler room feeling disconnected. Daily I search for work in the newspapers. An ad attracts my attention. Someone in San Carlos, an upscale community, is seeking telemarketing help. I feel intuitively drawn.

Following directions, my car climbs into the San Carlos hills to arrive at a posh cliff side residence over looking the San Francisco Bay. An attractive, wealthy looking man in his sixties opens the door. He has the vibe of a high-end con man. His name is Mr. Hyde. I cannot help my mind's association when it hears the name and wonders what is in store for me here.

He is a business consultant to the owner of a window company. They want a telemarketer to contact potential customers recently pitched by their sales force who failed to close the deal. The purpose is to get Mr. Hyde, the consummate closer, in the door to make them an offer they cannot refuse. He is slick, savvy, and smooth. I am to set appointments for him, offering a discount deal. We work out a script and he gives me a list of leads I am to call that evening.

I return home. My love is coming down the stairs as I walk in the door. I begin telling her about the interview and she breaks down sobbing for no reason. Shocked and puzzled, I demand to know what is going on.

"I have no idea. My body just reacted. It has nothing to do with what you said. I am sensitive, you know. I feel things, sense energies. This may be a dangerous situation."

"What do you expect me to do? Decline the job?" I feel frustrated. "This looks to be a lot better than the boiler room."

"No. Go forward with it. Let's see what it brings."

That night I make the calls and successfully set up several appointments for the following week. Mr. Hyde is successful in closing most of the deals and invites the two of us to the window factory to meet the owner. We learn he inherited the business from his father. It becomes clear he has little skill in running a business and is clearly in Mr. Hyde's predatory grip.

The moment the owner lays eyes on my dear one he is smitten. He immediately opens a flirtatious conversation with her right in front of me. She tells him she is an artist and is currently working on a commission to paint butterflies for the Ghana government. He lights up.

"I have a collection of mounted butterflies in display boxes," he beams.

He takes us to see the collection and insists she choose one for herself.

The owner's interest in her clearly changes the game.

We talk it over and decide to handle the situation. I continue working to develop closing appointments for Mr. Hyde, and am brought into the company's sales meetings where I am introduced as a psychologist, whose job is to evaluate their in-home sales performances, immediately placing me in an intimidating position. I feel sorry for them. They are locked out of the sale if they fail to close on the first visit. Hyde asks me to evaluate them and offer commentary on their sales techniques.

Each week I travel to his home on the hill in San Carlos where I receive instructions. The increased income enables us to consider moving out of the teaching house into our own apartment. We find a place just a few blocks down the hill from Mr. Hyde's house and move there.

Our business relationship continues to build. I am consistently successful at getting Hyde's foot in the door and he's good at closing the deals. The owner continues pursuing my woman. He calls her constantly and she manages to subtly elude him each time while he keeps up the pressure.

A few weeks later, there is a company dinner where we both are invited but intentionally seated apart. In the chair next to me is a young blonde woman recently hired as personal assistant to the owner. She gives me an abundance of semi-flirtatious attention, comments, and attitudes intentionally designed to hook my attention. My love is seated next to the owner who engages her in intense conversation. The game could not be more obvious. We joke about it later. Mr. Hyde does everything he can to put me with the assistant, apparently in the hopes I will stray in her direction. Meanwhile, the owner keeps up the pressure, calling our house almost daily.

One day I go the Mr. Hyde's house to find the owner

and the sales manager visiting him. They are sitting at the kitchen counter that is covered with an array of deli snacks. The sales manager is intimidated over being invited to the big house and goes on and on about the view of the bay, continually running to the picture window to gaze into a telescope. He is making a fool of himself, encouraged by the owner. Hyde reaches over and pulls a napkin off a covered plate, revealing several marijuana buds and rolling papers, looking me in the eye.

"You know what that is?" he slyly asks.

"Sure. It's marijuana."

"Can you roll a joint?"

"Absolutely."

"Let's give it a try."

I roll several joints and we all smoke. The drug is powerful, laced with some other intoxicant. The owner intensifies his harassment of the sales manager, playing the rich man's game, making the hired help dance, intentionally and obviously making a fool of him. He turns to me.

"You do it. Tell him he is an idiot. Make him grovel. Tell him to crawl on the floor." The employee is in a trance, held in thrall by his fear of the owner.

"No way! I would never do that."

"You have to."

I look him dead in the eye: "The only things I have to do are die and pay taxes. I have avoided paying taxes for several years and I'm working on the dying part." I smile back.

"I'm telling you to do it!"

"I do a job for you. You don't own me. I would never disrespect another person that way." I reply in an even tone.

"Fine. Come play chess with me." He bristles. Obviously he wants to make me do something.

"I love chess. You want to play. I would be delighted."

We sit down at a chessboard and begin. Four or five moves into the game an expression of irritation crosses his face.

"I don't want to play anymore." He says petulantly.

"OK. Do you have any leads for me this evening?"

"Yes."

"Great. I'll call Mr. Hyde later to tell him how it went."

It is the Friday evening before Easter weekend. For the first time I fail to make a single appointment. When I call Mr. Hyde to tell him this, he fires me. Somehow I am not surprised but relieved. We both feel the same way.

The whole scene with Mr. Hyde and the owner feels like a Faustian drama, an encounter with temptation and darkness. In the midst of extreme uncertainty we attract a play to test our commitment to walk the path of awareness and light. We literally dance with the Devil. Mr. Hyde is a white haired, sixty something patrician that does everything he can to tempt us with sex and money. We see it for what it is, meaningless distraction. Neither one of us comes close to considering what he offers as anything more than an archetypical game. Monday finds me back in the VFW boiler room selling plastic trash bags and feeling good about it.

One evening, a few weeks later, we are having an art class in the empty living room of our apartment. There are three or four of us sitting on the floor drawing with charcoal sticks. We begin to notice little dark spots appearing on our paper. They appear momentarily then disappear. I notice first but say nothing, pretending to myself that nothing is happening, not wanting to disturb the student artists.

A few days later she awakens to discover small black spots on her legs. We pull back the covers and find she is covered with fleas. Are we receiving another bug intervention? She looks at me.

"You realize, don't you, that they are all on my side of the bed. You don't have a single bite."

"I guess I don't taste good. They obviously like you. You must be tasty."

"Very funny. I am not having a good time!"

We eventually admit to ourselves that our first home together is infested with fleas. A few investigatory conversations with our neighbors inform us the previous tenants had cats. We begin obsessing about what to do. We are in a one-year lease.

That morning I go to work. Mid-morning she calls me. She tells me the student who had been designated the next "conscious being" by The Teacher has left The School. She is in a state of shock.

"Come home now!! We have to talk about this."

When I arrive she says, "I have an idea. My mother's cousin lives in Palm Springs. I visited her years ago. Go to the apartment manager and tell her about the fleas and what we found out about the previous tenants. This is a violation of our lease agreement. Demand a return of our rent and our deposit. Threaten to sue for damages if necessary. I am going to call my cousin and arrange to visit her. It is time to leave The School."

It all goes smoothly. The building manager is sympathetic and refunds our money. We borrow a truck from a student, put our belongings in a storage unit and head to Southern California. WE ARE OFFICIALLY HOMELESS.

CHAPTER FIFTY-SIX

Palm Springs

Her cousin is a woman in her late fifties, a millionaire widow. She lives in a fancy condo in an upscale Palm Springs neighborhood. She is initially delighted to have our company. We camp out with sleeping bags in her office. We go from struggling apartment dwellers to homeless vacationers.

We swim in the community pool, play tennis on their court, and are taken out to dinner at fancy restaurants. My love remembers that an old friend of hers from art school in Philadelphia is living in Palm Springs. She contacts her and we go to her house for lunch and spend the afternoon. She and her husband are a delightful couple. We have a great time and get invited to a gallery opening the following week, where we sip wine and view the work of modern artists.

It all feels surreal. We have no connection to a life. We

are homeless and directionless. There is no continuity, no stability. We are truly living in-the-moment, with no idea of what is to come nor any sense at all as to our life direction. It is exquisite and painful. My mind feels something is missing. There is no sense of social identity. We are non-entities, disconnected observers. We have no address, no phone number, no profession, and no job. It is a grand adventure, step by step into the unknown. All the normal illusions of certainty, the attachments that normally root a person into the world, are missing. All is well in-the-moment, but there is an edge of anxiety generated by the absence of the aforementioned illusion. We cannot see beyond the moment, something that is always true, but now, is painfully obvious.

Back at the condo, her cousin begins to have periods of strange behavior. We discover she is taking medication for some sort of mood disorder. She disappears for hours into the enormous bathroom off her bedroom. At lunch one day she tells us about the pain in her life. Her husband died several years ago, leaving her his fortune and real estate. She worries constantly about money. She has no capacity of her own to earn and was completely dependent on her husband. Now he's gone, she is insecure and confused. She feels the two or three million she has is not enough. She would feel better if she had five. She wants recognition from headwaiters at fancy restaurants as verification of her importance.

She likes us, is charmed by the story of how we met and, at one point, offers to take us to Las Vegas to get married. She also mentions an interest in selling her condo and wonders if we would help her with it.

Then her mood shifts. She becomes paranoid and

controlling. The Las Vegas offer disappears and is replaced by suspicion toward us, thinking, perhaps, we want to take advantage of her. She retreats into her bathroom for days at a time. We decide to go to Los Angeles to visit the teaching house there, hoping to see and interact with normalcy.

We arrive at the LA teaching house just in time for their Friday night meeting. The centre director is an old friend to us both and greets us warmly. He was her first teacher in Philadelphia. He seats us up front on stage for the meeting, introducing us as honored older students. I feel his expectation, his excitement that we are here and will contribute to his meeting that is filled with young students.

I sit there looking out on the student's faces. I have sat in audiences in meetings over the past eight years expecting the older students to share their experience of The Work. Now it is my turn and I feel nothing. I listen intensely internally. All I get is stillness. I have nothing to offer. The meeting is an agony. I realize at that point I am no longer a student. It is shocking to me. I used to believe I would always be a student. I have always wanted to be invited to sit on stage for a meeting, yet, now I am here, I can hardly wait for it to be over. I am speechless.

Finally, the meeting ends. We compare notes. Her experience is the same. The director comes over to us to ask if we would make ourselves available to talk with the younger students. We smile politely and agree, then visualize invisibility and disappear, speeding away into the night.

She pulls me aside and says: "We have to get out of here now! This is creepy. I feel so weird. Quick. We have to sneak out before we are caught here for hours."

Heading back to Palm Springs in the early hours of the morning we decide to pack up and leave the following day. It is 2:00 a.m. when we reach the downtown area to find a Spring Break riot. The streets are swarming with highly intoxicated college students, slowing traffic to a crawl.

The following morning we tell her cousin I have an important business opportunity in Northern California and we have to leave right away. We pack up and head north, deciding to take the scenic Route 1 up the coast. We stop at San Simeon to tour the Hearst Castle and continue the next day on to the Palo Alto teaching house where we crash for the night in sleeping bags on the floor, still homeless, living in trust.

CHAPTER FIFTY-SEVEN

Limbo Again

The next morning she contacts one of her old roommates from the Mountain View house on an intuitive whim. Her friend has her own apartment now, but is house sitting for someone the following week for seven days. She offers us her apartment to stay in during her absence, giving us a week to manifest our next move. I keep telling myself all is well, right now, each time my mind starts thinking fear thoughts about the future. Our situation is so precarious we cannot afford the luxury of fearful thinking. We are learning the value of truly living in The Now without any thought for tomorrow. We are compelled to trust tomorrow will take care of itself when it becomes today.

Later that day she finds an ad in the newspaper for a Holistic Expo being held that weekend in San Francisco.

"We have to go to this." She says emphatically.

"Why do we want to waste what little money we have on an Expo?"

"I don't know. I feel strongly we need to go there. You have to trust my intuition. It never fails me."

That weekend we go to the Expo, looking for the clue that leads us to our next step. We wander through the exhibits. I run into the directors of the health retreat where I spent two weeks healing. Then we turn a corner to see a young man playing New Age music on a piano.

"That's the boyfriend of my rebirth instructor! Remember, I told you about the prosperity group I attended last year in San Francisco? I met a woman there who helped me heal through a breathing process called Rebirthing."

We walk up to him as he pauses. She calls his name. He turns in recognition. She engages him with her gregarious charm and within minutes we discover his girlfriend is returning to Oregon and he's looking for a roommate. He lives in Marin and can't afford it on his own.

"Really!! We need a place to stay. Would you be willing to have us as roommates?"

"Sure. That would be great. She is leaving next week. You can move in the week following."

We leave the Expo with our next step. The synchronicity it of astonishes me. She, however, does not have a happy face.

"He's really weird. I do not want to live with him. There must be another answer."

"You followed your intuition. It took you right to him. Now you don't like what it gave you? I am reminded of what The Teacher said to you at that dinner we had with him. Remember? He said if someone throws you a life preserver when you are drowning, you do not quibble over the shape and color of it, you grab hold."

She persists: "There must be another answer. We have to keep looking!"

"I disagree. Keep looking if you want, but we must follow through on this lead. So far, there is nothing else."

We return to Palo Alto and move into her friend's apartment the next day. She scours every available resource in search of another answer, but none comes. During the week we visit the young man and his girlfriend to see the apartment. It over looks a park in Fairfax, a charming little town in Marin County across the Golden Gate Bridge from San Francisco. He gives us the master suite with a private bathroom and arcadia doors opening onto a balcony over looking the park. It is a slice of heaven.

The following Monday we borrow the same truck we used to put our belongings in storage and deliver our worldly goods to the Fairfax apartment. Finally, we are nesting, a breath of fresh air, no longer homeless.

CHAPTER FIFTY-EIGHT

Struggling in Fairfax

We spend the week settling in, getting to know the neighborhood. Marin is a gorgeous upscale area. On the one hand we feel grateful for this opportunity to live midst such beauty. On the other we are living in a candy store with very little money. We explore the little towns leading into Fairfax, the cafes, bookstores and gift shops. She goes to a beauty shop for a hair cut, taking paintings with her. She sells two of the pieces. Once again her manifesting magic helps meet our needs.

I answer a want ad and find my self in an upscale telephone room in Tiburon selling silver stock. The silver market is down and we promise it will soar again soon. It is a hard sell. Very few men in the room (and it's all men) make a deal on any given day. The pay is commission only. After a few weeks of this struggle I quit and find a VFW outlet locally that agrees to allow me to work out of my home. I begin spending my evenings earning our rent and expenses once again successfully selling plastic trash bags.

The student who left The School, the one designated the next conscious being, starts a transition group in San Francisco. There are many who have left the school with him. We begin attending weekly meetings, starting The Work all over again, like graduate school. Only ex-members of The School are admitted. Now we are no longer residents of the village at the foot of Mount Analogue, nor even of its suburbs, but are outcasts living on the fringes seeking a way to begin our climb. The group is our social network.

Each week we drive to San Francisco, receive a free Reiki energy healing at an ashram, have a vegetarian dinner in Chinatown, and attend the meeting where practical aspects of The Work are discussed, and our feelings about The School processed. It is a decompression group intended to facilitate reintegration into mainstream society.

We have an occasional art class at the apartment, but sell no more paintings. My earnings telemarketing supports us and we begin to save a little money. Still, any attempts of the mind to peer into the future are met with bleakness. Is this it? Is this what I gave up everything to do, to be in a worse place economically than before I began? I notice how my mind takes what is happening in the present and projects it into a permanent future, operating on the assumption that things will never change.

I find an advertisement for a course on how to become a millionaire buying and selling real estate with no seed capital and no money down. I study the course intensely, and we even take some spare time to look at properties for sale, feeling all the while a deep resistance to actually taking action by making an offer and leveraging the deal to have it pay for itself. The more I study, the more I realize I will be buying properties I will have to maintain. This realization is enough to take my attention off the idea.

Spring transitions into summer. She joins a health club down the street, another piece of manifestation magic. Our roommate's girlfriend visits a month after we move there. She happens to mention to her a lovely little health club for women only and how she would like to join but cannot afford it. Her friend smiles:

"I have a membership there which I am obviously not using. Let's go see if I can sign it over to you."

They visit the gym, which agrees to allow the transfer for a small fee. She begins daily workouts. As the summer proceeds she stays away more and more. When I ask her where she goes, she smiles: "Shopping, of course."

"But you haven't bought anything."

"I know. I just like to look."

This goes on for sometime until one afternoon she comes in and throws a huge handful of money on the bed.

"Where did you get that?!"

"I have been experimenting. A few weeks ago I was looking at clothes in a department store. There were several things I liked on the sale rack. I have a photographic memory. I remember everything I see. I went down the street to another department store and found the same items on the rack at full price. I went back to the store with the sale and purchased a few items on sale. Then I went to the other store and returned them for full price. They gave me cash for the returns."

"I don't believe it. Isn't that illegal?"

"I don't see anything wrong with it. I am buying and selling. We desperately need money. We cannot continue on this subsistence level, nor can we afford to move anywhere. Why don't you drop what you're doing and come help me do this. Take a notebook with you and copy down model numbers and sale prices. Look for something to specialize in, like knife sets, or silverware. We will watch the papers each day for sales."

"Don't you need receipts?"

"No. Just tell them you received the item as a wedding gift."

"What if they refuse to accept the return?"

"We keep the original receipt and return it."

The next day we dress up and go out. Our first stop is at a clothing sale in a department store. She looks at the blouses and skirts carefully. Then we go to another store down the mall and, sure enough, the exact same items are on display at full price. We go back and purchase a sweater for $25 marked down from $75 and take it down to the other store. She turns to me and says: "You return it. Just say your wife asked you to return it. It is a gift."

I walk up to customer service, my heart pounding as I work on appearing nonchalant.

"Hi. I'd like to return this."

"OK. Is there anything wrong with it?"

"No. It's a duplicate gift. I don't have a receipt."

"That's OK. Do you have an account with us?"

"No. I'll just take cash."

"Alright. It will just take a moment."

She hands me $75 cash. It cannot be this easy? I cannot believe it. Within a few minutes we have manifested an increase in our wealth. I am blown away. My reality is altered. We take the money and go out for an expensive lunch, after which we work the mall for several hours, netting $250 profit.

The next day we travel to another shopping center in the Bay Area. Some stores will not return cash, but mail checks. Others will only refund to an account. In the ensuing weeks we open accounts to handle that situation. We also open a post office box to receive checks. I stop my telemarketing activities and we focus our entire energy on the project, working to accumulate savings to get us out of the economic basement.

Over the next two months this activity escalates. We branch out into household gifts like knife sets and kitchenware, higher ticket items. The inevitable outcome is that department store management finally notices us. One day we receive a phone call from an investigator who interrogates us. We stick to the story that we are newly weds who have received duplicate gifts. The upshot is that our accounts get cancelled, the game is called, and I return to telemarketing. Now, however, we have a small nest egg.

Weeks after this happens we receive a surprise phone call from her daughter. She told me about the existence of her adult children, but rarely mentions them on a regular basis. I have the impression they are the source of considerable pain. Now, out the blue, her daughter calls saying she is coming from Colorado to visit with her new boyfriend. She is excited about her arrival.

A few days later they arrive. Her daughter is a stunning blond version of her dark haired beauty. Her boyfriend is a dark male version of her. He is a Ninja warrior who once was a security guard for the Dali Lama. They are quite a pair.

We spend the next week taking them on a tour of the magical places in Marin, the charming little towns, the redwood forests, and Jade Beach where the small pebbles that compose the beach contain water worn nuggets of Jade. Her daughter is an introspective, brooding, individual who is difficult to read. There always seems to be something brewing beneath the surface, she is always ruminating about something with furrowed brows. When she is outgoing she is utterly charming, having her mother's huge heart and gregarious nature.

We go to an upscale restaurant on the bay in Sausalito on a day when her boyfriend is away on some errand. I enter with one of them on each arm creating a palpable stir. The whole room looks up as we enter. It is a moment of memory. They are each so striking and similar that heads turn when they pass.

Her daughter shares her mother's intense creativity, channeling it into porcelain sculptures of fairies. She appears to have a great love for her mother, a love that is tainted, however, by some underlying angst that causes her to reach out to her mother then retreat into abandonment. It is a life long pattern that causes her mother great pain, a pain that mars the visit, creating underlying tension. Her daughter a is not a person who has the capacity to express her feelings, so the tension is never openly confronted but is ever present, making the visit bitter sweet. One evening just before they return to Colorado a momentous event occurs, altering our life course.

CHAPTER FIFTY-NINE

Another Sacred Message

It is early evening. I am once again telemarketing from our bedroom while she entertains her daughter in the living room. Suddenly she rushes into the room in an altered state of awareness.

"I just had a vision of a bird of flame arising from the ashes, a Phoenix!! I was telling her how we are in limbo waiting for a sign, when this vision of a Phoenix bird overwhelmed my consciousness. It was vivid, intense."

"It must be a sign for us to move to Phoenix!"

"Of course. What else could it be?"

We are excited. For fifteen months we have bounced around the state, torturing ourselves, at times, questioning the value of having done what we did to our lives by devoting them to our spiritual growth at the cost of our material existence.

What was that all about? I dreamt this big dream,

to spend my life in a seeker's paradise. I succeeded in creating a rich life there only to find myself once more plunged into the fray of life, struggling to gain a foothold in a world I had rejected, found unworthy of my attention. Now I stand outside that world seeking re-entry, and it says to me:

"Who are you? What do you want?"

I want a mission, a purpose, a next step. The Phoenix message seems to be it. The long awaited call has come. Now we are off to face the unknown, to meet the challenge of uncertainty at a whole new level, severing all connection to The School's support. This is it, the first step on the path leading out of the village at the base of Mount Analogue, a simple, singular instruction. Go to Phoenix.

CHAPTER SIXTY

Preparation for Departure

Making the commitment to move to Phoenix unleashes the appearance of new resources. The power of commitment is discussed in esoteric literature, but is never so apparent as in this moment. I find a steady job running a phone room for a roofing company. Our lease is up in six weeks, giving us a departure deadline.

She sets about selling everything that will not fit in our car. Her intuitive magic, innate charm and beautiful smile facilitate the transformation of our worldly goods into cash. She gets top dollar for everything. In the midst of cleaning out our dresser before selling it, I pull out all the drawers. Taped to the last drawer I find an envelope. Inside is $500 cash.

She gasps: "Oh my! I put that there last year for a rainy day and forgot about it."

In the final three weeks we work together in a phone

room setting timeshare appointments. We are so good at this the owner offers to set us up in our own phone room. This is something I noticed the last time I made a huge, life-changing commitment. Temptation shows up. Being given a business would be easier than going to a strange community and finding our way. When I was preparing to move to The Retreat, I was offered a high paying position in the insurance business.

Finally the day arrives. The apartment is empty. The car is loaded. Every last detail has been handled. We have an itinerary. It is fearful going directly to Phoenix. We have stops planned along the way to give the appearance we are on vacation, not migrating. This is where the instruction: live in the moment, consider the next step only, has extreme practical value. Attempting to see or even consider anything beyond that is to fall into an abyss of madness.

We head south, out through the East Bay into the San Joaquin Valley down Route 5, spending the night at a motel near Fresno. The next day we continue on to Santa Barbara where we meet with a couple, who are ex-students, spending the afternoon with them discussing their current relationship to The Work.

The challenge is to maintain one's connection to inner development without the support of The School's community. The School's propaganda was "lose The School, lose The Way". Clearly a fear based manipulation designed to keep students from straying. Still, our friends point out it is not easy to remember what is important in the face of the material demands of ordinary life. We resolve to each other to never lose our focus, our intention to Be Present to our lives, and to the larger, transcendent reality.

Our next destination is her cousin's house in Palm Springs. It is clear to us we are stalling, postponing the inevitable. We have burned the boats. There's no going back. Still, we drag our feet. Each day is a step into the unknown.

Her cousin is hospitable but we feel the same discomfort with her as before. The next day I call my father's sister and her husband in Los Angeles. They are glad to hear from us and welcome our visit. Now we are actually backtracking. Palm Springs is closer to Arizona than Los Angeles. We spend two days with them.

Finally, on the afternoon of the second day we head out.

CHAPTER SIXTY-ONE

An Empty Handed Leap

Leaving California for us is metaphor for leaving the village at the base of Mount Analogue. The final ties have been cut. We are ready to fly solo. We are scared but resolute. We have enough experience of the miraculous to know we will fare well, but this is the big test. We are going to a new town with little money and no contacts or jobs, trusting it will all work out, taking The Work with us as our internal guidance. Interstate 10 unfolds before us all the way to Blythe, CA, the border town between California and Arizona. We find lodging for the night.

That morning we cross the Arizona border. The highway, an undulating black ribbon, disappears into the vastness of the Sonoran Desert. It is beautiful, awe inspiring and desolate.

She says: "Pull over. We have to do something."

She turns to me, takes my hand and places it on her

heart. I take her hand and place it on mine. We look in each other's eyes.

"Never ever forget, our home is in our hearts. We will always find our way."

We merge back onto Interstate 10 and disappear into the infinite horizon of Now.

AFTER WORDS

"We shall not cease from exploration, and the end of all our exploring will be to arrive where we started, and know the place for the first time." T.S. Eliot

My journey to now is an inner voyage that takes place in the external world. It also is an oxymoron. There really is nowhere to go but Here, no other time but Now, there and then only exist metaphorically. To discover this truth required me to cut all ties with my imagined reality, my story, and release all my identifications with everything external: career, marriage, family and possessions. This withdrawal gave me the opportunity to live in a community of like-minded people in a cultural laboratory where I developed the skills necessary to climb Mount Analogue.

Leaving The Retreat and The School was the necessary next step. The part of me that wanted to live out my life in The School was the same part of me that seeks the illusion of security. The deeper truth is that once the skills are acquired it is necessary to re-enter the world and apply those skills to the ensuing life challenges.

I am thirty years into that process at this writing. We continue to find our way, part of which is, for me, becoming a psychotherapist and a corporate consultant. In my attempts to distill my years of study into sensible tools, I have developed a powerful, mind stopping, open-eyed meditation, an accurate self-assessment tool and seven principles/practices of mind mastery that have been remarkably successful. What follows is a pamphlet in which these tools are presented for your use should you wish to make your own Journey to Now.

TOOLS FOR THE SEEKER

A Handbook for Conscious Living
By James Westly MC LPC

INTRODUCTION

TOOLS FOR CONSCIOUSNESS

I come to the writing of this book having spent the last thirty-seven years living the life of a seeker, initiate and teacher of spiritual practices. These include exercises and philosophies that enhance Consciousness, spiritual aliveness, and facilitate a direct experiential connection to a larger reality, or higher power. In my opinion, this connection is the answer to humanity's search for meaning and purpose. It is the key that gives access to life's secrets, its hidden meanings.

In this essay I have compiled a set of powerful practices and ideas, synthesized from the world's wisdom traditions, which enable the user to make that connection. My challenge to you is simply to say that if you use the tools presented here, you will come to live more consciously. I know this to be so from my own experience and from the experience of the thousands of individuals I have taught.

If you do the work, it will produce results. And, work it is! Some say it is life's most difficult task, the work of inner self-transformation. Presented in the pages to come is a set of learnable skills. Any sufficiently motivated person can learn to use them, but it is like the light bulb joke about therapists. How many therapists does it take to change a light bulb? One, but the light bulb has to want to change. What kind of light bulb are you? Motivation is an essential ingredient!

> Motivation is an essential ingredient!

The foundation of my spiritual journey was an eight-year mid-life withdrawal into the retreat of a school built around the teachings of George Gurdjieff and Peter Ouspensky, called The Fourth Way. Eckhart Tolle, Neale Donald Walsh, and many others have also contributed significantly.

I was asked to lead a Fourth Way group in Phoenix, Arizona in 1986. Individuals in the group had problems they could not share with the group. They requested one-on-one assistance with their psychological issues. Treatment tools were developed out of the practices I taught. This eventually led to entry into mainstream mental healthcare where these tools have been refined into the seven principles for conscious living offered here, along with a powerful assessment tool and an intense meditation capable of immediately producing a state of no-thought.

> ...any individual can connect to life's meaning and purpose.

In my opinion, any individual can connect to life's meaning and purpose, but only through the elevation of consciousness. Knowledge, is necessary, perhaps, but not sufficient. Applying these precise tools will help you to live passionately now.

James Westly, MC, LPC, Phoenix, Arizona 2014

Creating Presence Therapy
Self-Healing

In August 1979, two months before going to live in the retreat mentioned above, I received a head injury in an auto accident which impaired my automatic memory functioning, that part of my brain that reflexively registers impressions and takes action without my conscious participation. The consequences of the injury did not immediately manifest, but developed gradually over time, and, were subtle. Short-term memory, as an automatic function, slowly deteriorated. This was accompanied by a profound physical depression, a flattening of affect, and chronic exhaustion. As the post injury weeks, months and years unfolded, these effects deepened, making my daily life one of effort to merely maintain sanity.

The consequences of this were devastating. Small agreements made were instantly forgotten. I struggled daily with fatigue. The concept of effort was reduced to literally, physically taking the next step. Memory loss devastated my personal life, plunging me into my darkest period, a period of profound aloneness, which would have been unlivable without inner work, and the support of the retreat community.

Making a Distinction between
Consciousness and Functions

Establishing Presence in the moment is the primary intention of my practice. To accomplish this requires making a distinction between functions and Consciousness. "Consciousness can exist without functions, and functions can exist without consciousness", wrote Peter Ouspensky, author of The Fourth Way.

This means that functions; thinking, feeling, perceiving, moving and sensing, can do their work automatically, without our awareness, like flying an airplane on autopilot. This phrase also says that Consciousness exists independent of functions. If Consciousness is my true identity, then that identity is separate from my functions, my ability to 'do' in the world. Perceiving this distinction became the foundation for my sanity in the face of subtle brain injury.

> ...true sanity is a state of consciousness.

In the 35 years since the accident it has become clear to me that true sanity is a state of consciousness. To achieve that state requires the establishment of an aware existence separate from the thinking mind. This requires one to constantly monitor thoughts.

As we are, mind is dominant; Consciousness is passive. We are led around by the mind with its programming and its ego (the mind's sense of identity, who we "think" we are). The objective of Presence Practice is to reverse this relationship, making Consciousness dominant, and mind passive. To accomplish this requires Consciousness to become aware of itself as separate from mind. Inner self-observation is the beginning of that process. Socrates, an ancient Greek philosopher, said: "The unobserved life is not worth living."

Rendering mind passive requires constant inner vigilance. The moment you relax, mind resumes dominance, overwhelming Consciousness with its fear-based agenda. When one is not observing mind, it is in charge, making inappropriate, sometimes devastating, life decisions.

> Rendering mind passive requires constant inner vigilance.

Eckhart Tolle, Twenty-First Century consciousness teacher, wrote in The Power of Now how he awoke one early morning with his mind repeating the sentence "I cannot live with myself any longer." His Consciousness awakened the moment he realized that sentence contained two entities, I and myself, one of which had to be false. He could no longer live with the decisions his false 'self' was making. Making that distinction permanently changed his life.

Using this Distinction in Mental Health

People with issues like depression, anxiety, panic attacks, obsessive thinking, compulsive behavior, various forms of psychosis and substance addiction, are experiencing the consequences of allowing their mind to be the arbiter of their personal reality, rather than their Consciousness.

Rene Descartes' famous dictum: "I think, therefore, I am" is a core societal belief. Most people I have encountered in treatment know this phrase no matter what their educational level. It places personal identity in the operations of the mind, The Thinker, the voice in our head that is hardly ever silent. Identifying with this voice cuts off our connection to the larger organism we reside within, the larger mind of which it is but an isolated fragment.

Presence Training

Presence Training has as its intention the development of a new relationship to our thought process, one in which the individual learns to objectify their mind and experience it as a powerful, reality creating tool. By withdrawing identity from cognitive process, focusing attention fully into the moment, and practicing the art of surrender to what is, the mind is taught a new, more functional role, that of service to Consciousness.

Consciousness teachers of all eras understand the incorrect operation of the mind to be the primary obstacle to elevating awareness, and have devised techniques to assist initiates in withdrawing from their identification with 'The Thinker'. All self-awareness exercises have the same objective, to create inner stillness, freeing Consciousness from its addiction to thought, and allowing aware connection to a deeper reality. Where that connection is made, is Here. When it is made, is Now.

> All self-awareness exercises have the same objective, to create inner stillness.

In a moment of connection, or Presence, psychological symptoms diminish, or may even vanish. The individual relaxes into a state of well being, using their concentration to focus their entire attention into the present moment. From this vantage point problems cease to exist. They require a past and a future. When time disappears, so do "problems". Situations are discussed from a next-step perspective, while acknowledging life's uncertainty.

This shift in perspective is simple, profound, and confrontational. It is accomplished by moving attention out of the mind into the body using the senses. When the mind is empty of attention, it becomes quiet, fears and regrets vanish, and the voice of "The Thinker" is stilled. This leaves pure Consciousness, unimpeded by the mind's programming, opening the individual to their inner guidance and connection to a deeper, richer, way of life.

> This shift in perspective is simple, profound, and confrontational.

This is what spontaneously happens the moment an individual learns to consistently quiet the mind, no matter what their belief system or knowledge base. In the 1950's the Central Intelligence Agency (CIA) of the United States government, in order to spy on the Russians, attempted to train people with psychic ability in techniques of remote viewing. Learning to do this required the person to quiet their mind. In many cases, when they accomplished this they experienced a spontaneous connection to a deeper reality, a spiritual awakening.

Making this connection on a regular basis and following

its direction, resolves inner conflicts, leaving a healthy interaction with the life process. The "doing" of life is then driven by the individual's deeper intentions, and decisions are made by Consciousness not by mind (programming). Wide varieties of psychological symptoms diminish or vanish in the face of this process, setting the person free to be their authentic selves.

The tools of Presence Training have been developed to accomplish this intention. I first used them to survive brain trauma. Later they were developed further in private consultation. Finally I evolved them into a systematic approach that has the capacity to empower the individual and enable them to be more effective in all areas of life. Learning to operate your mind as a powerful tool is a basic life skill no one ever taught us.

> Learning to operate your mind as a powerful tool is a basic life skill no one ever taught us.

Fragmentation of Consciousness

We live in a multitasking society. We are proud of our ability to perform a multitude of mental tasks simultaneously. We carry out routine chores while we 'think' about other things. We play back scenes from the past. We worry about what is to come. We make plans and have fantasies about how the plans will play out. We rehearse important future events and then wonder what went wrong when what we rehearsed turns out to be ineffective. We unconsciously conduct internal conversations that often have conflicting values, then wonder why we feel stressed and overwhelmed. Each one of these mental activities consumes a portion of our energy and attention. The older we get the more we have to multitask about and the less attention we pay to what is occurring in the one place and time where life is actually occurring, Here/Now.

I recently asked a client where she had the majority of her attention. She gave me a long list of 'important' concerns: she was: worried about her children; having discrimination in the workplace; concerned about how this would effect her pregnancy; she wanted to quit and find work elsewhere but 'knew' that no one would hire a pregnant woman and give her maternity leave; she feared not being able to maintain her family. All legitimate concerns. Each one of these 'concerns' held a fragment of her consciousness outside the present moment. She said she was so stressed out she would get overwhelmed by the slightest challenge. I asked her what percentage of her attention was Here/Now.

"Hardly any of it" She sighed.

Her presenting issues were depression, anxiety and panic attacks. It does not take much of an intuitive leap to see the connection between her presenting symptoms and how she was operating her mind.

Cognitive Psychology

In psychology we know that the mind and body are intermeshed, hard wired together, such that the body reacts to every thought the mind thinks. We call this complex physical reaction emotion. Think a thought, have a feeling.

If I am thinking fear thoughts about some possible catastrophe befalling me in the future, my body reacts immediately. The reaction may consist of such symptoms as elevated heart rate and blood pressure, muscle tension, and increased adrenaline. All this occurs as the body's response to thought. Apply this idea to the thought patterns of the woman mentioned above and we begin to see how thought patterns may have produced her presenting symptoms. Cognitive-behavioral therapy teaches people to think different thoughts. Presence Training teaches how to objectify mind and reduce thinking.

Conscious Living Defined
Recognition of mind as a tool

Have you heard the phrase mentioned above: "I think, therefore, I am"? Each person is asked this question in his or her first session. The majority acknowledges their awareness of the statement regardless of education level, demonstrating it to be a part of Western group mind, an underlying cultural belief.

What does this mean to you: you think therefore you exist? Your thought process defines your reality? Does it mean your mind is who you are, the voice in your head that incessantly talks? Is that the voice of your true identity? The common answer is affirmative. As a culture we define ourselves by our thought process.

How is it possible then, that we are able to observe thought? Who is observing? The Buddha said:

"You are what observes, not what you observe."

Eckhart Tolle realized this at such a profound level that it permanently shifted his Consciousness. He realized his mind was not his true identity. This realization is the foundation of all that follows.

Our mind is not who we are, it is a function of the body. Who we are is the awareness that exists prior to thought, the Consciousness behind The Thinker. I consider the mind to be a powerful tool, a computer that orchestrates the operation of the human body. It is the tool of reality creation. It decides which elements in the stream of incoming data are relevant. It is a lens through which Consciousness directs the energy of attention. Whatever we attend to becomes personal reality.

Giving the computer (mind) the power of identity is a dangerous mistake. When we fail to recognize the power of thought and mistake it for Consciousness, we are courting disaster. Believing the voice in our head, which we call thought, to be us is a failure to recognize the power of mind and the need to educate ourselves in the use of the tool. The ideas and techniques given here are designed to help the reader master the use of that tool. It is a basic life skill no one ever taught us.

Educating the mind to understand its place

When a significant portion of our attention is absent from the moment, the mind is in charge. Each day, moment-to-moment, we make decisions large and small. Allowing the mind to multitask our awareness outside the moment leaves these choices in the hands of our programming, our automatic reactions, robbing us of our creativity, and setting the stage for psychological dysfunction. Even if the programming is not defective, this process makes creative solutions impossible. The computer (mind) cannot generate original thought.

> The computer (mind) cannot generate original thought.

The difficulty is that, since our attention is absent, we have led the computer to believe it is in charge. This is not its true function. Since it is not performing its intended function, it feels anxious, fearful. The mind runs on fear. A glance at the daily headlines in the media confirms this.

To be free from the debilitating effects of fear requires us to re-educate the computer and install new software that teaches the mind to understand its true role, that of service to Consciousness. The seven principles outlined in the pages ahead are that new software.

Developing the ability to focus full attention Here/Now

These principles are designed to facilitate the user's ability to bring all their attention into the present moment. The concept is simple. Doing it is challenging, at least in the beginning. We are faced with the habitual momentum of thousands of years of mind dominance. Taking up the practices outlined here requires the release of those of habits.

Experiencing full attention Here/ Now reverses the relationship between mind and Consciousness, bringing Consciousness into an active dominant position, making mind passive. Many ancient teachings have developed practices designed to place full attention onto

> Being fully present to the moment cannot be relegated to special occasions.

the mundane activities of ordinary existence. Being fully present to the moment cannot be relegated to special occasions, but should be practiced daily, and applied to every life activity.

Most of life consists of mundane tasks. Bringing full attention to ordinary behaviors enables us to live fully and passionately in the Now. It is the difference between black and white television and vivid color. We knew this as innocent children. We have forgotten it as mind addicted adults.

Releasing ego: mind-based identity

What we did not have as children was a mind-based self, a collection of thought patterns representing who we 'think' is us, beginning with the thought of our name.

The phrase 'I am...' is the language equivalent of identity. Repeat this phrase many times placing different nouns and adjectives behind the 'I am' each time. I am (my name), I am (smart/stupid), I am (male/female), I am (loved/not loved), I am (white/black/Latino/Asian), I am (poor/rich), I am (worthy/unworthy)... and on until you run out of options to put behind the 'I am'. This will reveal the contents of your ego. It is who you 'think' you are. Notice how you repeat your answers to this exercise to yourself throughout the day, reinforcing this false identity. Observe the emotions they produce. This is your mind created personal reality, your ego.

> In a state of full Presence we cease perceiving Life through our mental filters.

In a state of full Presence we cease perceiving Life through our mental filters and are fully focused on present-moment reality. Mind recedes, assuming it's proper function of service to Consciousness, and ego vanishes, leaving pure awareness.

Learn to intentionally create personal reality

Learning the skills of Presence brings with it new experiences of personal truth. You learn to view your life directly without the encumbrances of personal need and desire. Being fully Here/Now is our natural state, a state of innocence. Innocence is simply awareness without thought.

> Innocence is simply awareness without thought.

The facts of the moment are perceived directly without placing value (right or wrong, good or bad). Decisions arise naturally without the imposition of mental process (analysis, worry, fear, guilt, regret, and concerns over the opinions of others). In this state, you are Awareness in a body directly experiencing life. You do what obviously needs to be done. Ask a hero how they found the courage to take whatever risk they took and they will tell you they just did what was obviously needed in-the-moment, without thought. They were totally present.

Connecting to true or conscious identity

The hero did not have the thought he/she would be a 'hero'. Something larger operated thru them. When you achieve a state of total Presence you are immediately connected to that greater reality. This is why we seek Presence, not knowing what it is we seek.

> When you achieve a state of total Presence you are immediately connected to that greater reality.

What do drug addicts, skydivers and Buddhist monks have in common? They are all seeking release from their mind, seeking that connection. Drug addicts seek to 'blow their mind' with drugs. Skydivers seek the thrill of total Presence through physical risk. Monks engage in internal exercises designed to free them from thought. I once met a skydiver whose tee shirt read: "If you're not living on the edge, you're taking up too much space". The edge is the moment, called the razor's edge by some, the thin slice of no-thing between past and future. It is here your find your Self.

Making life decisions based on inner-guidance

Jesus said the kingdom of heaven is within. Neale Donald Walsh, author of the Conversations with God series, said, "If you don't go within, you go without." I am writing these words by listening to inner guidance rather than 'thinking'. My mind is passive, doing its job of supplying words and phrases chosen by inner guidance. This is our direct personal connection to a larger reality that immediately emerges the moment we achieve inner-stillness. The mind is free from trying to "figure out" solutions and answers and is in a quiet receptive mode.

When we are honest with ourselves, we acknowledge the mind has never been capable of producing original thought. All creative people know their creations arise from a source outside their mind. We always have been and ever will be personally connected to a larger reality. Our

> We always have been and ever will be personally connected to a larger reality.

problem has been in believing otherwise. As we learn to listen, and objectively observe, we discover the Universe is responding to every thought we think. Learning to use this power consciously is the basic life skill we never learned. This is what the principles and practices given here are meant to accomplish. Listening to, trusting in, and following the direction coming to us from a larger reality sets us free from the fear based mind with its 'concerns', free to live passionately now!

THE PRESENCE METER
An Assessment Tool

The Presence Meter is an assessment tool that accurately measures the degree of attention focused Here/Now. Ask yourself this question right now and listen internally for your reflexive first response. It's the first thought that comes to mind. The question is:

"What percentage, zero to one hundred, what percentage of my attention is Here/Now?"

Look for the fast answer. What is your number? Is it less than 100%? The common response is 50%. A person with this level of attention has only half of their resources available to deal with life in the only place and time it is happening, the present moment. This gives new meaning to the phrase: "Playing with half a deck."

It also means the mind is dominant, and Consciousness is passive. Someone has to run the store, make the myriad of life decisions we each make moment to moment. When attention is not entirely focused

> ...the mind is dominant, and Consciousness is passive.

Here/Now, and it rarely is, then it is mind that chooses. This is the 'self' Eckhart Tolle could no longer live with, the mind-based identity or ego, who we 'think' we are.

Now ask your self the question: "What is the non-present attention doing?" The answer is frequently some kind of negative thought pattern, and generally not just one, but several, often conflicting thought patterns. Worry, fear, concern, and anxiety are common responses to this question. These are all thought patterns focused on an imagined future. There also may be regret and frustration over events that happened or decisions made before now, or you may just wish the moment to be different. Maybe you are bothered by the weather, or who you are with, or your life situation.

Your first answer to the presence meter question is your baseline, your degree of presence-in-the-moment before any inner work. The lower the number, the more fragmented your Consciousness. If you have a high degree of attention focused outside the moment, you may be experiencing fear based thought patterns. If your programming, your automatic functioning, arises from an upbringing that was in any way abusive, you may be enacting self-destructive dramas.

Ask yourself this self-assessment question repeatedly throughout your day. Notice that when you are able to generate a higher number, or 100% or more, your feeling experience of the moment improves, even though your life situation remains the same.

> Presence brings with it a sense of wellbeing regardless of circumstances.

Presence brings with it a sense of wellbeing regardless of circumstances. Examine how it feels to be more present. Assessing yourself this way gives you direct feedback.

The answer to the second question (What is my absent attention occupied with?) gives you clues as to where you need work. Typical answers may include:

"I'm worried about how I'm going to pay my bills."
"I'm afraid something will happen to my children."
"What if...?"
"I'm afraid that..."
"I regret that stupid decision I made ten years ago and fear I'll do it again in the future."
"I'm worried what my relatives will think."
"I feel guilty about the bad investments I made."

One of my clients, whose response was 10%, said she wanted everyone around her to be happy, and was willing to do whatever it took to accomplish that. Wherever she went, everyone's wellbeing became her personal business. She was a vacant house, available to be taken over by anyone. No wonder she was depressed and exhausted.

Another client reported zero percent of her attention Here/Now. This person confessed they hated their life and had deep regrets over all the choices they had made in the past. She sat mindlessly in front of the television everyday. When she conversed, it was about all the things she had regrettably done, or how unhappy she was with the way things are. She focused all her attention into the past, reliving the emotions that arose from re-stimulated painful memories. When confronted with this tendency she resisted giving up this practice, saying she would not know who she was without this identity. She resisted giving up her pain, fearing to lose the only 'self' she knew.

An Intervention

The Presence Meter question also is an intervention. It brings to awareness our poverty of attention in the moment. The answer is a call to action, a prompting to intensify Here/Now focus. The answer to the second question gives direction to the work needed to increase awareness. The principles of mind mastery provide tools with which to accomplish that intention.

Fragmented attention is the result of multitasking thought outside the moment. A person's attention is divided among many mental tasks. Each task is producing its own emotional response, which may be in conflict with the emotional response of some other task (inner conflict). This is a formula for mental/ emotional distress.

> Fragmented attention is the result of multitasking thought outside the moment.

Ask yourself what feelings those thought patterns outside the moment are generating. Notice how they interfere with your experience of life in the present. Your moment may not contain any conflict, but you feel conflicted. It may not contain any difficulty but you feel stressed. Everything may be going well right now, but you feel anxious about what might happen next. Notice how your thought processes negatively effect your overall sense of well being and generate psychological symptoms by removing your attention from the Now.

Summation

The Presence Meter (PM) is a simple question that measures the degree of our attention focused Here/Now. It is both an assessment and an intervention. It determines the quality and focus of our Consciousness, and alerts us to the need to alter the subject of our attention.

ENTERING THE NO-THOUGHT ZONE

The No-Thought Zone is a meditative technique that drains the mind of attention, placing it in the senses. Its purpose is to attain a state of inner-stillness with attention focused entirely into the Now. The benefits of this experience are enormous.

The most apparent benefit is an enhanced sense of wellbeing. You feel good. When inner-stillness is achieved, even for a moment, profound, subtle shifts occur within. Your mind ceases its endless processing with all its consequent bodily reactions, and negativity. Tension and anxiety vanish, leaving a deep sense of ease. In this state of awareness, Consciousness is dominant, mind is passive. You experience an alert inner stillness with an absence of thought. Pain may vanish, depression diminishes, and anxiety dissipates.

> The most apparent benefit is an enhanced sense of wellbeing.

> Consciousness is dominant, mind is passive.

Experiencing this for the first time is often described as weird, peaceful, or different. Though I believe most people have experienced moments of pure Presence, it is usually in a context, like skydiving, an auto accident, giving birth, or some intense unique event that galvanizes attention. Evoking a state of full attention internally thru effort, in an otherwise ordinary moment,

> ...transforms the base metal of forgetting into the gold of remembering.

transforms the base metal of forgetting into the gold of remembering, the true meaning of alchemy. Presence is never forgotten, absence is never remembered.

Accumulating the gold of remembering creates wealth far greater than that of any earthly illusion. It is this wealth that has the power to heal internal divisions and transform suffering. The experience of Presence itself does this, regardless of mental model or belief. Closely examined, all true teachings, ancient and modern, have a common intention, to produce this profound state of awareness. Entering the no-thought zone offers that opportunity, the opportunity for connection, for at-one-ment.

The No-Thought Zone

The meditation is best done in dyad, sitting face-to-face a short distance from another person. However, it can also be performed alone using a candle flame or some neutral object as a focal point.

As you sit facing each other, direct all your attention into the left eye of the person across from you (this will be on your right side). The left eye is said to be the eye of essence, one's true Self. The right eye is the eye of personality (ego). Hold this gaze throughout the exercise, resisting the urge to blink. If you are alone, stare at the focal point, a candle flame, spot on the wall, or even you own left eye in the mirror.

While you are gazing into the eye of your partner, feel the physical sensation of your feet resting on the floor.

Wiggle your toes a few times to make sensory contact, then continue feeling your feet throughout the meditation.

Now, if seated, feel your body pressing into the cushion of the chair, while you are feeling your feet and maintaining eye contact. So, feel your feet, feel your seat.

Next become aware of sound in your environment. Do not focus on what you hear, or respond to or label the sounds. Just be aware of sounds, while you are feeling your feet, feeling your seat and maintaining eye contact.

Then expand your peripheral vision to its fullest extent and hold it there while maintaining eye contact. Now you are simultaneously feeling your feet, your seat, being aware of sound, maintaining eye contact and expanding your vision.

Finally, turn your hands palms up on your knees and feel the palms of your hands without touching them. Feel them from the inside. Feel the energy of Life circulating in the palms of your hands. There is blood pumping through them. Electrical energy is circulating from the millions of nerve endings in your fingertips to your brain. If you really concentrate and intensely focus, you may begin to feel a subtle tingling or pulsation in the palms of your hand. You are actually experiencing the Life force circulating in your hands.

Pull it all together now! Feel your feet, feel your seat, feel your hands, open peripheral vision, be aware of sounds, maintain eye contact! Concentrate on all this all at once, intensely, for two minutes. Use your mind to count 120 seconds. Now assess.

Are you still thinking? What percentage of your attention is Here/Now? You have succeeded if you can honestly answer your mind is quiet and your attention Here/Now is 100% or more. If your answer is yes, you are still thinking, and less than 100%, redouble your efforts to focus attention on the elements of the meditation. Continue to sit in dyad practicing the focus of attention described above. Sit for four or five minutes. Continue counting internally. It helps keep the mind focused on the task.

As you do this, you may notice your vision change. Exactly how varies by individual, but most have some effect. If you have visual effects, don't try to correct them or allow them to disturb you. Just allow it to occur.

The change comes from expanding your vision to see all it can see, in combination with performing an exercise designed to enhance Presence. The more present a person is, the more energy they bring to the moment, which, at times may produce visual anomalies.

SEVEN PRINCIPLES FOR CONSCIOUS LIVING

Key Words

BE

OBSERVE

LISTEN

DIE

EXPECT

REMEMBER

SURRENDER

B.O.L.D.E.R.S.

Take the 'u' (ego) out of the boulders of life
and you get a bolder way of living.

First Principle
BE
Here/Now
Full Attention into the Present Moment

Second Principle
OBSERVE
Inner Self-Observation, Mind Watching

Third Principle
LISTEN
Deep Inner Listening
To the Voice of: Intuition, Gut instinct,
Conscience or Inner Guidance

Fourth Principle
DIE
To the Past, Every Moment

Fifth Principle
EXPECT
The Unexpected

Sixth Principle
REMEMBER
Your Self, the Awareness Behind The Thinker

Seventh Principle
SURRENDER
To What Is, Complete Acceptance,
Release All Resistance

FIRST PRINCIPLE

BE
Here/Now
Full Attention into the Present Moment

Simple Presence, a state of awareness in which one's entire attention is concentrated into the Now moment, is what we all seek. It is the underlying quality all 'special' occurrences have in common. It separates ordinary forgotten moments from moments whose memory will live in eternity. It is what makes them memorable. Memory is an indicator of Presence. It is created through the intensity of an experience, and intensity is determined by how much of one's attention is focused Here/Now. Whether it is a beautiful sunset, a moment of terrifying danger, giving birth, being in an auto accident, winning a contest, meeting someone special, the significance of such moments are ultimately defined by the Presence they create.

Sue's Story

I once treated Sue, a young woman in her twenties, who told me how she had been abducted as a teen and held for seven months by her captor who raped her daily and threatened her life. Every moment of those seven months she was at risk. The reality of death was constantly present. She never lost her determination to survive and eventually escaped, returning to her high school class where she found the concerns of her classmates superficial. She began using drugs and came to counseling for post-rehab treatment, seeking the cause of her addictive behavior.

She told the tale of her abduction matter-of-factly, without much emotion, like it wasn't relevant to her treatment. To her it was history and had nothing to do with her addiction. We had this conversation after she had received Presence Training but hadn't taken it seriously. As she told her story, her intensity escalated.

I realized she had been totally present the entire time of the abduction. Extreme danger has the potential to bring us to this state of awareness. It shows us a unique state of consciousness in which we are more powerful and have greater resources than in 'ordinary' moments. It became clear that this was a peak experience. She had been profoundly present the entire time. Her attention was entirely focused Here/Now, driven by her determination to survive.

> ...a unique state of consciousness in which we are more powerful and have greater resources.

Returning to ordinary life, with its past/future orientation, was intolerable. She became drug addicted and suicidal. Back in high school, she unconsciously sought ways to recapture the intensity of the abduction experience through association with a rebellious crowd. When she understood how her experience had created Presence, all her motivations to use went out the window. She realized it was present-moment focus she sought. When she was shown this, she began practicing the principles of mind mastery daily and now she works to help others find Presence.

Presence is life changing.

It is a profound shift in awareness that has life changing potential. I once treated a 17-year-old young man who was living in a group home after being taken to court by his father and legally ejected from his family. He had no interest in therapy and refused to respond to my efforts to engage him. He told me his story of rejection, saying he just wanted to die and was waiting for the opportunity to end his life.

I led him into the No-Thought Meditation without explanation. Within a few minutes he was in a state of inner stillness. His suicidal thoughts vanished and he felt at peace. I told him about the value of present-moment focus, a place of aliveness and inspiration where he could create the life he wanted. In subsequent sessions he confirmed the value of the practice and how it changed his life.

Multitasking: The Fragmentation of Consciousness

Multitasking outside the moment is the norm. As I write, fragments of my thought process chip away at my resolve, making the task more difficult. Part of me resents having to rise at four A.M. Another fragment is 'thinking' how tired I will be mid-day. Some other part is wondering if this effort is worth it. My inner work is to continually refocus my full attention on the task at hand, releasing the distractions created by thought.

> Multitasking outside the moment is the norm.

If you have your attention focused anywhere but Here/Now, to the degree it is so, your life is diminished, Consciousness is fragmented. Ask yourself the Presence Meter question.

"What percentage of my attention is Here/Now?"

If it is less than 100% your life is living you, the programming in your mind is dominant. The simple effort to focus all one's attention into the Moment is all that is required. In this shift Consciousness becomes dominant and mind becomes passive, a servant to Consciousness.

> If it is less than 100% your life is living you.

Attaining this state of awareness, however, is not always easy. It is a process fraught with obstacles. The six principles that follow address these obstacles.

> Sustained effort, consistent intention and deep commitment are required.

They are practices that facilitate attainment of Total Presence. Sustained effort, consistent intention and deep commitment are required. These principles form a practice that supports and maintains mental, emotional, physical and spiritual wellbeing.

Most, if not all, of us have had experiences of being fully present, but they were externally imposed. The skydiver mentioned earlier attains full Presence through risking his/her life. The drug addict puts his negative thoughts to sleep with a substance, giving him a moment of freedom from painful thinking. Traumatic experiences, accidents, significant life events, tragedies, giving birth or witnessing it, all galvanize our attention. Once the experience is over, however, the mind returns to its habit of multitasking thought outside the moment.

Death Is Part of Presence

Life is completely and totally uncertain. We never know what will occur next. The biggest uncertainty of all is how much life we will have, a fact the mind diligently works to deny. What would change if we consciously acknowledged it, if we lived each day as if it were our last?

> Life is completely and totally uncertain.

I recently sat in the circle of an over sixty men's group. One man said he had a new electronic watch that could tell him how long the battery would last. He realized the battery would probably outlive him. He went to a pet store to buy his grandchildren turtles and asked how long they would last. They too would outlive him he discovered. This sparked a round of commentary from the group members in which everyone spoke about what they were going to miss.

I read a story recently about a highly successful businessman who went to his doctor for a check up and left the office with a terminal diagnosis. The news sparked a spiritual awakening in him. He realized that everything in his life he considered important wasn't, and everything he had previously considered unimportant was indeed valuable. He began to live what life he had left from this new perspective. Then he received a second medical opinion that reversed the first and began weeping bitter tears. The astonished doctor asked why he grieved. The man replied he feared he would lose what he had gained when he thought he was dying.

What he had gained contemplating his own death was Presence. The shock of being told he was dying disrupted his past/future mind set. He was confronted with the truth of his mortality, a fact the mind-based ego denies or avoids. Notice how, when someone we know dies, our values shift temporarily. We drop our ordinary activities. They momentarily cease having any importance. In the dying of someone else we are forced to confront the temporary nature of our own lives.

Suppose you were able to maintain that awareness of death in your moment-to-moment consciousness? How would that change your life, your values? Would you not become like the businessman with a terminal diagnosis? Awareness of the uncertainty of life itself brings attention to the moment. After all, this moment could be the last moment of your life.

Outside In, verses Inside Out

We cannot rely upon external events to make us present, especially when we do not realize Presence is what we seek. It is like expecting to finance your life by finding money in the street. It is living life from the outside in. Most of the examples of Presence mentioned above were the consequence of some external event or influence. If we value Presence, and the evidence says we do, then we need to find our way to it internally, through our own efforts. Anything else is inconsistent and unreliable.

> ...we need to find our way to it internally.

The mistake we make is identifying our state of consciousness with the external event, influence, or substance that evoked it. Following this logic you will continue to pursue whatever activity it is that produces the experience. We give our power away to external events and circumstances, becoming winners and losers, victims and villains, not realizing what we seek lies in the experience of Presence, not in the circumstance that created it.

The alternative is to live life from the inside out. This is an empowered approach in which you assume total responsibility for the events and circumstances of your life, even when you cannot logically 'figure it out'. Our mind is actually not equipped to 'figure out' anything. Einstein was once asked how he figured out the theory of relativity. He replied it came to him. It was

> ...assume total responsibility for the events and circumstances of your life.

not the consequence of thought. We are all capable of receiving in this way. It is a learnable skill. But we cannot access that skill as long as our Consciousness is fragmented.

When you take responsibility on principle for your life, you recognize it as your creation. Break down the word responsibility and you get the ability to respond. When you are living life from the outside in you are not responsible (response-able). It is someone else's 'fault'. You have no respond-ability. When you own it, it becomes within your power to change it. Is it not true that your life now is the consequence of every decision you ever made? You may say others influenced you, or coerced you, even forced you to make many of these decisions, but you were the one who decided. Even if you were 'victimized' as a child, you decided how to respond to or interact with that experience. Some people, given an abusive, hard upbringing, become drug addicts and prostitutes. Other people, given a similar upbringing, become Oprah (a highly successfully television celebrity).

You are in charge, whether you acknowledge it or not. Who is going to live for you? Who is going to die for you? How often do we allow the influence of others to make decisions for us while we fail to listen to our inner guidance?

> You are
> in charge,
> whether you
> acknowledge
> it or not.

Living from the outside in requires no internal effort. Here mind is dominant. Whatever is programmed rules Consciousness, which is passive, a victim of external influences. Living from the inside out is about internal effort, the effort of disciplining the mind to be in service to the Awareness behind The Thinker. Consciousness becomes the active force, directly experiencing Here/Now reality without mental filters.

What is a Healthy Mind?

> A healthy mind is fully present.

A healthy mind is fully present, is not manifesting thought patterns outside the moment (worry, fear, resentment, wanting the-moment to be different, wanting to be somewhere else). These disconnected thought patterns create mental health issues like depression, anxiety and panic attacks. When you fully realize the preciousness of the moment, when you cease taking it for granted, when you really get what a valuable gift life is no matter what your life situation, you make Presence your first priority. All the other 'concerns' of daily mundane existence are handled. Lao Tzu, who founded Taoism twenty-five hundred years ago, called this a state of non-action, where less and less is done, yet nothing is left undone.

> ...make Presence your first priority.

We live in a society that focuses on worry, fear, and non-acceptance of the contents of Now. The global political situation reflects this state of group mind. Humanity is in spiritual crisis. Everywhere we turn television, newspapers, political issues, all are infected with the mental disease of fear, worry, concern, analysis of what may happen, predictions of future calamities, and victim thinking. The instant one focuses attention in this direction the precious present is lost, solidifying the ego's illusion of separation from all that is. Our brother becomes the enemy against which we must defend our-selves (ego).

Being consistently and completely Here/Now experientially opens you to your connectedness to everything and everyone. Wholeness, oneness (at-one-ment) ceases being a philosophical theory and becomes a practical personal reality. Make Presence your first value and all life concerns fall into place behind it. The drama of life is then perceived as material for spiritual development, and you find gratitude for the opportunity it provides.

What we do with the material is the question. Material can include abuse (mental, emotional, physical, and sexual), traumatic life events, intimate or familial relationship with someone drug addicted, alcoholic or psychotic. Life provides an abundance of material. That is its job. Initially the material may use us, spinning us into psychological/ emotional challenges like depression, anxiety, panic attacks, suicidal thinking and substance abuse. Adjusting perception through developing greater degrees of awareness facilitates the discovery of opportunities hidden in our suffering.

> ...the discovery of opportunities hidden in our suffering.

Spiritual teachers, artists, poets, philosophers, composers, writers and playwrights from all eras have left traces of this singular intention, Presence. Jesus coached his disciples to be attentive. Be like the servant waiting the master to come. "Be ready!!" he advised. I can only be ready now, or be attentive to the moment.

Shakespeare wrote: "To be or not to be, that is the question." It truly is the question for each one of us in every moment, to be here/now, or not? How often do we choose not to be? Other teachers and philosophers have left pointers toward the Now:

- "Make the divine present your destination." Al Ghazali, 12th Century Islamic jurist, theologian and mystic.
- "Give value to your time, live in the present moment. Do not live in imagination and throw your time away." Ibn Arabi, one of the world's great spiritual teachers, born into the Moorish culture of Andalusian Spain, 1165 AD.
- "The most subtle awakening comes through moment-to-moment attentiveness." Buddha
- "The personality comes into being by memory, by identifying the present with the past and projecting it into the future. Think of yourself as momentary, without past or future and your personality dissolves." Nisargadata Maharaj, I Am That, 1973, Hindu spiritual teacher.
- "Price of admission, your mind!" Herman Hesse, Steppenwolf
- "One moment in annihilation's waste, One moment of the well of Life to taste." The Rubaiyat, Omar Khayyam, born 1048CE, Persian mathematician, scientist, astronomer, philosopher and poet.

The present moment is a portal.	The present moment is a portal, a gateway to a deeper reality, another level of consciousness available to all,

but accessed by few. It is through this portal that a person discovers what is true, what is real, and what is illusion.

We hear about illusion from all the wisdom traditions. They say all is illusion, a dream we are dreaming, yet the mind is incapable of grasping the significance of this statement or directly experiencing it. In fact, it is cognitive process (thinking) that contributes to or directly creates illusion. Thought filters and interprets incoming data, shaping it to our mind's model of reality, creating a false, mind-based illusion devoid of awareness.

Direct experience is only available through stepping outside the mind. This cannot be described with words. Words point to a reality the mind cannot experience, a reality unknowable, unspeakable, unthinkable, beyond mind, accessible only from a no-thought perspective.

If you get this, not because it is written in a book or someone said you 'should', if you get this because it resonates with something deep in you that you cannot deny, it becomes your obligation to live passionately now. You can no longer sleep comfortably. If you get this, you will dedicate your existence to Presence. If you get this!

SECOND PRINCIPLE

OBSERVE
Inner Self-Observation, Mind Watching

"The unobserved life is not worth living." Socrates

"Awake! Be the witness of your life! You are what observes,

not what you observe." Buddha

The fundamental intention of these principles and practices is to establish an experiential separation between Consciousness and mind, realizing, at the feeling level, that mind is not Self. For this to happen, a new internal entity must be created, a Witness Self, an observer. The mind is described here as a powerful, hence dangerous, tool, yet we have never been told what is generally said in the face of dangerous power tools:

"Watch what you are doing! Be careful, you may hurt yourself."

The process of thinking is infinitely more powerful and dangerous than a shop saw. Yet no one says:

"Are you thinking? Be careful! Thinking is dangerous! Watch your thoughts or you will manifest your life in chaos and disorder. You may even hurt or kill yourself!"

> Thinking is dangerous!

I have never encountered a suicidal person who is present-moment-focused. Suicidal ideation arises from defective thinking, thinking depressive thoughts; thoughts that regret some past decision or action, find some current situation unacceptable, or fear some negative outcome. Opportunities for healing any situation are available Here/Now. The healing process begins when attention is removed from the 'problem'. This requires an attentive awareness of mental process. The mind must be disciplined to be responsive to the intentions of Consciousness, to be in its service, and know it is **not** in charge.

For this to occur, Consciousness must become the dominant factor, not mind. This means full attention into the present, First Principle. The current situation for most of us, most of the time, is one in which the mind is dominant and Consciousness is passive. Reversing this relationship entails a struggle. After all, Consciousness has given its power over to mind for thousands of years. Most minds have the discipline of a three year old. The moment attention drifts, the mind leaves the moment, causing suffering. It wanders into the past, the future, or day-dreams.

Most people's answer to the Presence Meter question is 40% to 50%. This means 50% to 60% of their inner resources are not available to address the challenges of present-moment reality. In addition to depleting resources, the absent portion of our Consciousness is thinking thoughts that are emotionally disruptive (remember, thought stimulates emotion), making our present-moment experience miserable. So, not only are we not working at full capacity most of the time, we are also allowing our mind to disrupt our joy of living.

Whatever your life situation, whatever challenges are in your past/future illusion, you are reading these words currently, do they have your full attention? If they do not, what is the point of reading? Are you performing any other task right now, mentally?

Multi-tasking

The mind is always multi-tasking. A human being in the wilderness uses this ability to survive. Being aware of where you are stepping, while maintaining auditory and visual omni-directional awareness for signs of danger, are all parts of surviving in the wilderness. Peripheral vision is used to maintain vigilance, while hearing is attuned for sounds of potential predators or other dangers. All the senses are engaged in present moment awareness in order to survive. All of this is multitasking in the moment.

'Civilized' people multitask outside the moment, causing themselves no

> 'Civilized' people multitask outside the moment.

end of grief as their mind torments them. This is why Australian Aborigines call them mutants. When we are in the wilderness, survival demands full attention, probably the reason many of us are fond of camping and hiking. These activities evoke Presence because we have placed ourselves in a dangerous situation.

Self-Observation

Another way to teach the mind the value of Presence is to assign a portion of Consciousness to constantly watch the mind. Call this the Observer, or Witness Self. Its task is to monitor thought patterns and keep the mind's activity focused on the present moment. To succeed at this exercise is to tolerate a high rate of failure. One has the intention to watch astutely, then becomes identified with a thought and forgets the aim of observation, only to awaken some time later to the memory of the intention and have to start over, without recrimination.

Buddhists call this process "beginner's mind", they are constantly beginning anew their efforts to attain and maintain Presence. It is a struggle in which the mind will constantly attempt to regain

> ...constantly beginning anew.

its dominance. This mechanism is a fail-safe device. When Consciousness is absent, the mind is left to take care of the details of living. This is running on autopilot. However, the more an individual develops valuation for Presence, the more the mind will come to understand its true role, that of service to Consciousness.

Mouse Hole Visualization

Here is an exercise. Imagine your Consciousness is like a cat stalking a mouse hole. It sits intent, single minded, staring at the mouse hole, waiting for the mouse to emerge. Visualize your Consciousness being the cat watching the mouse hole, your mind, waiting for the next thought to appear. Watch intently! Watch now! Don't attempt to generate a thought, just watch attentively, waiting for a thought to emerge.

Executed with sufficient intensity this exercise can have the effect of freeze framing the mind, like a fly pinned to the counter by the intensity of your attention. Watching your mind intently has the effect of slowing its process, or stopping it entirely. This is another way to enter the No-Thought Zone.

Studying your own mental process in this way enables you to see it in action, to see how your mind distracts you from what is important, your focus on the moment. You become familiar with your thought patterns as an objective phenomenon rather than identifying them as 'self'. Study how your mind connects you to negative feelings. Observe what your ego deems important.

Socrates, ancient Greek philosopher, declared: "The unobserved life is not worth living", making clear the essential need to maintain vigilance, watchfulness. Jesus often, throughout the Gospels, counsels his disciples to watch as a spiritual practice. It is likely he is referring

> ...essential need to maintain vigilance, watchfulness.

to a similar exercise. The moment one relaxes vigilance over the mind, it resumes its dominance and we are again overtaken by illusion.

When you BE, Here/Now, and OBSERVE your mind intently to maintain focus, you open to direct contact with your inner-guidance.

THIRD PRINCIPLE

LISTEN
Deep Inner Listening
To the Voice of Intuition, Gut Instinct, Inner Guidance
Listen and Respond
The Choice-less Choice

"The Kingdom of Heaven is within." Jesus

"If you don't go within, you go without." Neal Donald Walsh

Efforts to focus full attention into the moment, in combination with mind watching, have the potential to produce Inner Stillness, a state of alert Presence with an absence of mental activity. An active effort to listen internally deepens this state, facilitating connection with either personal divinity or inner guidance; also known as intuition, conscience, gut instinct, Higher Self or the Holy Spirit.

Jesus said: "The kingdom of heaven is within." The kingdom of heaven is a metaphor for an elevated state of awareness. It is not a geographical location in time and space, but rather, an intensified state of Consciousness outside of time and space.

Have you ever experienced intuition, or gut instinct? You just instinctively know something without knowing how you know it. Most have. Ever ignore it? What was the consequence? Every person I have asked these questions agrees, ignoring intuition is a choice that often leads to undesirable consequences.

The voice of intuition is the expression of our spirit's intention. Not paying attention to this inner voice results in non-alignment with that intention. Living life non-aligned

> ...intuition is the expression of our spirit's intention.

with spirit is doing things the hard way. It is not being true to Self, which makes everything that follows difficult and fraught with unintended consequences.

Becoming more aware, or enlightened, does not make one complacent or passive. It rather engenders a state of enlightened self-interest, where everything you do is connected with your intention to BE, Here/Now. Setting boundaries, learning to say no, when that is the direction from inner guidance, is a part of empowering one's behavior through aligning it with spiritual intent.

Payment for this is giving up the need to please others. Taking the actions suggested by inner guidance may require one to behave in ways not understandable to significant others. Jesus did not teach family values, he taught spiritual empowerment, being true to oneself. He said he came to separate child from parent, brother from brother, friend from friend. He encouraged all to drop what they were doing and follow the promptings of the Holy Spirit.

> ...produces immediate connection.

Listening deeply, with full attention focused in the present, produces immediate connection. How that connection manifests specifically is unique to the individual. For some it may be an inner voice, for others an image, or a sense, or an instinctive knowing. It can even be something overheard in the supermarket. You will recognize it by the feeling it evokes. Quieting the mind through meditation, listening to the resulting inner stillness, while making efforts to focus full attention into the present, cannot fail to align you with deep inner wisdom, your spiritual intention, your life's in-the-moment purpose.

I came to write this book through this process. While attending a continuing education seminar (a professional requirement) on Spirituality in Psychotherapy, my inner voice prompted me to talk to the presenter at the break, and get his opinion on my approach to therapy. He advised me to write this book and offered help in making it happen. It was out of the writing process that B.O.L.D.E.R.S. emerged.

It is through the use of this principle (Inner Listening) that I conduct therapy. My intention is to be fully present to my client, watch my mind to keep it still, and listen internally for direction. This is my preparation for therapy. I listen internally for how to proceed. For me it has become a clear inner voice that is concise and confidant. It directs the session through questions and uses my mind as a resource (advises what stories to tell or examples to use). I become a conscious conduit for something beyond mind.

> ...the mind's job is to simply listen.

Making this connection consistently has profound practical implications. First, the mind is freed from the burden of 'figuring out' life. Much of what we define as stress involves the mind attempting to: calculate right action; analyze situations; think things through; all descriptions of ineffective mind activity. Now the mind's job is to simply listen and comply with Spirit's intention. When this is accomplished, the 'doing' of life becomes obvious and effortless.

Most 'heroes', when asked how they found the courage to perform their heroic acts, say it had nothing to do with courage but was simply a response to what obviously had to be done in the moment. You don't have to 'think it through' when confronted by a life-threatening situation. What needs to be done is apparent. This is true generally anytime our attention is focused entirely in the Now. The next step is obvious.

There is an old formula for conscious manifestation: BE, DO, HAVE. Being is the first step, the very same Being discussed here, complete attention on the Now. When this is accomplished, there is immediate connection to inner guidance that dictates the doing and the having. It is a joyful alignment with our higher power. We are aligned with the script of the Holy Spirit, not the script of the ego (mind). Then the having is in full alignment with spirit and is not dysfunctional or conflicted.

Beware, though, how mind will attempt to cast aspersions, raise doubts, or argue with inner guidance, weakening resolve, defeating purpose. Poet William Blake wrote:

"He who replies to words of doubt
doth put the light of knowledge, out."

Shakespeare wrote in Hamlet's soliloquy:

"... thus the native hue of resolution is sickly o'er
with the pale cast of thought, and enterprises
of great pitch and moment, in this regard, their
currents turn awry and lose the name of action."

Reasonableness will try to displace, question or argue with intuitive knowing, be it a large issue, like who you marry, or something mundane, like locating something you cannot find.

At a conference recently, I was comparing notes on the use of intuition with a therapist. She told me how she had been traveling in a strange city using a rental car and needing to get it washed. Her intuitive voice chimed in with "go down there, and turn left." Her mind argued that she was in a residential neighborhood. "We'll just have to fumble around and find something." After twenty minutes of no success with that strategy, starting over, she went down and turned left, and, of course, there it was. The message is clear, use intuition all the time.

Intuition is our direct, in-the-moment connection to our deepest intention. It knows next steps, but it neither gives reasons nor persuades. You may choose to disregard it and it will be there the next time you choose to listen. The more you listen, the stronger your connection to deep wisdom. When we ignore inner direction, we are choosing not to be. We have chosen the ego's script over spirit's direction. This produces inner conflict. Listening to and aligning with intuition, inner guidance, invokes inner harmony, then life cannot help but become better. The ego's script is based on the fundamental emotion of Fear; Spirit's script is based on the other fundamental human emotion, Love.

> ...intuition, inner guidance, invokes inner harmony.

Ask yourself how many fear motivated decisions you have made and what they brought you. We spend money on products designed to alleviate our fears; insurances, alarm systems, financial investments to provide for our 'future', a future that does not exist, a mind-based, fear motivated projection of some imagined something that may never appear in our Now. Living in Love, Trust and Acceptance opens an internal space for the miraculous to manifest. Aligning one's actions with spiritual intention is true security. We are open to and in agreement with the Will of the Universe. We become its instrument.

FOURTH PRINCIPLE

DIE
To the Past, Every Moment

Yesterday is a concept of the mind, a linguistic tool enabling us to discuss something that happened in some previous Now. It is notable that many indigenous languages lack past and future tenses. 'Primitive' people live entirely in the present. This makes them naturally intuitive. The ability to be connected to the world of Spirit is a given, is not considered to be 'extrasensory' or mysterious, and is certainly not questioned, or doubted as it is in 'civilized' societies. The fact of constant change is a given. There is no delusion that remembrance of past events will be a predictor of future realities.

It is important to not confuse memory with learning. You may 'think' you need to remember how you learned something, but truly, once something is learned, it becomes integrated into who you are Now. You are permanently changed at the DNA level. Do you remember how you learned to walk, or learned how to drive, and do you need to remember how you learned them in order to do them? The obvious answer is no.

Our tendency to dwell on past events is what ages us. The older we get, the more baggage we carry from the past, sapping our ability to keep our attention Here/Now. Plus, remember, the body reacts to every thought we think with an emotion. Replaying the past is reliving it again, Now. Shakespeare reminds us of this in his thirtieth sonnet:

> Replaying the past is reliving it again, Now.

When to the sessions of sweet silent thought
I summon up remembrance of things past,
I sigh the lack of many a thing I sought,
And with old woes new wail my dear time's waste:
Then can I drown an eye unused to flow,
For precious friends hid in death's dateless night,
And weep afresh love's long-since cancell'd woe,
And moan the expense of many a vanish'd sight:
Then can I grieve at grievances foregone,
And heavily from woe to woe tell o'er
The sad account of fore-bemoaned moan,
Which I new pay, as if not paid before.
But if the while I think on thee, dear friend,
All loses are restor'd, and sorrows end.

The thee that is 'thought on' here is our connection to a higher power, the Higher Self found in the present-moment. Shakespeare eloquently describes the torment the mind can subject us to when we allow it to take us out of Now and replay a memory. Not only is the moment lost in this excursion into the past, but so too is our sense of wellbeing. It is said the coward dies a thousand deaths, the hero dies once. We are the coward when we allow fear to dominate our thoughts. We become the hero when we access the moment.

Our ability to record events in our memory is useful, but also, like other tools of the mind, dangerous. The mind tends to ignore the reality of constant change and believes it can predict what is to happen tomorrow by knowing what happened yesterday. Being unaware of its creative powers, the mind forms thought patterns not knowing those patterns create realty. This is true at both the psychological and the quantum level.

Consider the last time you had to tell someone close to you negative news, like not getting a raise. Since you "know" that person, your mind predicts their reaction, and then reacts to that reaction. You are already angry with them as you confront them, stimulating the very behavior you predicted. This used to be called self-fulfilling prophesy. The mind feels justified in having accurately predicted the future, unaware it created that future.

At the quantum level we create through focusing thought on a particular potential in the quantum field. Physicist Werner Heisenberg first discovered this in the 1930s when he attempted to determine whether light was a particle or a wave. When he experimentally tested to confirm the particle theory, the result was positive, but the same was so also when he tested to confirm the wave theory. Both phenomena existed in potential and were drawn forth by the intentions of the experimenter, producing what

> The act of observation changes what is observed.

we now call the participant/observer phenomenon. The act of observation changes what is observed.

This is why practicing Principle Two, mind watching, is so important. Our moment-to-moment experience is continuously created by our focus of thought. This is called The Law of Attraction. We are literally making it up as we go along. When we allow our mind to run its fear-based agenda, an agenda supported by our global media culture, we are summoning the experiences we fear. A headline in my local paper once read: "Man Struck By Lightening, Thing He Feared Most". This man's mind obsessed intensely each time a thunderstorm occurred. Eventually he experienced what he feared.

The good news is our mind is a creative instrument. This is a key to conscious manifestation. We live in a quantum universe. This translates into what you put your attention on manifests. Ever notice how the 'unlucky' person habitually has negative, cynical, critical thoughts about their world. They say "_____ happens, and if it is going to happen, it will happen to me." For such a person everything goes wrong, they have misfortune after misfortune. Their mind builds an ego around it, an identity. It is a habitual thought pattern. The ego forms a victim persona. This person is unaware they are creating their misery, and if confronted with it, will go to great lengths to defend that position. I once had a client say to me:

"You mean you want me to give up my pain? I wouldn't know who I was!!"

This was someone I failed to reach. Her ego was so entrenched, she so deeply believed she was her mind, that it successfully resisted every attempt to redirect her attention. If we want history to stop repeating itself, we must let go of our memory of what was and create a new future through doing it differently Now.

Otherwise the past is a sack of rocks we carry that grows as we age. We accumulate memories. More and more of our attention goes to maintaining those memories through inner replay and unnecessary talking, telling our stories to ourselves and others, leaving less and less attention available to attend to life in the Now. Many of these memories are negative or painful in character, material the ego uses to form identities.

> ...the past is a sack of rocks.

We also collect negative accounts (memories) against the people in our lives. The closer we are to them, the more accounts we have. We also have accounts against ourselves, our perceived failures, and mistakes. When assessing our percentage of attention in the moment, that fraction that is outside the moment is maintaining the accounts in our rock sack, which gets larger and heavier with each passing day.

To be free from this misery, we must constantly let go of the past each moment. Otherwise we are, to a greater or lesser degree, defined by its contents. Many people I see in my practice have sacks filled with horrific contents. Their minds have made identities from this material. Such a person has a low percentage of attention Here/Now. They are living in their past of painful traumatic experiences. First efforts have to be directed toward getting their attention out of yesterday. Later, when they are able to establish a presence in the Now, work can proceed on reframing (redefining) the contents of the sack.

Dying to the past is a daily, moment-to-moment, effort. It entails letting go of identities connected to past events. Many people I encounter in mental health have firm attachments to the painful events of their past, like the lady who refused to give up her pain. Much of what therapists define as secondary gain arises out of identities created out of past experiences. Secondary gain is the benefit we receive from being dysfunctional, from hanging onto our victim identity. Eckhart Tolle, in his book The Power of Now, calls it the pain body. It is the personal and collective thought patterns mind develops around our painful life experiences. We all have an identity built around our pain, both our individual experiences, and our group experience.

> We all have an identity built around our pain.

Some examples of collective pain bodies are the African-American experience, the Jewish experience, or the female experience. Many individuals in these groups have an identity, a series of thought patterns, linked to their group. The mind forms identities out of these thought patterns which effect everyday behavior and influence decisions.

Identifying and releasing attachment to the past must be an ongoing practice. It is part of the benefit of the information collected by practicing Second Principle, inner self-observation. As you watch your mind, you will detect attention going to past

> The idea that time heals is a myth.

experiences, be they ones that occurred yesterday, or fifty years ago. I have a relative who was badly treated by her mother-in-law sixty years ago, yet when she speaks about it, she goes into white-hot rage as if it happened yesterday. The idea that time heals is a myth. When a well-maintained memory is evoked, it is as fresh as the day it happened and the body reacts accordingly. You can be certain that anger is having an effect on her present-moment reality, on her physical, mental and emotional wellbeing.

Releasing, forgiving, the events of the past is essential to maintain mental health. Forgiveness is one of the most powerful practices Jesus Christ demonstrated. He forgave his tormentors as they were putting him to death. Failure to release the past results in more and more vital attention being lost to the moment, not available to meet the challenges of life in the one place and time it is actually occurring, Here/Now.

FIFTH PRINCIPLE

EXPECT
Expect the Unexpected

One legitimate use of the mind is the making of plans. A plan is a command the mind sends to the body to take action. It can be as simple as saying stand-up to yourself if you are seated. We cannot move without a plan. The mind, however, believes a plan to be a prediction of the future. In the process of formulating a plan the mind visualizes the plan unfolding. It then identifies with the visualization, expecting the plan will unfold according to its fantasy. In my therapy practice I often encounter people who are depressed because their life did not go as they expected.

"I'm so depressed. I never expected to be in this situation at my age."

This is the consequence of allowing the mind to form expectations. They arise when the mind identifies with visualization, wanting an event or outcome to occur the way the mind conceives it. Formulate a plan. Once the actual work of planning is done the mind automatically creates, and identifies with, a fantasy about how the plan will go.

Identifying is merging one's sense of self (ego) with some external object or event. When identification with a fantasy occurs, the mind creates an identity around an outcome, making it personal. Then when reality fails to match the fantasy, one's sense of self is damaged or offended, evoking resistance to what is with its consequent negative feelings.

Now, what happens to plans? This question usually evokes laughter. Most of us know events and processes rarely go as they were initially conceived. Our projection of thought into the quantum matrix interacts with all the other projections of thought, at all levels (i.e. conscious, subconscious, super conscious), to give back to us a manifestation that frequently is not an exact match with our visualization. The differences can be positive, negative, or just different than "expected".

Most experiences we pursue have extra-added bonuses we had not anticipated in our thought process when formulating our plans. It's like meeting and marrying the love of your life to find out later he/she has pathological mood swings and you met them on an up swing. The 'extras' have the potential to become the material that fuels spiritual growth when we

> ...nothing is what it appears to be.

remember that nothing is what it appears to be and there is always a balance.

We are planning constantly. We cannot move without a plan. Lying in bed at dawn, I need a plan to start my day. The next step, getting out of bed, is the plan, the thought that says 'get up!' As I set my foot down on the floor, I step on the hairball my cat deposited there sometime during the night. Unexpected!! This was not part of the plan. I now have to stop and make a new plan. Clean up the hairball.

When expectations are not met by present-moment reality, we go into resistance mode, addressed in Principle Seven. Resistance is a thought process ('Oh no!!' was my first thought upon

> ...we go into resistance mode.

encountering the hairball). Remember, thoughts evoke emotions. Frustrated expectations produce a wide variety of negative feelings: anger, rage, sadness, depression, and anxiety are a few examples. When we resist the contents of Now we have exited the moment. We fail to see the gift that is there. It becomes a missed opportunity.

> No mind is capable of predicting the future.

No mind is capable of predicting the future. It does not matter how smart you are, you only know what you know Now. Life is constantly changing and completely uncertain, the ultimate uncertainty being the length of life itself. The when, where and how of the death of the body we are traveling in is an unknown factor. The mind dislikes this. It wants certainty, so it fools itself with expectation. I have people in my treatment room frequently complaining how they are depressed over how they did not expect to be in their current life situation at their age, or at all.

The solution is to train the mind to expect the unexpected. It shows up everyday. Teach yourself to find delight in surprise and challenge, giving up the mind's pleasure seeking pain avoiding roller coaster. The best way to encounter life is to meet its challenges head on, eye to eye, in full Presence. To do this, we cannot arrogantly assume we know what is going to happen next. Recent history has some fine examples of this. September 11, 2001, a person working at the World Trade Center Building in New York City having their morning coffee, did not expect that moment to be their last. The same was true for individuals vacationing on the beach in Thailand on December 26, 2004 when the tsunami hit.

The unknown, the unexpected, is showing up moment by moment, though it is not always as dramatic as these examples. The best way to deal with surprise is to show up too, manifest Presence. Anything else is denial and avoidance.

SIXTH PRINCIPLE

REMEMBER
Your-Self
A Spiritual Being Having a Human Experience

The implications of this statement are huge. It assumes, as a premise, that Consciousness precedes matter rather than arising from matter. The Institute of Noetic Sciences, an institution devoted to integrating Consciousness and science, says it this way:

> Consciousness precedes matter rather than arising from matter.

"Instead of assuming matter to be the primary reality, we need to turn our model of reality inside-out and put Consciousness firmly at the center of things."

In this model Consciousness exists prior to occupying a body, and will continue to exist when that body wears out.

This may seem theoretical, or philosophical, but it has important practical implications.

For starters, it implies purpose. On the surface, life can seem meaningless, random, disconnected, and chaotic. Yet, when we make efforts to raise our level of awareness, to bring more of our attention into the Now, we directly discover meaning, purpose and order. Nothing is what it appears to be. There are no accidents. What appears to be chance or coincidence exhibits purpose and connection when awareness in the moment is deepened.

The more an individual practices focusing full attention into the Now, watches their mind to keep it passive and focused, listens for and follows inner guidance, lets go of the past and expects the unexpected, the more they directly perceive the interconnectedness of all there is and realize their conscious role in the unfolding drama. It is a shift in perspective from focus on apparent chaos to an experiential awareness of a larger reality.

Mental Models

What is being expressed here is a mental model, a theoretical representation of reality. Every mind I have encountered in my life and work has one, a belief system that structures their perception, deciding which elements of the incoming data stream have importance. Place an American Army general in the same room with an Aboriginal shaman and enact some event. What the minds of these two individuals consider relevant, what they perceive, what conclusions they draw from the event and what behaviors they enact will differ dramatically based upon their cultural conditioning, their mental model.

Mental models enable us to organize and prioritize the incoming flow of data from the senses. They are the operating software of the mind. They are **not**, however, The Truth. It's when an individual, or a group of individuals, decide to make their mental model right and everybody else's wrong, that mental models become dangerous and dysfunctional.

I make no claims on The Truth, capital 'T'. If I believe anything, it is that either there is no capital 'T' truth, or if there is, it is inexpressible in language and incomprehensible to the mind.

At best, mental models are conceptual filters designed to focus attention, or Consciousness, on the elements of incoming data deemed important. Our personal and cultural conditioning determines importance. Reading this

> ...mental models are conceptual filters.

book may change what you consider important, in fact that is my intention in writing it. When we recognize our mental models for what they are, subjective approximations of a greater, unknowable truth, they become flexible and changeable, a work in progress.

I Am a Spiritual Being Having a Human Experience

"I AM a unique, individualized unit of Consciousness seeking to know its own Light through a journey into darkness. I intentionally agreed to fall asleep in the flesh in order to Awaken to a greater Realization of my Self".

This is the current statement of my personal relationship to the Unknowable. The global aspect of this belief is that every individuated Consciousness, whether it knows it or not, is that, a Spiritual Being having a Human Experience. This is the opening premise; the core belief upon which all that is to follow is founded.

While it is recognized that this premise is a theory, a belief, or an assumption, for the purposes of this discussion, it is considered to be a truth. Notice the lower case "t". Everything that follows is deduced from this premise.

Non-Materiality

> Spiritual is non-material, immortal, beyond space and time.

Spiritual, or metaphysical, implies non-material, or beyond physical. Material is mortal, bound by space and time. Spiritual is non-material, immortal, beyond space and time. Spirit is the non-physical, the un-manifest, the context within which the manifest exists, the motion picture screen upon which the drama of life is projected. It is the universal Life force itself, the unifying single Consciousness that contains all Consciousnesses, infinite worlds within worlds. This implies that the I AM that I am, my Consciousness, exists outside of time and space, and is immortal.

On the level of linear time this would indicate a continuity of

Consciousness from pre-incarnation, through incarnation, to post-incarnation, a continuity of Awareness that includes one of the most basic characteristics of Being-ness, the ability to choose and decide.

Life is movement. Movement involves decision or choice. Choice requires intention. I made a dozen choices in writing these sentences, including the decision to perceive life as movement. We make thousands of choices daily, from what clothing to wear, or what food to eat, to what career to pursue, or who to marry, major and minor choices. The ability to choose, then, is an aspect of the continuity of Consciousness.

Choice involves purpose. We cannot make a single move without purpose, intention. We choose clothing with the intention of protecting our body from the elements and to socially accommodate. We choose food to sustain our physical structure and/or please the senses. It follows then, that prior to incarnating, or taking a body, a complex series of decisions was made motivated by an overall intention. These decisions included space-time variables such as what historical era and culture to show up in, and were not made in social isolation.

> ...a complex series of decisions was made motivated by an overall intention.

If I am a Spiritual being having a human experience, then everyone, without exception (including history's 'bad' people), is the same. Planning an incarnation then would occur in a social context in which agreements are negotiated with other units of Consciousness intending to have a human experience. It might go something like this.

An individual intends to manifest a human life for the purpose of developing forgiveness. They make a deal with another being to be an abusive parent, giving them material to work with. That agreement, of course, cuts both ways. It matches some corresponding intention of the other individual. Maybe they need to work on taking responsibility for their actions. Carolyn Myss, PhD, a medical intuitive, celebrated author and presenter, wrote a book entitled Sacred Contracts on this topic, detailing how such agreements operate. Johann Goethe, Eighteenth Century poet, novelist and philosopher, wrote a novel entitled Wilhelm Meister's Apprenticeship about a young man's search for life's meaning. It leads to a script and a secret society that has access to the deeper meanings of Life.

> ...everyone in my life serves a purpose.

From this perspective everyone in my life serves a purpose connected to my intentions for this lifetime. Every drama is a contract, the outcome of choices and agreements made at the Spiritual level. Have you ever met someone who seemed familiar, like you already know them, especially someone who provides a major drama? Maybe that feeling is correct. You do already know them. You have an agreement with them to enact some play for mutually beneficial purposes (spiritual growth is always the benefit); purposes you agreed to when planning the incarnation.

The choices made at the level of Spirit are then intentionally forgotten and we play out the drama without conscious awareness of its true significance. This supports the idea that there are no accidents. What appear to be accidents are actually the outcomes of decisions made outside the incarnation.

Forgetting is part of the plan. It maximizes the growth potential of the experience. We would not take our incarnations seriously if we were aware of their true nature. The enculturation process facilitates forgetting. We slowly become lost in thought and identify with our mind based false identity, ego. The human body is a highly complex mechanism, a machine, containing an on-board computer, the mind, used to manage and coordinate the complex array of systems that come together to make a human being. It is the programming of this computer that I call the enculturation process. Learning language and appropriate behavior, developing relationships, learning society's rules, acquiring belief structures, learning how to operate the body, drive a car, use a computer, are all layers of programming that cover over our true Spiritual nature, creating distractions and false identities.

We lose direct contact with our true Self, and our identity becomes our mind's idea (ego) of self that is the product of the enculturation process. We lose conscious touch with who we truly are and exist on the basis of who

> We lose direct contact with our true Self.

we think we are. The mind and its contents, its programming, then, becomes the source of our identity. The game, recognized as such by 60's writer Robert De Ropp in his book The Master Game, is to regain that lost contact with our true identity, to search for and find what we don't know we have lost or what it is we seek.

The programming is powerful, not to be taken lightly. It is the mind's job to enable the Being to negotiate the complex, mystical experience we call Life. Losing our Selves in the process is part of the game we came here to play. We engage in the drama through identifying with the roles we enact. Forgetting allows us to do this. If we were in memory of our true nature, we would be less able to commit to participating in the drama. We wouldn't take it seriously. And, you know, seriousness is required!!

> We enact a script we wrote.

We enact a script we wrote, in conjunction with others. It is a plan for a drama rich in disguised intention, personal meaning and purpose. Nothing is what it appears to be. Everything has a hidden meaning and purpose that is not fathomable to the thinking mind.

> The plan is not predestination.

The plan is not predestination. It's just a plan. We all have experienced how plans are simply devices to signify an intention, a direction. We know that once we enact "the plan" it changes moment-to-moment as it interfaces with the reality of Now.

A simple plan like "today I go north" encounters unexpected situations along the way, requiring new decisions. As I head north I encounter an unanticipated mountain, decisions are remade based on this new information. As I head around the mountain, I encounter a canyon. Again decisions are remade. Direction changes arise out of these decisions and now I'm heading south and it all makes sense. How could plans made anywhere be otherwise? The script written at Spirit level is probably as vulnerable as plans made anywhere else.

This is where free will and choice comes in. When we exercise our free will in a state of forgetting, we choose the illusions, the surface appearances, the ego's script. If these choices are not in alignment with Spirit's script, and they

> ...in a state of forgetting, we choose the illusions.

frequently are not, we experience the inner conflict that arises when mind is in disharmony with a larger intention. One of the barometers for measuring that disharmony is emotion.

Emotions are reflections of thought patterns. They are a litmus test for how in or out of alignment a particular thought is with an individual's deepest intentions. This is the secret of our capacity to emote, it tells us how aligned we are with Spirit. The more there is alignment, the more positive the emotion. The converse, of course, is also true. The more out of alignment, the darker the emotion.

> ...it tells us how aligned we are with Spirit.

The resolution of this inner conflict can become a strong motivating force to identify and make new choices that are more in alignment with deeper intentions. We call this Spiritual awakening.

Frequently the inner conflict is not resolved, or is temporarily resolved by a closer approximation, though still missing the mark. This will produce another existential crisis further on down the line of time. I used to place my identity in career, a common Western man's mistake. I didn't feel good about the one I had. I thought my angst would resolve itself if I had a career I thought was cool. After having the new career for a while, the angst returned. We may go through many iterations of this process, each bringing us closer to our true intentions, each redefining what we believe to be important.

Spiritual Reframing

In psychotherapy, reframing is developing a new, healthier perspective on the facts and events of our lives. The assertion I am making here is that all life experience has meaning and purpose on the level of Spirit. Beginning to see one's life as a journey of spiritual development, in which all the events and circumstances are precisely designed to facilitate the emergence of new strengths, is a shift in awareness that finds importance and significance in what was formerly considered shameful and painful.

> ...to see one's life as a journey of spiritual development.

Many people find themselves involved in mental health treatment as a consequence of abuse, trauma, or just poor programming from their family of origin. Their thought patterns are fixated on the consequences of their negative or painful experience, and their minds have formed identities around these painful experiences.

Begin asking yourself questions like:

How did I survive these experiences?

What new strengths did I develop to help me cope with my pain? I am not dead or institutionalized, what kept me going?

> What new strengths did I develop?

Developing answers to these questions usually reveal character strengths, qualities of being that were developed in the fire of difficult or adverse experience. With the recognition of these strengths comes a sense of appreciation for the events and experiences that enabled these qualities of being to emerge.

Could you have developed these qualities any other way? No? Then, and this may be a stretch, you can begin to find gratitude in your heart for the person or persons who made the development of these qualities possible. Here forgiveness can arise out of a shift in perception that actually appreciates the painful events or circumstances, and clearly sees the gifts that arose out of the experience. I've heard people say:

"Cancer was the best thing that ever happened to me."

The implication is that everything that happens to us in life serves a deeper purpose, no matter how horrific the experience. I recently read a quote from the Dali Lama saying how the loss of Tibet to China was the best thing that ever happened for Buddhism, placing it and him on the world stage.

This is an alternative approach to the mind's pleasure seeking pain-avoiding strategy. Rather than avoiding the challenge and difficulties that come with life, embrace them and be transformed by them. Through this process we begin to appreciate the friction we encounter in life. Adversity becomes a friend whose challenges we welcome.

It is essential to attain and maintain this perceptual framework. It is important for you to see the growth opportunity in your suffering to free yourself from the victim role. When the trials and tribulations of human existence are viewed through the lens of this perspective, we begin to find value in all life experience, no matter how traumatic or painful. Gurdjieff was fond of saying: "We always make a profit" meaning there is a hidden benefit to every experience. Develop the ability to see the benefit in all your life experiences, without exception. This attitude gives order and meaning to the, at times, apparent chaos of life challenges.

> ...begin to find value in all life experience.

Remembering your Self as a spiritual being raises you above the fray of life, altering perspective. Remembering those around you as spiritual beings helps you to not identify with or resist their behavior. Being spirit-occupying matter implies the I Am that you truly are existed prior to entering the body, and will continue to exist upon departure from the body. The death of the body is then perceived as change, not annihilation. And, of course, this all takes place within the illusion of linear time.

This is another huge can of worms that asserts that there is no linear sequence of events, that all is happening simultaneously Now. Everything in this perspective is

> Everything that ever has been, or will BE, IS, NOW.

simultaneous, all events and lifetimes are occurring as we speak. Everything that ever has been, or will BE, IS, NOW. Adopting this attitude releases our hold on illusion, enabling us to see through it to a deeper reality.

The heaven and hell spoken about in many religions refer to states of Consciousness. Heaven is Presence in the Now, and Hell is the lack of that quality of awareness, autopilot. Heaven is being single minded, possessing a unified consciousness (Jesus said, let thine eye be single) focused entirely into the Moment. Hell is fragmentation of Consciousness; thinking about this, worried about that, fearing something awful may happen, punishing oneself for past "mistakes", with the consequent unpleasant emotional states these thought patterns evoke.

In the gospel of Matthew it is said: "straight is the gate, narrow is the way that leads to the Kingdom of Heaven." The straight gate, the narrow way, is that thin slice of nothing between the past and the future, the Now, also called the razor's edge. Conventional wisdom dictates the narrow way to be living an obedient life, following the rules, and the Kingdom of Heaven is one's reward in the after life for this obedience. But truly, the narrow way is the Now and the Kingdom of Heaven is a single-minded state of Consciousness.

Keep in mind this is a mental model, a working theory. It is not the Truth. The subjective experience of the perceiver is all there is. There is no capital 'T' objective truth, only lower case 't', subjective truth. It is said in ancient esoteric wisdom that objective truth may be experienced during a state of intensely elevated Consciousness, but for most of us, most of the time, objective perception is a myth and the experience of ultimate reality would be unbearable.

> ...objective perception is a myth.

The closest we come to objective, is consensus perception (called consensus trance by one writer), which is bound by culture and language. A primitive tribesman would probably perceive the desk I am writing on right now as shelter. Perform some simple action in front of a group and interview them privately about what they saw, you will get as many versions as there are people, especially if they arise from different cultures. An Army general will perceive an action one way, an Aboriginal shaman another, a New York street hustler yet another. Which is 'the truth'? They all are. Truth is in the eye of the beholder.

I find this working theory to have a high degree of positive explain-ability. It is loving in its essence, and is flexible and open to learning. It gives meaning to meaninglessness, order to chaos. It enables me to embrace my enemy as another version of me I have formed an agreement with to facilitate my inner development. With it I am able to accept and find meaning in the difficulties and challenges I encounter, and value in hardship.

SEVENTH PRINCIPLE

SURRENDER
To What Is
Release All Resistance

Surrender is the unconditional acceptance of the circumstances or contents of the present moment. It is being at peace with What Is. Of all the principles, this is the most difficult. This is where life constantly challenges us, offering up the unexpected every moment, daring us to accept it on its own terms. Anything else is denial, with its consequent unnecessary suffering, not to mention the loss of the Precious Present.

Eckhart Tolle advises there are three things we can do with What Is. We can change it, leave it or accept it. In addiction recovery communities we encounter the Serenity Prayer:

"God grant me the serenity to accept
the things I cannot change,
the courage to change the things I can,
and the wisdom to know the difference."

Unnecessary suffering occurs when we attempt to change the unchangeable, or fail to find the strength to make doable changes. Stress is the distance between what is and what we think it should be. We cannot, for instance, change another person, past actions or decisions, or the contents of this moment. Begin noticing your resistant attitudes, your thought patterns that produce unpleasant emotional reactions like anger, rage, disappointment, frustration, depression, suicidal or homicidal thinking and more.

Emotion sets the stage for action. Thought produces feeling, feeling produces emotion, and emotion stimulates behavior. E-motion is short for energy in motion. It both stimulates and directs behavior. Resistant attitudes and beliefs (habitual thought patterns) produce negative and potentially violent destructive behaviors. They reject some aspect of the Now, wishing it were different.

> E-motion is short for energy in motion.

Consciousness is fragmented. A segment of attention is splintered from the Now, rejecting the contents of the moment. When you fail to focus attention fully Here/Now (First Principle), neglect inner self-observation (Second Principle), argue with the promptings of Spirit (Third Principle), have attention linked to past events or deeds (Fourth Principle), have expectations (Fifth Principle) and forget we're all spiritual beings, particles of the one Consciousness (Sixth Principle), resistant thought patterns arise.

In the extreme, the Now is completely rejected, producing thoughts like: I hate myself; I don't want to be where I am; everybody is incompetent. Look at all the license plate holders that say "I'd rather be _____", anywhere but here.

Resisting or rejecting the Now, or previous Nows, or some aspect of your life path, will predictably produce negative emotions, misery. The ego, the mind's false self, will form identities around this resistance, tormenting your very soul. This is how victim thinking arises. The ego blames other people or circumstances for its current life situation, rather than taking responsibility. It fails to find value in the life path it is living and wants some other life path. Giving our power away to the lives of celebrities, watching them, idolizing them, invading their privacy with cameras (a multi-million dollar business), is a distraction from and a rejection of our personal drama, wishing it to be different.

> The ego... will form identities around this resistance

We are not victims but creators. We have created our personal drama by how we have chosen to focus attention and pattern thought. We have at least potential power over the subject of our attention. This is taking responsibility (the ability to respond). It is a learnable skill. With responsibility comes the ability to create our life drama consciously (we have been creating it all along unconsciously).

We cannot create consciously however, when our Consciousness is fragmented with denial of the moment, or is in resistance to what is and blaming others. Giving up the blame game requires complete acceptance, complete responsibility, even though we cannot logic it out, or see exactly how we did it. Is it true or false that your life Now is the consequence of every decision you ever made? Especially when you include the ideas of Principle Six?

Complete acceptance of the facts of the moment is required to attain full Presence. If there is not acceptance, there is resistance, thought patterns that reject some element of the Now, wanting What Is to be different, including your history of previous Nows.

> Anger is the emotional consequence of resistant thinking.

In my work as a therapist I encounter many who are referred to treatment for anger problems. Frequently the referral is court mandated. Anger is the emotional consequence of resistant thinking. While it appears to be connected to specific circumstances, anger is frequently the outcome of deeply held attitudes and beliefs which have been generated by experiences in our earlier life, experiences to which we are still attached.

Abuse of any kind, perpetrated against a helpless child, has the potential for generating deep anger that then plays itself out in adult existence. I have treated many individuals who have criminal backgrounds. Their crimes are frequently the consequence of the anger they feel about how they were treated as children. Resentment, frustration, helplessness, suicidal thoughts, wanting revenge, arise from resistant thinking, mind based identities created around being a victim, which then perpetuate themselves by attracting more victim experiences, confirming the ego's theory about life.

It is impossible to manifest full Presence in the moment if the ego rejects its contents. The mind resents change, the universal constant, because it short-circuits predictability, confronting the mind with its inability to forecast events. It judges, or resists, trying to impose its agenda on the moment, a formula for obsessive thinking and compulsive behavior.

Surrender is the realization we cannot 'control' anything. We can only master the moment. Surrender is required for mastery to occur. Otherwise we remain resistant victims.

> Surrender is the realization we cannot 'control' anything.

USING THE TOOLS

Now you have tools:

- The Presence Meter
- No-Thought Meditation
- B.O.L.D.E.R.S., the seven principles of mind mastery

They are the distillation of thirty-seven years of seeking, practicing and teaching Consciousness, and are a basic, generic set of proven inner practices. Feel free to add to them, or add them to what you already have in place.

Now the question is using them. This means learning and practicing the principles, following the discipline of daily meditation, and monitoring Consciousness through self-assessment. Your challenge is to integrate these tools into your moment-to-moment existence and find the willingness, desire, and motivation, to actually do it. These are proven principles that work when they are practiced. Anyone I've given it to who practices it has succeeded. Success is definable as a practice that brings inner peace and facilitates conscious living.

Before considering using them, consider carefully your motivation. To live consciously in a predominantly unconscious world requires consistent, focused, intent. Make Presence in-the-moment the most important intention in your life, placing it before all other concerns, including; family, relationships, children, livelihood, possessions,

> Make Presence in-the-moment the most important intention in your life.

pleasing others, even survival. These are all relatively important, Presence is absolutely important. With this decision, all that is relatively important falls in line behind your dominant intention. Then, everything is done and there's no doing. In pure Presence we are instruments of a larger reality operating through us.

An initiate once asked a Buddhist monk what level of motivation it would take to become enlightened (live consciously). He told him to kneel in front of a bucket of water. Plunging his head into the water, the monk held it there for three minutes. Finally, letting him up, the monk asked how much did he want to breath. That is the level of motivation required.

You have been presented a set of learnable skills, basic tools for inner work. With clear intention, persistence and willingness to do what ever it takes (no job too low or too small), you can live your version of a connected life, a life filled with meaning, purpose and fulfillment.

Each of these principles is a process and a practice to be implemented in the context of our moment-to-moment existence. Each requires effort, and supports experiencing mundane existence as meditation, transforming daily life into spiritual adventure, a way of living that turns the ordinary into the extraordinary through the simple act of Presence.

> ...turns the
> ordinary
> into the
> extraordinary.

When we work to **BE**, Here/Now, **OBSERVE** our mind to keep it compliant with the intention of maintaining that

Presence, **LISTEN** to and comply with inner guidance, **DIE** to the past without regrets or recriminations, **EXPECT** the unexpected that is showing itself to us daily, **REMEMBER** our true nature as spiritual beings and **SURRENDER** to the facts of the moment, we live a life of inner peace and harmony. We truly experience connection with a larger reality and set ourselves free to live without fear.

The challenges we encounter, the temptations we face, arise from the distractions of the material illusion. Saying all is illusion may seem intellectual, experientially trivial. Having actual illuminating glimpses of non-surface reality is moving and powerful. Being able to consistently focus your entire attention Here/Now, to truly be the simplicity of a Consciousness in a body, gazing out of the portals of sight into an Eternal Now, is an experience unequaled by any other. It turns your perception of reality inside out. Everything formerly held to be of worth turns to dust, and what was before considered meaningless is now alive with significance.

> ...an experience unequaled by any other.

There is a payment. We must give up our addiction to mind (thinking) to go where mind cannot go. Words cannot take you there. They only point the way. We must die to mind (ego) to be reborn into Spirit. Then mind is transformed into a powerful servant, like the genie in Aladdin's lamp ("Your wish is my command"), and it forms an identity

> ...mind is transformed into a powerful servant.

around the effort to acquire Consciousness. The mind becomes devoted to facilitating Here/Now awareness, understanding and accepting it's own limitations.

The payment also includes our attachments, our identifications, the objects and relationships in the illusion we have made into identities. This includes roles, relationships, possessions, wealth, careers, positions and attainments. In a moment of pure Presence we see clearly none of this is real or important. Then we can Be and Do more effectively.

Constant vigilance is required

Use the Presence Meter frequently to assess your degree of focus. Make anything less than 100% attention in the Here/Now unacceptable. Turn it into a game. Can you acquire and hold 100% in an otherwise idle, ultra mundane, moment, like waiting in line, or using the restroom?

Give yourself daily healing using the No-Thought Meditation, five minutes in the morning, five minutes later on in the day, or any time you feel the

> Give yourself daily healing.

need. Stopping thought on a regular basis has enormous healing capabilities. It gives you a whole brain experience. There is even scientific research indicating brain cell growth arising out of meditation.

Daily life as meditation

When you are not sitting in meditation, take the elements

of the meditation with you on your life's journey. You can always be aware of your feet. Hold your peripheral vision open continuously, being sensitive to your entire visual field. Maintain auditory connection with your physical surroundings, feel the air on your skin, smell the smells. The senses are the key to maintaining constant awareness of Now. Remember, every moment is precious, is significant. The only difference between special moments and mundane moments is **Presence**.

> The senses are the key.

Each B.O.L.D.E.R.S. principle is a practice. All practices take place in the Now. Now I **BE** fully Here. I **OBSERVE** my mind to keep it performing its correct function, present-moment focus. Now, I **LISTEN** for guidance from Spirit. I **DIE** to the last moment Now, I **EXPECT** the appearance of the unknown. Now, I **REMEMBER** my true nature in this moment, and continue to **SURRENDER** to the unfolding of Life's mystery Here/Now.

To engage in these practices is to go against the habitual momentum of a lifetime. We are self-indulgent creatures. We enjoy our trauma/drama. Our mind would feel bored if we gave up our addiction to thinking.

I consider the material presented in this book to be new software. Reading this book and engaging in these practices is installing the new software. Then the challenge is to remember to click onto the new program and forget the very existence of your old programming, which then naturally decays until it no longer exists in conscious awareness. Once this connection is clearly made there is no going back. The ego's defense mechanisms will not work as before, old addictions used to avoid the pain of reality will not have the power they once possessed. You will no longer be able to sleep (go through life without awareness) comfortably in automatic functioning. Making this

> You will no longer be able to sleep comfortably.

transition is difficult to the extent you encounter and identify with internal resistance. Obviously, the more you commit your entire being to the process, the better it will go for you.

Conscious Creating

When you become proficient with focus, when your Consciousness is defragged, you will automatically begin using the mind consciously as a tool for reality creation. This is the function it is constantly performing, with or without your awareness. With increased awareness and greater degrees of attention focused Here/Now, comes greater power to create personal reality from a place of conscious intention.

> Thinking creates.

The mind operates according to the Law of Attraction, which declares: like attracts like. This operates on the level of thought, and is the major reason thinking is dangerous. Thinking creates. Whatever the mind places attention on becomes an attractor that brings the experience out of quantum potential into physical reality. If your attention is fear based, it will bring forth the feared experience.

The good news is, when you focus attention upon a

positively expressed desire, the desire manifests, the more intense the focus, the faster the manifestation. The

| Ask, Visualize, and Receive |

process has three steps. Ask, Visualize, and Receive. Ask for what is desired, visualize it happening, and be open to receiving.

A positive expression of desire has no doubt or fear attached to it. Doubt that it cannot or will not happen; fear that it is not possible. You cannot say to the universe, I want a new car, and then say, but I cannot afford it. Each is a creation; one cancels the other. Trust the universe to respond to your asking, visualize it happening and feel worthy of receiving the desired outcome. When your mind is single (100% Here/Now), you have the power to create miracles.

Actor Jim Carey is said to have written himself a check for five million dollars at a time in his life when he and his family were homeless, living in a car. Each day he looked at the check and declared someday he would be paid this amount to make a movie. This combined asking, visualization and openness to receiving. His current level of success is a testament to the power of this law.

The challenge for some is in the asking. I have asked many people what they want and they give me a list of what they don't want. 'Thinking' this way, focusing attention on what is not wanted, brings more of what is not wanted, perpetuating victim thought patterns. It is based in fear. When I am given a list of what is not wanted, it is a list of fears. I don't want poverty, ill heath, disaster, and unemployment. Many have great difficulty formulating what is wanted out of a life long habit of thinking fearfully.

If you have difficulty expressing a desire affirmatively, start with something small as an experiment. Ask for a parking place directly in front of the place you are going. Just to see what happens. Visualize a car pulling out just as you pull up. Be open to the possibility of it happening.

Use second principle, **OBSERVE,** to monitor your thoughts and connect those thoughts to events occurring around you. You will eventually begin seeing directly how you are creating your drama. Add third principle, **LISTEN,** and your thoughts will begin aligning themselves with your deeper intentions, bringing to you more and more moments of peace and fulfillment. Continue to **DIE** to the past moment to moment and **EXPECT** the unexpected as you witness your thought projections interacting with other thought projections and quantum potential to produce a manifested reality, reminding you to **REMEMBER** your true nature as you **SURRENDER** to the moment. Walking the razor's edge of Now is the straight gate and narrow way that leads to the Kingdom of Heaven, a state of awareness fully focused Here/Now.

> Walking the razor's edge of Now is the straight gate and narrow way.

I offer you these simple tools that have emerged out of my 37+ years of study, practice and teaching. This is not a belief system to be taken on faith, but a generic set of practices that are applicable across all cultures. My motto, taken from The Fourth Way, the foundation of my studies, is: Believe nothing, verify everything. Work seriously with these tools, become skilled in their use, and verify for yourself their effectiveness. Use them to reveal your Self. Use them to discover and develop the gifts you bring to life. Use them to connect to the Divinity within you. I use them daily and have witnessed miracles in my psychotherapy practice as a result of their application. Open to your miracles!!

> ...connect to the Divinity within you!

Good Luck on your Journey To NOW.

GLOSSARY

In order of appearance:

Is There Life On Earth, by J. G. Bennett

The Psychology of Man's Possible Evolution, Peter Ouspensky

The Fourth Way, Peter Ouspensky

All and Everything, Beelzebub's Tales to His Grandson, George Gurdjieff

Sacred Contracts, Caroline Myss

Theory of Eternal Life, Rodney Collin

The Master Game, Robert De Ropp

Mount Analogue, Rene Daumal

The Power of Now, Eckhart Tolle

READERS GUIDE

This book is ideally suited to group reading and discussion, both the story and the tools. The work of elevating one's self-awareness can be greatly enhanced by working in groups to help each other see them Selves.

ABOUT THE AUTHOR

JAMES WESTLY currently resides in Phoenix, AZ with his wife Allura, the artist he met while living in The Retreat. They co-led a Gurdjieff Group for ten years, which led to James' career involvement in psychotherapy, where he is currently in private practice.